To the Other Towns

But he said to them, "To the other towns also I must proclaim the kingdom of God."   LUKE 4:43

"Parece que no es nacido para estar quedo en una parte—He seems to have been destined to be ever on the move."

Letter of Father Bartholomew Ferron to
Father Santa Cruz, *February 19, 1546*

To the
Other Towns

a life of Blessed Peter Favre

first companion of St. Ignatius

by WILLIAM V. BANGERT, S.J.

The Newman Press
in Westminster, Maryland
1959

Imprimi Potest: Thomas E. Henneberry, S.J.
Provincial, New York Province

Nihil Obstat: Edward A. Cerny, S.S., D.D.
Censor Librorum

Imprimatur: Francis P. Keough, D.D.
Archbishop of Baltimore
August 12, 1958

Library of Congress Catalog Card Number: 58–11030

Printed in the United States of America

*To the Scholastics of the Society of Jesus
whom it has been my privilege to teach.*

Preface

FATHER JEROME NADAL, Saint Ignatius' *alter ego* in the promulgation of the Constitutions of the Society of Jesus, had the practice at the Communion of his Mass of praying for the grace to imitate Ignatius, Peter Favre and Francis Xavier. In Nadal's mind they were three names to be grouped together. The one suggested the other two. He was of course thinking as a contemporary of the events that had created this trio at the very origins of the Society. In the four centuries since Nadal's time there has been a change, and people who now reflect on Jesuit beginnings usually think of them as the achievement of Loyola and Xavier. With the passage of time clarity of perspective has been lost, and the sharp, clear lines of Favre's part in the foundation and extension of the Society, so distinctly seen by Father Nadal and others, have become blurred.

Peter appears of course in all the biographies of St. Ignatius and St. Francis. Invariably he is presented as an especially attractive and congenial companion—gentle, modest, loveable. But once his story takes him away from Rome in 1539 and his immediate association with Ignatius, hardly a word more is said about him until the recording of his death on August 1, 1546. Yet during those seven years of ceaseless travel, with journeys into northern Italy, the Netherlands and Portugal, into Spain twice and Germany three times, Peter was hard at work helping to lay Jesuit foundations in all those countries. Surrounding him in his constant labor there was ever an aura of prayerfulness which made him *par excellence* the "contemplative in the midst of work" envisaged by St. Ignatius as the ideal for his sons. Father Nadal's perspective is the true one; it is the purpose of this work to recreate, in at least a partial way, that perspective.

The only full scale life of Blessed Peter in English is the translation by Father H. J. Coleridge, S.J. of Father Giuseppe Boero's *Vita del Beato Pietro Fabro*, published in 1873. Father Boero's *Vita*, as well as the works by other nineteenth-century authors, such as Maurel, Prat, Cornely, contains some rather seriously misleading errors. The present work, attempting as it does to correct these errors, is nevertheless not the definitive biography of Blessed Peter. Before that can be written much research must yet be done in Europe's libraries. St. Peter Canisius has had his Braunsberger. St. Francis Xavier has his Schurhammer. Blessed Peter still awaits the scholar of like competence and industry to round out the task that has been so excellently begun by the editors of the *Monumenta Fabri*.

The chief source for the material of this biography has been the volumes of the *Monumenta Historica Societatis Jesu*. The number of people in Europe to whom I am in debt for kind help is proof of how difficult it has been to write this work on this side of the Atlantic. M. R. Avezou, Chief Archivist of the Département de L'Isère, and M. François Cochat, late Director of the Musée Municipal de Thônes, were most generous and exquisitely courteous in supplying me with information about the geography, the history and general background of Villaret, Blessed Peter's birthplace. Father Otto Pies, S.J., Tertian Instructor at Münster, loaned me an essential work, *Ein Seelensoberer: Lebenserinnerungen des ersten flämischen Jesuiten Kornelius Wischaven*, by Alphons Kleiser, S.J. Father Georg Schurhammer, S.J. put me on the trail of an important unpublished document in the

Jesuit Archives in Rome. Father Olphe-Galliard, S.J. graciously had microfilmed for me the notes of Father Cros now in the archives of the Toulouse Province of the Society of Jesus. Father Lehergne, S.J. did the same with several pages of Blessed Peter's notebook, presently preserved in the archives of the Province of France. M. Alain Dufour, Librarian at the Bibliothèque Publique et Universitaire de Genève, kindly sent to me the microfilmed copies of the notes of Théophile Dufour on the book *Modus Componendi Epistolas,* written by Peter Veillard, Blessed Peter's teacher in Savoy. Canada has also made a contribution. Father Emile Papillon, Tertian Instructor at Mont Laurier, P.Q., let me see a precious work I could not find in the United States, Nicholas Orlandini's *Forma Sacerdotis Apostolici expressa in exemplo Petri Fabri,* the second edition of the first life of Blessed Peter ever written.

I have also had the unstinted help of the man who is probably next to no one in his knowledge of Blessed Peter's *Memorial,* Father William J. Read, S.J. Intractable passages of Peter's awkward and difficult Spanish yielded their meaning only after they were subjected to the not-to-be-denied probing of Father Herbert A. Musurillo, S.J. To all I express my sincere gratitude.

Saint Francis de Sales, who was enchanted by the memory of Peter Favre, once observed that Peter's life, when written, would be "all honey and sweetness of devotion." No surer way of achieving that peculiar *dulcedo* can be found than to let Peter speak for himself in his letters and his spiritual diary or *Memorial.* This is the justification for the many and lengthy quotations.

WILLIAM V. BANGERT, S.J.

St. Andrew-on-Hudson
Poughkeepsie, New York

Contents

To the Other Towns

I. Of Books and of Sheep

IN THE increasingly nationality-conscious world of the early sixteenth century there rested on France's southern borders two territorial anachronisms, remnants of the passing feudal world, the Kingdom of Navarre and the Duchy of Savoy. Both lay astride great mountain ranges, Navarre touching France and Spain on either side of the Pyrenees, and Savoy touching France and Italy on either side of the Alps. On April 7, 1506, in the castle of Xavier, secure in the mountain passes of Navarre, Doña Maria Xavier gave birth to her third son, Francis. Six days later, in the village of Villaret, hidden in the Alpine defiles of Savoy, Marie Périssin Favre brought into the world a boy whom she named Peter. Nineteen years later Francis, the nobleman, and Peter, the shepherd, left their homes for the University of Paris. At the University they became roommates and dear friends. There it was that Ignatius of Loyola met them both and won them to his intensely ardent ideal of following Christ. Ignatius quarried well when he cut from the mountain sides of Navarre and Savoy the first stones for the edifice that one day would become the Society of Jesus.

The heart of Savoy—the fringes had changed frequently with the ebb and flow of the medieval world—stands like a great feudal castle between the valley of the Po and the stretches of Burgundy. The giant bastion of Mt. Blanc and its entourage of lesser peaks stand guard to the south and southeast; the long water line of Lake Geneva and the River Rhône to the north, west and southwest. Save for the valley

3

of the Isère, Savoy stands securely closed in by its Alpine wall and moat of the Rhône waterway.[1]

Twenty-eight hundred feet up in that lower section of Savoy known as Les Hautes-Chaines du Genevois, in the valley of Grand Bornand, in the venerable old parish of St. Jean-de-Sixt, lies the hamlet of Villaret.[2] Resting on the River Borne just about two miles from where the waters abruptly change their westerly direction and turn northward to meet the River Arve, Villaret looks eastward toward the great strong wall of the Aravis chain of the Alps. Mt. Pointe Percée, 9,000 feet in height, reigns as king of the Aravis. The fields about Villaret are rolling and broad, breaking off abruptly at the foot of a great cliff or some large patch of forest land. Clusters of pine trees, dark and solemn, stand like battalions of soldiers in close formation, with points glistening like lances, in the presence of their generals, the Aravis. Under the timeless gaze of the mountain peaks, sparkling with their snows, the deep silences of the valley of the Grand Bornand speak of eternity and peace unending.

Here Peter Favre spent his childhood with his mother, father and two brothers, Louis and Jean.[3] The Favres had their roots planted deep in the soil of the valley of the Borne. Records of 1408 show that Jean de Fontaine, Lord of Thônes, made a notation that he had received land rent from Mermet Favre, Berthet Favre and Pierre Favre, all of Villaret.[4] Peter's mother, Marie Périssin, was from the neighboring parish of Le Grand Bornand. Soon after his birth Peter was taken to the parish church, whose *curé* was Antoine Agniellet, and there received the sacrament of Baptism.[5]

In this undisturbed and tranquil world about Villaret Peter passed the first ten years of his life. Here in the spring he saw the fields that rose sharply behind his home and fell away in the direction of St. Jean-de-Sixt become green again

4

with the melting of the winter's snows, saw the periwinkle, the anemone, the jonquil and the myositis bring their white and blue and yellow to the ridges, knolls and fells about the River Borne. On these fields, smooth and fresh, Peter spent the beautiful summer days watching his father's sheep. Under the wide open skies and under the vigilant gaze of Pointe Percée he walked where the marguerites, the corn-flower, the cyclamen grew. Autumn came all too soon. The royal blue of the gentians, the red of the martagan lily, the white and blue of the colchium announced that it would not be long before the winds from the east would bring their broad blanket of winter snows. And when the snows came, Peter felt the sharp cold and crisp stillness of the winter nights under the white and yellow stars. This was the world that Peter saw, felt, grew to love.

As he advanced in years another world became to him just as real as the world of rivers, fields, mountains and trees. It was the world of Almighty God, the Blessed Virgin Mary, the saints and the angels. One neighbor of the Favres re-called that Peter, at the age of five, was able to recite the tiny children's catechism from memory.[6] Peter's parents were good pious folk and they opened the eyes of their boy's soul to the realities of God the Father, God the Son, God the Holy Ghost, of Jesus Christ lying in a manger and dying on a cross, of heaven as a reward for good done on earth, of hell as punishment for evil. Marie Périssin told her son about the beautiful life of the Blessed Virgin Mary. Peter's young and impressionable mind became accustomed to think about our Lady receiving the Angel Gabriel, kneeling at the manger at Bethlehem, standing at the foot of the cross, re-ceiving from her Son the crown of Queen of Angels and the hosts of heaven. So beyond the beautiful world that Peter could view from the doorstep of his little home there opened

5

up to him the other, even more beautiful world of the invisible.[7]

One day in 1621 Saint Francis de Sales happened to be visiting a monastery at Tailloires, a village of Savoy near Annecy. Francis threw open the window, looked out over the splendor of the mountains and fields that lay before him and exclaimed: "What an exquisite site! Here noble and beautiful thoughts will come to us as thick and fast as the snows that fall in the winter." [8] Seventy-five years before, in the midst of the natural splendor of his own corner of Savoy, on the mind and heart of young Peter the shepherd boy there fell the flakes of countless noble and beautiful thoughts. "When I was about seven years old," Peter recalled, "I several times felt an especially strong attraction to a devout life, as though God Himself from that time on clearly willed to take possession of my soul as its Spouse." [9] Neighbors of the Favres looked back over the years and recalled how Peter, when about six or seven years old, would seat himself upon a rock and there, surrounded by twenty or so boys and girls of his own age, taught his young audience how to say the rosary and to recite the prayers he had learned from his mother. Fifty years after Peter's death, George Bertin, then an octogenarian, could show visitors to Villaret the rock that Peter used. People of the village referred to him as *"petit prédicateur"* and *"petit docteur."* On Sundays and feastdays even the older folk stopped to listen and then rewarded the young preacher with some apples and nuts. These Peter distributed among his young friends. His popularity with the other shepherd boys and girls did not suffer for his being made the center of attraction. George Bertin remembered how loved and revered he was by them. Nor was his piety of a soft and sentimental kind. Early he had learned the hard lesson of self-abnegation, for twice in the week he used to

6

fast. Louis Blanchet drew a picture of a boy, comely, charming in manner, fluent in speech. George Bertin was impressed by Peter's quickness to learn and the retentiveness of his memory. People in Villaret did not hesitate to predict that the son of Louis Favre and Marie Périssin would one day be a great man.[10]

* * *

When Peter was ten a desire began to burn in his pure soul with the intensity of the evening star in a clear sky. He wanted to study. His parents refused, Louis Favre probably having his eye on keeping his boy at home to care for the sheep. But Peter's tears of disappointment won the day. "I wept so much," Peter said, "in my great desire to go to school that my parents felt constrained, contrary to their intentions, to send me." [11] So off to the little town of Thônes he went. Thônes was about seven miles from Villaret on the River Fier. There Peter learned to read, to write, to master the elements of grammar. Among his schoolmates were two future priests of Savoy who had reputations for unusual holiness, Antoine Duborjal and Jean Lamottaz.[12] After a short period of time at Thônes, Peter changed to the school at La Roche, about ten miles northwest of Villaret on the road between Annecy and Bonneville.

The school at La Roche was run by a pious Swiss priest named Peter Veillard. For perhaps seven or eight years Peter was under Veillard's direction, advanced in the study of Latin literature, and even dipped into a bit of theology. Veillard had made his mark as an author, having published in 1517 a volume entitled *Modus Componendi Epistolas* which he dedicated to Claude de Chateauvieux, Archbishop of Tarentaise.[13] The book was off the press of J. Vivian of Geneva only about a year when Peter enrolled at La Roche.

7

More than likely Veillard "introduced" his *opusculum* into the school and saw to it that Peter and his fellow students became expert in the art of the elegant letter. Veillard was exactingly systematic in his methods and he took great pains to show his students that each letter has seven parts, the Salutation, the Exordium, the Narration, the Petition or Reply, the Conclusion, the Signature, the Address. He pointed out the innumerable types of letters there are to cover every conceivable situation, whether it be to offer solace, to make a request, to blame, to express affection, be it maternal, paternal, or filial, to pacify, to encourage, etc. For his tyros Père Veillard drew up a certain number of stock phrases that became part and parcel of the epistolary art. In a letter of a child to its parent such phrases as the following would be most appropriate: *Nihil eorum parvi faciam quae iusseris, pater; Jussa tua omni exequar nisu; In dies atque in horas tibi obsequissimus ero.*

In his religious instruction Veillard believed in giving his older students a diet that befit their age. He put the catechism aside and taught some of the more intricate problems of the faith as outlined by the famous twelfth-century schoolman, Peter the Lombard. At nineteen years of age Peter had filled one hundred and fifty pages of a notebook with an abstract of the Fourth Book of Peter the Lombard's *Sentences* as well as with certain enlargements taken by Veillard from Saint Thomas and other authors. The subject matter was on the sacraments and sacramentals. This notebook, now preserved in the archives of the Jesuit Province of France, begins on a pious note with a prayer evidently dictated by Veillard:

O Good Jesus, Most Gentle Jesus, Most Sweet Jesus, Son of the Virgin Mary, full of mercy and love, graciously wash away

8

our injustice. For you, my students, I have with the divine assistance made this extract from the Fourth Book of the *Sentences* in order to provide you with the help of the Divine Physician.

Peter relieved the sombre appearance of his copy book by some decorations in the style of the sixteenth century. Along the margin of the page he sketched some flowers. Around the capital letter of the first word he drew some elaborate flourishes. And from behind these flourishes he made four not so pious faces to peer with jaunty grimaces.

Père Veillard may never have met the Brothers of the Common Life, those classic representatives of the widespread *Devotio Moderna*. The Brothers never seem to have settled in Savoy, their nearest residence being at Strasbourg in Alsace. Be that as it may, Veillard's teaching and approach to learning had a close affinity to the devout, simple piety found at Deventer and Windesheim and in the pages of the *Imitation of Christ*.

Surely, high sounding words and polished phrases make a man neither holy nor just; but a good virtuous life makes a man dear to God and loved by everyone.—If I knew all things in the world and had not charity, what would that profit me before God, Who will judge me according to my deeds?—A good life makes a man wise according to God, and experienced in many things.

These sentences from the classic of Thomas a Kempis would have been wholeheartedly received at the school of La Roche. Peter recalled too how Veillard took the ancient writers and poets, gave them such an interpretation that they breathed the very spirit of the Gospels, *"ut faceret evangelicos."* [14] Peter learned to love his teacher and in later years he always kept green the memory of him.

9

One of Peter's friends at La Roche was another Savoyard, about two or three years older than himself, Claude Jay. Claude was born at Mieussy, about fifteen miles north of Villaret in the valley of the River Giffre, a tributary of the Arve. Early in life, Claude, influenced by the example of his uncle Peter, a priest, decided to be a priest himself. He did his schooling under Père Veillard and was ordained in 1528.[15] Out of this friendship of youth there grew in later years the deep union of desire and purpose in the Society of Jesus.

God's grace continued to draw Peter to a life of holiness. In 1518, at the end of the school year, he closed his books and returned to Villaret for the summer months. He was then twelve years old. Out in the fields with the sheep one day his soul was swept by the beauty of the idea of a complete dedication to God. "One day when I was filled with intense joy," Peter recalled, "and when I was carrying out the chores of a shepherd (it was the vacation period) I felt an intense desire of purity and I made a promise to God of perpetual chastity." [16] Attraction to holiness did not mean freedom from temptation and the difficulty of preserving that purity of heart he so much desired. Temptations there were and sometimes Peter fell.

At school for nine years I grew in age and knowledge. But I cannot say the same for that wisdom which is of a part with holiness of life and the chaste watchfulness over my eyes. It is sufficient here to say simply that I have every reason for giving thanks to God as well as for having sorrow and contrition of heart for my daily sins, some of which I was only then learning, and then repeated with increasing frequency.[17]

Over the Aravis, on a tributary of the River Arve, seven miles northeast of Villaret, stood the Chartreuse of Reposoir.

10

A twelfth-century foundation, Reposoir was a tribute to those early sons of Saint Bruno who had come with crucifix and axe into this wild country. Aimon de Faucigny long had the desire of bringing the Carthusians to Savoy and finally established a group at a place called Béol. But the monks beat a hasty retreat before the rigors of cold, snow and rain. They came back, however, a second time under the tenacious Blessed John of Spain. To prove that he intended to stay, Blessed John changed the name of the place from Béol to Repausatorium—Reposoir—a place of permanent abode. In 1508, when Peter was two years of age, Dom Mermet Favre, brother of Peter's father, became the Prior. With him he brought a background of wide experience as superior, having been Prior at Val-Sainte and Oujon. Peter found in Dom Favre a wise counsellor from whom he received constant guidance and advice.[18] When Dom Favre died in 1522 he was succeeded by Dom Claude Périssin, Peter's cousin on his mother's side. In the monastic annals of Reposoir Dom Claude is called "a man of singular piety, extraordinary skill, gifted by nature and grace for the office of governing." [19] There was, therefore, good reason for Peter to feel close to the monks of the monastery on the other side of the Aravis. All of the inhabitants in the region of Grand Bornand, in fact, had reason to feel that Reposoir was their very own because their valley was a veritable granary of vocations on which the monastery fed. After Dom Claude Périssin, the next three Priors all came from Grand Bornand. The names Favre and Périssin were frequently written into the monastery's roster among the many others who came from the area around the River Borne. There were Dom Pierre Fournier, Dom Jacques Bastard, Dom Pierre Favre, Dom François Perillat, Dom Pierre Banchet, Dom Jacques Favre, Dom François Périssin. Peter learned to love the Carthusians and

11

gave Saint Bruno a select place among his favorite saints. Years later he always kept in touch with the various charter-houses located in the cities where he was working. Probably even more surely than did Père Veillard, the monks of Reposoir brought Peter within the spiritual influence of the school of Gerard Groote, Ludolf of Saxony, Henry Herp, and Jean Ruysbroeck, since it was the Carthusian monasteries at Treves, Mainz, Cologne, Louvain, along with the Brothers of the Common Life, that were the important pegs which held the web of the *Devotio Moderna* spread out over the Low Countries and the Rhineland.

When Peter came to his nineteenth year, the time had arrived to say farewell to his parents and brothers at Villaret, to his cousin Dom Claude at Reposoir, his friends Père Veillard and Jay at La Roche. His hope was to continue his studies at a university. In his desire to learn he recognized what he felt was a providential means of rescuing him from further falls into sin.

Many more sins would I have committed were it not that the Divine Majesty permitted to grow up in my soul a certain selfish desire of knowledge and study. By this impulse to learning the Lord led me away from my native land where I could no longer serve Him the way I should have. May You be eternally blessed, O My God, for the great blessing You gave me in lifting me out of the appeal of the flesh, out of my nature, corrupt and at war with the spirit, and in drawing me to an intimate knowledge of Your Majesty.[20]

Nine years earlier the star of learning had led Peter from Villaret to Thônes and La Roche. Once more it went before him. This time it stopped over Paris, the beautiful city on the Seine far to the north.

✿   ✿   ✿

12

About six months before Peter set out for Paris Charles de Lannoy, commander of the imperial troops in Lombardy, sent off posthaste a special messenger to the Emperor in Spain with the resounding news of the Battle of Pavia. Not only had the French gone down in defeat, but Francis I himself had been captured. And all this on Charles' twenty-fifth birthday. In England the first impulse of Henry VIII, his head filled with ideas of regaining the Provinces of France that Edward III and Henry V had conquered, was to go straight to Paris, take the French crown and divide the land of the Valois among his allies. These three young rulers, Charles, Francis, Henry, whose fortunes were so vitally touched by that great battle of February 24, 1525, were the Big Three in whose hands lay the fortunes of early sixteenth-century Europe and its unity.

In 1509, when Peter was three, Lord Montjoy wrote about the heavens laughing and the earth rejoicing on the accession of eighteen-year-old Henry to the throne of England. In 1515, when Peter was nine, France received as her king the twenty-one-year-old Francis, over whose extravagance Louis XII used to shake his head, and say that it would be the undoing of all he had accomplished. One year later in the Cathedral of Sainte-Gudule in Brussels, amid the splendor of the Burgundian ceremonial, sixteen-year-old Charles took a sword from the Bishop of Badajoz, raised it to heaven and heard thousands hail him as king of Spain. The Europe that Peter was to know was a Europe dominated by the Tudors, the Hapsburgs, the Valois. These three young men were on their thrones when he left Savoy for Paris. They were still reigning when he died in Rome twenty-one years later.

In this age Peter's own Savoy cut a sorry figure on the

13

European scene. It was then deep in the valley of ignominy between the peak of late medieval prestige, when in 1416 Amedius VIII received the title of Duke, and the peak of early modern influence at the accession of Duke Philibert in 1553. Trouble had started for the duchy in 1419 with the annexation of Piedmont. Territorially a great acquisition, Piedmont nevertheless carried with it the seeds of discord, for it meant that Savoy was now a state with two clear-cut areas on either side of the Alps, each with its distinctive language and regional feeling. The Piedmontese gained, in time, the ascendancy, and Chambéry, age-old capital of Savoy, was practically effaced in the transfer of the government to Turin. Political ill fortune continued to plague the Savoyards. The event that dominates their history in the first half of the sixteenth century is the loss of Geneva. Geneva had been closely tied to Savoy ever since the end of the thirteenth century, but the shortsightedness of the royal family created antagonisms between the great city and the duchy. The dukes carefully saw to it that one of their own held the episcopal see of Geneva; they repeatedly interfered with the local liberties of the citizens. The Genevans began to lean toward a policy of union with the Swiss Confederation and this they effected in 1526. Religious separation followed in the wake of this territorial division and the arrival of Zwingli with his troops. The Bishop went into exile and Annecy became the heir to the great medieval see of Geneva. Shortly after Peter left Villaret for Paris, the duchy of Savoy, lying on the path of the warring armies, was invaded by Francis I and for twenty years existed in name only. Fifteen years later Peter was to meet the Duke, Charles III, in exile in the Holy Roman Empire.

Sixteenth-century Europe was of course more than just

14

a theatre of war for three young men of rival nations. In 1506, the year of Peter's birth, Bramante began the Basilica of Saint Peter's in Rome. In 1512, when Peter was six, Michelangelo finished his famous ceiling of the Sistine Chapel. In 1515, when Peter was nine, a girl named Teresa was born in Avila and a boy named Philip Neri was born in Florence. The next year, 1516, was hailed as a golden year in Europe's history by men who sought Church reform in the way of a deeper and truer life of learning. It was the year that John Busleiden ran off his press the great achievement of Erasmus, his *Novum Instrumentum*. Erasmus' spirits were running high and they carried into 1517, when he wrote to his friend Wolfgang Capito, "But at the present moment I could almost wish to be young again, for no other reason but this, that I anticipate the approach of a golden age. . . ." [21] This was in February. Eight months later the hopes of Erasmus were chilled by the shadow of a hand tacking a challenge on the church door of Wittenberg. In 1521, when Peter was fifteen, the French and the Spanish fought a battle at Pamplona and one of the casualties was a Basque soldier, Ignatius of Loyola. The year following, Cardinal Cajetan wrote finis to his monumental *Commentary on Saint Thomas*. These were the currents that crossed and recrossed in the world that stretched out before the great natural fortress of Savoy: the divisive jealousies of new nations and the traditional faith in the order of a united Christendom; the crushing burden of Luther's despair of human goodness and the serene confidence of a reawakened Thomism in the dignity of man; the flourish of the aesthetic Renaissance in the Italy of da Vinci, Michelangelo, Bramante, and the great surge of the Biblical Renaissance of the North in the writings of Erasmus; the canonization of evil

15

by Machiavelli and the proof of God's presence among men in the heroism of an extraordinary number of saints. These were the things that went into the fabric of the world into which Peter moved when he left Villaret for the north of France.

II. A Decade in the Land of the Fleur-de-lys

JOHN OF SALISBURY, that great Englishman of the twelfth century who loved the University of Paris so intensely, once put into metrical form his thoughts on the ideal conditions for the student who would grow in learning.

> A *humble mind, a life by strife untouched, a*
> *zeal to understand,*
> A *quiet room, poverty's cloak, a foreign land.*[1]

If Paris could assure Peter of nothing else she could at least provide him with the *terra aliena*, "the foreign land." In place of the timeless and unchanging mountains and valleys about Villaret, Peter found in France's capital city a perpetual pageant of buildings and monuments that spoke in the language of stone of the ever changing, growing, restless Paris, the Paris of the Romans, the Merovingians, the Carolingians, the Capetians. Within the very boundaries of the Latin Quarter where he was to spend most of his university life, Peter walked in the shadow of such edifices as the Church of Saint-Séverin with its memories reaching back to the burning of the original chapel by the Norsemen and to the voice of Foulques de Neuilly-sur-Marne preaching the strange Fourth Crusade. On the hill along which the schools of the University were clustered, Saint Geneviève kept her watch over her dear city from the simple unadorned church, originally Clovis' memorial to the victory of his Franks over the Visigoths at Vouillé. Down the hill, off the old Roman

17

road christened Rue Saint-Jacques, was the assembly place of the University since the thirteenth century, the Church of Saint-Julien-le-Pauvre. Near Saint-Julien there was the unforgettable view of Ile de la Cité and its noble Notre Dame that told of the days when Paris had been embraced by the great movement of the Gothic with its characteristic heights, points, delicate arches. The ridges of the roofs were "points innumerable, ends always tapering upward. It was as though the city had adopted an attitude of prayer, and as though the buildings looked above them and joined their hands together."[2] This, in its externals, was the Paris that Peter came to in 1525. But the spirit that had put up those buildings had withered and died as it came in contact with the mad era of François Villon and the Spider King. And now, even while Peter was in Paris, the new Hôtel Dieu was rising according to the design of its Italian architect, Domenico de Cortona, and heralding the invasion of France by the men and the ideas of the Italian Renaissance.[3]

If Saint-Séverin, Saint Julien-le-Pauvre, the Hôtel Dieu, made a *terra aliena* for Peter, they were but a reflection of the strange new world of thought into which he moved. The ideas of traditional Scholasticism, Nominalism, Humanism, Protestantism all crossed and recrossed in the narrow streets of the Latin Quarter, echoed and re-echoed in the halls of the University's sixty colleges, were thrashed out by the four thousand turbulent students.

It was an abrupt break, this change from the country school at La Roche and the pious teaching of Père Veillard to this cosmopolitan guildhall and center of ideas. In this intellectual *terra aliena* appeal was still made to the authority of the *Doctor Angelicus,* the *Doctor Seraphicus,* the *Doctor Subtilis,* great constructive thinkers and the inspiration of what came to be known as the *via antiqua.* But the

18

men who came after were not equal to the great initial impulse of their leaders and brought Scholasticism into disrepute by their sterile and formalistic dialectics. Strong positions were also held by men of the *via moderna*, those followers of William of Ockham who broke apart the synthesis that was one of the thirteenth century's great achievements. Despite the shreds of outworn thought, there appeared signs of hope that Paris would rededicate herself to sound scholarship and to an ennobled concept of the function of philosophy and theology. The influence of the great Dominican General, Thomas de Vio, reached into the ranks of his order in Paris and gave a new orientation to theological studies through an idiom that was intelligible to the men of the Renaissance.[4]

The infiltration of Italian humanistic ideas did not ease the situation. Tension mounted between the traditional theologians, strongly entrenched in their citadel of the Collège de Sorbonne, and the humanists, who found asylum in the Collège Sainte-Barbe and other schools of the University. The former, adamant in their viewpoint that *belles-lettres* were but steppingstones in the educational advance to the ecclesiastical career, rejected the program of the humanists for whom *belles-lettres* were an end in themselves. So deeply rooted was the antagonism that Gaguin had good ground for his observation: "Our University is a two-headed thing."[5] But the new humanism was not to be stopped. The ascendancy of Guillaume Budé and the foundation of the Collège de France for the presentation of courses in the ancient languages according to the spirit of the times were signs that France was replacing Italy as the *maîtresse* of the literary movement, even though the theologians at the Sorbonne thundered that "the new teaching was scandalous, temerarious, heretical and tainted with Lutheranism."[6]

19

Nor were the Protestants idle. Formed in a giant arc about France's capital, the printing houses in the great cities of Antwerp, Strasbourg and Basel kept the University under fire with the ammunition supplied by the latest heterodox developments in Germany.

There was no telling to what limits a lover of the University of Paris would go to express his enthusiasm. One writer did not hesitate to call upon his readers to imagine all the sky as parchment, all the sea as ink and all the stars as the Masters of Paris. Not to be outdone, another exclaimed that Paris was the mill where the world's corn is ground and the oven where the world's bread is baked.[7] For eleven years, from 1525 to 1536, with one interruption of seven months, Peter tended his scholastic mill and oven on the left bank of the Seine. He enrolled at the Collège Sainte-Barbe, a sort of Portuguese enclave presided over by Diogo de Gouveia. There is very little to indicate just what stand Peter took in the battle of the schools. He showed superior ability in the study of Latin and Greek.[8] His College was especially sympathetic to the new humanism. "We thought," Peter recalled years later, "that studies, which really are but a means, would in themselves be sufficient to teach us about their source and their last end." [9] These are but straws in the wind, but they do indicate that Peter had placed himself on the side of the enthusiasts for *belles-lettres*.

❉ ❉ ❉

Of all that Sainte-Barbe gave Peter during his early days at Paris, nothing could compare with the blessing of having as his roommate a young nobleman from Navarre named Francis Xavier. This gentleman, six days older than Peter, tall, slender, well-built, with handsome countenance, black hair and black eyes, enrolled at the University in the fall

20

of 1525, the same time as Peter.[10] He came to Paris with memories of the castle of Xavier dedicated to Saint Michael, of his father moving in the highest court circles, of his mother gathering the children for evening prayers before the great crucifix in the castle chapel, of himself and his two brothers chasing after the shepherds who refused to pay the toll when they crossed the Xavier property with their flocks. His memories were of Navarre caught in the conflict between Francis I and Charles V, of the castle razed to the ground after the abortive rebellion of 1515 against Spain, of the capture of Pamplona in 1521 despite the spirited defense by a Guipuzcoan soldier, Ignatius of Loyola, of the French disaster at Noain and the price the Xaviers had to pay for their loyalty to the cause of Navarrese independence. And now in his nineteenth year, when the fury of the storm had subsided, he was able to leave home for his university training at Paris.

In contrast with Francis, Peter was a blond. Manly and attractive in his appearance, of medium height, soft in his speech, Peter had a most friendly and open manner of dealing with others.[11] In 1577 Father Simon Rodrigues, one of the first Jesuits, looked back over his long life and singled Peter out as unmatched in graciousness, affability and the power of attracting others.

There was an especially rare and delightful sweetness and charm in his relations with other men which I must confess to this very day I have not discovered in any other. In some way or other, he so won the friendship of other men and gradually stole into their souls that by his whole manner and the gentleness of his words he irresistibly drew them to a love of God.[12]

Between the nobleman from Navarre and the shepherd from Savoy a friendship was formed which was to deepen with

21

the years and which the distances of continents and oceans would not diminish.

In October 1526, after a year of preparatory studies, Peter and Francis began their three and one-half years' philosophy course under the direction of a Spanish Master of Arts, Master Juan de la Peña. Peter did well in philosophy and Master Juan was not above asking his student for help every now and then in clearing up a doubtful point in Aristotle, probably because Peter had a good command of Greek.[13] Sometime between November 11th and Christmas of 1528, Peter and Francis faced the first major ordeal of their scholastic career at Paris when, under the supervision of Master Peña, they engaged in disputations at the Schools of the Nation of France on the Rue de Fouare and then at their own Collège Sainte-Barbe. Soon after, in January, they again went to the Rue de Fouare and faced five examiners. Peter and Francis came through the tests successfully and on January 10th they received their Baccalaureate.

One year later there were more exams, this time for the Licentiate. On February 3rd these examinations began at Sainte-Geneviève in the presence of the Chancellor in his private chambers. There were four examiners, one from each Nation of the University. When the questioning was over, all the candidates were arranged in order according to the grade they had received and were then placed in groups of eight. Then each month two groups, or sixteen students, were called up for a second examination. Francis outdistanced Peter by two positions, he himself placing twenty-second and Peter placing twenty-fourth. This meant that they were together in the same third group, not at all a bad standing, since normally there were eighty candidates, or ten groups, each year. In the beginning of March they had to return to Sainte-Geneviève to face four new examiners. When this examination was completed, the Chancellor instructed the candidates when and where they were to assemble, clothed in the prescribed ceremonial dress, for the ritual of conferring the Licentiate.

March 15, 1530, was the big day for Peter and Francis and the six companions of their group. They gathered together at the Cloister of the Trinitarians and, led by the Beadles of the Four Nations, they marched with the Rector and the Procurators of the Nations in solemn procession to Sainte-Geneviève. The Chancellor, Jacques Aimery, sat awaiting them in the choir of the Chapel of Our Lady of Mercy. He then gave to one of the Beadles the list of eight candidates to be read out, had the candidates introduced to him individually, gave a short speech, and then had them swear on the Gospel that they would be faithful to their duties as teachers. He then arose and pronounced the solemn formula which authorized them to teach "at Paris and anywhere else in the world."

The only thing that now stood between the new Licentiates and the Master's degree was a matter of francs and sous. The Master's grade was not so much a sign of intellectual accomplishment, since no strict examination was required, as it was a proof of an individual's ability to meet the endless expenses involved, payment for the testimonial letters, gratuities to the Regents, provision of the banquets that were expected to be given for friends and teachers. Peter's purse could not stand the strain and he postponed taking the Master's degree until the spring of 1536. Francis, however, had the wherewithal and in that same month of March 1530, he became Master Francis.

By this time Peter and Francis had completed nearly five years of study at Paris. The reception of the Licentiate highlighted the need to think about the future and to decide whether to stay on at Paris for specialized training in one of the three higher faculties of the University, Theology, Law and Medicine. For Francis the way was clear. He had decided to be a priest and had received the tonsure for the Diocese of Pamplona. His eyes were fixed on a canonical benefice which would assure him a congenial and comfortable future amid the surroundings he had known as a boy. For Peter things were not so easy. All his academic success could not compensate for the utter loss of interior peace that for so long a time had been causing him so much distress. Doubts, scruples, temptations had been making a plaything of his soul.

Fears of having made bad confessions assailed him. "I was so tormented by these scruples," wrote Peter, "that I would have willingly retired into a desert and there lived the rest of my days on naught but herbs and roots just to find peace." [14] Impure thoughts, vainglorious, suspicious and uncharitable thoughts plagued him. Molehills reached the proportions of mountains. One time he could not make up his mind whether to give the barber a *double,* worth one sixth of a sou, or a *liard,* worth one quarter of a sou.[15] But if he was unable to come to a decision about a mere fraction of a sou, still less was he able to settle a question of such major importance as his vocation. Like the weathercock swinging with the prevailing wind Peter changed with the mood of the moment. At one time it was marriage that attracted him, at another the study of medicine, at still another the study of law. Nor was that all. The teaching profession, a career as theologian, the monastic life, all made their bid for his affections. He lost his bearing even in his intellectual objectives. The lessons he learned from Père Veillard on the relation his studies should have to the Divine Wisdom were crowded into the background. Twelve years later Peter congratulated the Jesuit scholastics at Paris on their clarity of perspective in their studies, so much in contrast with his own shortsightedness.

I am delighted no end in the Lord that you are enjoying such a great advantage over what we had at Paris. Mind you, I am speaking at least for myself. This advantage is that, even before you start out on your studies, you have a predetermined goal toward which you direct them by the straight line of a well-ordered intention. Since you already know the Source of all wisdom your study has been directed to It alone. Since you have chosen the proper means you are assured of your destination once your period of studies is over . . . But because from the very beginning we were without that true understanding of the Source of all knowledge which would guarantee a promising start, and because we were in ignorance of the final End of all knowledge in which the anchor of intention should be fastened, it was beyond us to make a choice of the right means in an ordered and tranquil way. We did not know how to discern in the light of truth what was good in our intellectual pursuits, and as a consequence we often took to be an end what was really a means and vice versa. We were also beset by another difficulty. Again, keep in mind that I am referring at least to myself. It was this. We did not think that the Cross deserved to have a place in our studies. . . . No small advantage that you have over us is your appreciation of the place that the Cross holds in human life. . . .[16]

Peter was, therefore, a totally confused, sorely tempted, deeply distressed young man. And strangely enough, unable as he was to help himself, he was nevertheless a pillar of strength to Francis Xavier. His holiness and attractiveness of character kept Francis from many a pitfall that awaited the university student at Paris.[17]

In his *Confessions* Saint Augustine tells how God had used him, albeit unknown to himself, to bring about the spiritual cure of his spiritually sick friend Alypius. "You use all men with or without their knowledge for a purpose known to Yourself—and that purpose is just. Thus of my heart and tongue You made burning coals to cauterize and heal a mind of such promise though it lay sick." [18] At the beginning of the school year of 1529, Peter and Francis were joined by another roommate who, unknown to himself and both of them, was to be God's instrument for the drastic changing of their lives. The name of the newcomer was Ignatius of Loyola. Ignatius' heart and tongue were burning coals that were to heal Peter's distressed soul and sear the narrow scope of Francis' ideals.

*　*　*

The new student at Sainte-Barbe, thirty-six years old, short and strong of body, with roundish face, aquiline nose, high forehead, deepset, lively and cheerful eyes, came to Paris with a background filled in by the chivalry of Spanish court life, the toughness of warfare, the mystic experiences of a soul especially chosen by God. Ignatius himself characterized his life up to his twenty-sixth year as one given over to the vanities of the world, the enjoyment of military exercises, the winning of a reputation.[19] The year 1521 was just another year in the monotonous roll call of dates in the story of the warfare between France and Spain. But for Ignatius it was a year of decision. The story of Ignatius and the siege of Pamplona has often been told, the story of the rebellion of the Spanish *Communeros,* the rally of the Navarrese to the side of the French, the terrible six-hour bombardment by the best artillery men of Europe, the stand made by Ignatius with drawn sword in the breach of the walls against the French infantry assault, the fall of Ignatius when a cannon ball crushed his right leg and a piece of flying masonry injured his left, the surrender of the city, the gracious courtesy and inept surgery of the French captors, the not much better "butchery" of the Spanish doctors.

Then followed his long convalescence at Loyola Castle, his readings in the *Life of Christ* by Ludolf of Saxony and in the *Golden Legend*, his enchantment by the story of the saints in their love for Christ, his night-long vigil before Our Lady of Montserrat, his awesome and mighty spiritual struggles at Manresa, his laborious pilgrimage to the Holy Land, his relentless assault on the citadels of learning at Barcelona, Alcalá, Salamanca, Paris. More than any place else, Manresa was the *atelier* where Ignatius served his apprenticeship in the art of the spiritual life and where God Himself acted as the Master. And never was a Master more exacting and at the same time more generous. A period of piercing temptation and blackest distress of soul was followed by spiritual blessings and ecstasies of the highest kind. Ignatius himself said "that he was transformed as it were into another person and his intelligence was completely made over." [20]

Père de Guibert could find but one expression adequate to describe what had happened at Manresa: *invasion mystique.*[21] Ignatius was transformed in the wake of the endless waves of extraordinary graces that kept sweeping across his soul. The apprentice had been a docile learner and for that reason became the better master, and, in fact, one of the greatest masters of the spiritual life in the history of the Church. His masterpiece was a twofold work: first, his own person, moulded anew through his generous co-operation with the designs of the Divine Master, and second, a little book called the *Spiritual Exercises*, which, although not given its final touches until years later, was nonetheless substantially put together at Manresa.

It was, therefore, with the most amazing of backgrounds that this new student at Sainte-Barbe came to room with Peter and Francis in the fall of 1529. But for the future of Favre and Xavier, the most important thing of all was the fact that, in receiving into their company this soldier, pilgrim, penitent and scholar, they were welcoming one of the greatest mystics in the history of the Church. "He will never comprehend Saint Ignatius," says Père de Guibert, "who does not keep before his eyes this fundamental fact, that he had been from the very first a mystic in the most forceful sense of the word and of the same stature as a Saint Francis of Assisi or a Saint John of the Cross. . . ." [22]

* * *

It was arranged that Ignatius should do his course under the direction of Peter's Master, Juan de la Peña, and that Peter should lend a helping hand by going over Ignatius' lessons with him. During these meetings for discussion on the meaning of Aristotle and the Scholastics they laid the foundations of a lifelong devotion of each for the other. It was inevitable that with souls so sensitive to the interior life of grace their conversation should take a turn in the direction of things spiritual. Aristotle was soon relegated to a secondary place in their attention. Ignatius recognized that his studies were suffering, and in his determination to keep first things first he made a pact with Peter not to speak for the time being on the things of God. [23]

The moment came, however, when Peter could contain his suffering no longer, and he revealed to Ignatius the cross that he had been secretly carrying. Ignatius, a veteran of the same humiliating experience, could not but deeply appreciate the agony of his friend's pure and generous soul. Someone remarked about Ignatius years later that, whenever he

28

met a fellow Jesuit, he was accustomed to see in him Christ, the Price of his Redemption, and that this practice filled him with a great interior joy. "This joy, obvious in the tenderness shown in his countenance, shone like a light on those who approached him so that it seemed that he wanted in some way or other to draw them into his very self." [24] Ignatius now took Peter to himself and with the finesse of the expert he set about the task of putting order into his distracted interior life. Ignatius the student now became the master. His directions were simple. He told Peter to make a general confession to Dr. John Castro, a Spanish friend of his and future Carthusian, to confess and receive Holy Communion every week, to make a daily examination of conscience. He then drew up the long range strategy of an aggressive campaign against the causes of Peter's spiritual setbacks. He instructed him on how to understand the voice of conscience, how to meet temptations, how to recognize scruples, what means to take against feelings of sadness. He showed Peter how, in the light of his self-knowledge, he should concentrate his forces on the eradication of those habits that had been an obstacle to God's grace, not combatting all at once but one at a time, and giving priority to those that were the strongest. Then he was to focus his energies on the building up of positive virtues. This strategy of *divide et impera* worked magnificently, and Peter gradually disentangled himself from the web of his scruples. He wanted to enlarge the program of prayer. Ignatius refused, and for four years held to that decision.

Peter's victory did not mean the cessation of temptation, nor did it mean the complete extinction of the tendency to scrupulosity as had been Ignatius' experience at Manresa. He was now, however, master of the situation and opposition no longer dismayed him. The hanging on of the old difficulties, in fact, had a value all its own. "For God," remarked Peter, "had left with me some spurs which were never going to permit me to be tepid." Through this period of trial Peter developed a delicate sensitivity to the ways by which the Spirit of Light and the Spirit of Darkness work in the souls of men. Ignatius' great proving ground had been at Manresa; Peter found his at Paris. The future guide of souls, to be famous for his wisdom, his prudence, his power of discernment, his sureness of touch, was in the making at Collège Sainte-Barbe. He later wrote:

> I can say with truth that I never had any difficulty, scruple, anxiety, doubt, fear—in fact, any feeling that is of the Spirit of Evil—for which I did not immediately or within a few days discover the remedy in Our Lord. All the while the Lord was giving me the grace of insistent prayer. With His remedy for my difficulties there came countless graces which enabled me to recognize the movements in the soul suggested by different spirits. Each day saw me grow more and more in this power of discernment. Never, as far as I can tell, did the Lord permit me to be deceived when it was a matter of looking into and forming a judgment about the workings of the Evil Spirit; nor did the Lord permit me to go astray when it came to making a decision about spiritual things, whether it be my own personal problem or that of my neighbor. In every instance, through the lights given by the Holy Angels and the Holy Spirit, I was just at the right moment freed from my uncertainty.[25]

Peter's indecision about his vocation also came to an end. Sometime during these years of intimacy, while Peter was imparting to Ignatius the wisdom of the Stagirite and Ignatius in turn was communicating to Peter the wisdom of Manresa, Peter discovered Ignatius' plan to walk in the footsteps of Christ in poverty and apostolic zeal. That was enough for him. Doubts about his future disappeared. He decided to become a priest and to make Ignatius' ideals his own. Favre and Loyola formed an *entente cordiale.* "We became one in will and desire," Peter observed. It was the first link in the formation of that association of men to gather about Ignatius and to receive in seven or eight years papal approval as the Society of Jesus.

Now that the skies were cleared of all clouds of doubt about his vocation, Peter decided to return to Savoy for a time before going on with his theological studies. His mother had died and he was anxious to see his father and brothers. Before he left Paris he saw Ignatius win two other students of the University to his ideals. The first was none other than their roommate, Francis Xavier. The other was a Portuguese resident at Sainte-Barbe, Simon Rodrigues. It was a masterful piece of strategy that Peter witnessed as he observed Ignatius, patiently, gently, skillfully, change the spiritually aloof Xavier into the most ardent adherent of all that he stood for and started him on the road that eventually led half way round the world. Simon Rodrigues, born at Vouzela in the Diocese of Viseu in northern Portugal, was four years younger than Favre and Xavier.[26] His parents, Gil Goncalves de Azevedo Cabral and Doña Helena de Azevedo, were both of the nobility. As a boy Simon was put in the service of Diogo Ortiz de Vilhejas, Dean of the royal chapel. In 1527 he came to Paris, matriculated at Sainte-Barbe, and around October of 1532 this black-haired, olive-skinned gentleman of exquisite graciousness became quite friendly with Ignatius. Inspired by Ignatius' aspirations, Simon placed himself at his side and gave every promise of being an ideal apostolic priest. There was nothing to indicate that this young man of polished manners and pleasant appearance would one day become a storm center in the Society of Jesus.

Peter started for Savoy in early June of 1533. During the

31

months that he was back in his home country, besides visiting his relatives, he called on his former schoolmate at La Roche, Claude Jay. Claude had stayed on in Savoy and started at least some part of his theological studies under Père Veillard. He was ordained March 28, 1528, at Geneva and said his first Mass at the little town of Faverges near the southern boundary of the See of Annecy. At Faverges Claude was conducting a small college when Peter came to see him and tried to persuade him that he should go to Paris to round out his theological studies. Claude, however, held back and waited about a year before he acted on Peter's advice.

Peter was back in Paris once more in January of 1534. Ignatius was able to welcome him with special pleasure because he had three more students to introduce to him as his disciples, all Spaniards, James Laínez, Alfonso Salmerón and Nicholas Bobadilla. James Laínez, small of body, cheerful looking, a quiet smile playing about his mouth, with large aquiline nose, large, exceptionally clear and lively eyes, was twenty-one years old. He was from the town of Almazán in High Castile and, despite his far from robust body, had, as Peter was to see, the heart of a lion. He came to Paris by way of Alcalá, where he had taken his Master's degree more than a year before on October 26, 1532. He placed third in a list of twenty-five candidates, but everybody knew that he had been edged out of first place in order to make way for the son of the Royal Treasurer.[27]

With Laínez there came from Alcalá Alfonso Salmerón, a beardless youth of eighteen, of medium height and with a body tough and sinewy. The youthful, open countenance, the animated and penetrating eyes of this Toledan revealed a soul serene and free from every trace of guile. He was

32

understandably not so far advanced in his studies as Laínez and was still on his way to obtaining the Master's degree.

The third was the twenty-four-year-old Nicholas Alonso y Perez, usually known as Nicholas Bobadilla because of the place from which he came, Bobadilla del Camino in High Castile. Nicholas, a genuine product of that rough country, believed in nothing if not in straightforward and uncomplicated speech. An out-and-out enemy of hypocrisy and flattery, he never left any doubt about what was on his mind. Never did Nicholas turn the expression of his face into a cover for his inner thoughts. With the complete guilelessness of Salmerón and the uninhibited bluntness of Bobadilla in mind, Ignatius once jokingly remarked some time later that there were but two dissemblers in the Society of Jesus, Salmerón and Bobadilla.[28] Nicholas did not give promise of becoming exactly a soaring eagle in the skies of the philosophical world, having had his difficulties in attaining the Bachelor's degree at Alcalá on June 20, 1529, when he placed fifty-first out of fifty-eight candidates. He came to Paris in the fall of 1533, met Ignatius, and was won by his ideals.

＊　＊　＊

Peter hardly had time to become acquainted with these new friends before he began the *Spiritual Exercises*. At least four years had passed during which Peter had been under Ignatius' direction, and it was only now that Ignatius felt that he was prepared for the demands of a thirty-day retreat. He retired to a house in the Faubourg Saint-Jacques with all the good will and thoroughness of a Saint Anthony slipping off into the Thebaid. About a week after he started, Ignatius came to see him and discovered that he had not eaten for six days, was without a fire, was sleeping on planks, and was making his meditations out in the yard in the snow. Parisians

33

remembered the extreme cold of that particular winter because the Seine had frozen so hard that the carts could be wheeled over on the ice. Ignatius told Peter that he had gained much merit by his generosity, but that he was not too sure that he should continue such great mortifications during the rest of the retreat. Ignatius decided to pray over the matter and left Peter with the assurance that he would be back in less than an hour with instructions for the remainder of the *Exercises.* He went to a nearby church, prayed, decided that Peter should keep a fire lighted and otherwise discontinue his extreme austerities.

During these days Peter had ample time to linger over and feel the strength of Ignatius' straightforward and direct phrases in the *Spiritual Exercises.*

For it is not much knowledge that fills and satisfies the soul, but the intimate understanding and relish of the truth.—Our one desire and choice should be what is more conducive to the end for which we are created.—What have I done for Christ? What am I doing for Christ? What ought I do for Christ?—Whenever the praise and glory of God would be equally served, I desire and choose poverty with Christ poor, rather than riches, in order to imitate and be in reality more like Christ Our Lord; I choose insults with Christ loaded with them, rather than honors; I desire to be accounted as worthless and a fool for Christ, rather than to be esteemed as wise and prudent in this world. So Christ was treated before me.—For everyone must keep in mind that in all that concerns the spiritual life his progress will be in proportion to his surrender of self-love and of his own will and interests.

The ideas of the *Exercises* were certainly not new to Peter, so close had he been to Ignatius for four years, but this was his unique opportunity to experience the impact of their unity, their order, their peculiar puissance.[29]

The retreat was more than just an opportunity for Peter

34

to grow in his appreciation of the principles of his spiritual father. It was a special preparation for the reception of the sacrament of Holy Orders. On February 28, 1534, in the main chapel of the Bishop's Palace near Notre Dame, Peter was ordained subdeacon. In the absence of the Bishop of Paris, Jean du Bellay, then in Rome about the business of the divorce of Henry VIII, the ordaining prelate was Milo d'Illiers, Bishop of Luçon. On April 4th he was ordained deacon by the Augustinian, Lawrence Alamandis, Bishop of Grenoble. Du Bellay was back in Paris by the end of May and on the 30th he ordained Peter a priest. This was probably the first time that this prelate, a minor light of the Renaissance, had any dealings with any of the future Society of Jesus. Years later, when he was in Rome after his falling-out with Henry II, he championed the Jesuits against Eustache du Bellay, his cousin and successor in the See of Paris and no admirer of the new Society. Peter waited a month and a half before offering his first mass on the feast of Saint Mary Magdalene, "my patron and patron of all sinners." [30]

By mid-summer of 1534 all except Xavier had made the *Spiritual Exercises*. Fixed as they were in their determination to follow Christ, they still needed to resolve a number of difficulties on just how they were to go about realizing their hopes. Their discussions were long and serious. They prayed and performed penance. Finally they decided to vow themselves, *ad maiorem rei firmitatem*, to follow Christ in poverty and chastity, and to go to Jerusalem, where they would work for the conversion of the Turk. Should the journey to the Holy Land prove to be an impossibility, they would then go to Rome and place themselves at the disposal of the Pope. During the three years that they calculated would be required to finish their theological studies, they would keep their external manner of life unchanged.[31]

In the morning of a mild summer day, the feast of Our Lady's Assumption, the seven left the Latin Quarter, crossed the Seine, passed Notre Dame, traversed the market section of Les Halles, went through the city gate to the Chapel of Saint Denis on the height of Montmartre. In the small, dark crypt of the chapel it was solitary and still. Here Peter, ordained less than three months, offered the Holy Sacrifice. His friends followed his actions at the altar as in his soft voice he broke the silence with the words of Our Lady's Mass. *Gaudeamus omnes in Domino—Let us all rejoice in the Lord, celebrating the feast in honor of the Blessed Virgin Mary, for whose Assumption the angels rejoice and join in praising the Son of God.* At the Communion Peter turned to the kneeling group and held the Sacred Host before them as each in a clear, audible voice pronounced the vows. He then gave them Holy Communion. Peter himself turned to the altar, pronounced his own vows and consumed the Blessed Sacrament. It was a simple ceremony, without pomp and circumstance, but it has become inlaid into the very history of Paris, that beautiful Crossroad of Saints, with its memories of Saint Geneviève calming the panic of the townspeople in the face of Attila sweeping from Metz; of Saint Thomas of Aquino replying, when asked by his students whether he would like to own beautiful Paris, that he would much rather have a particular text of St. John Chrysostom; of Saint Thomas of Becket remarking after his interview with Henry Plantagenet in the Chapel of Saint Denis, "Would to God that the Church might be delivered, even by my blood"; of Saint Louis, dressed in his camlet coat, mantle of black taffeta, and hat with white peacock feathers, sitting with his courtiers in the royal gardens and administering justice to his people; of Saint Jeanne d'Arc felled by an arrow shot by the garrison at the Porte Saint-Honoré. Saint Ignatius Loyola, Saint Francis Xavier, Blessed Peter Favre joined the company of those wonderful saints of the medieval world who peopled the streets of Paris before them. And as Paris turned with the rest of Europe to face the new era of the modern world, they became part of the very fibre of the city's past.

After the Mass Ignatius and his friends went to a fountain on the side of the hill and there had their repast. Here they spent the rest of the day, chatting and enjoying the gladness of heart that visited them in their consecration. "These Fathers," wrote Simon Rodrigues forty-three years later, "vowed themselves to God with a genuine and unlimited spirit of dedication. They made their offering with a spontaneity, a surrender of self-will, a trust in the Divine Mercy, that whenever I think back on the occasion, as I have often done, I am filled with intense fervor, renewed with a growth of piety, overtaken by wonder unspeakable." [32] Canon lawyers are correct when they insist that this was not the founding of the Society of Jesus. The establishment of a religious order had no part in their thoughts. There was of course not the faintest hint of anything like papal approbation. But there are things that elude the formulae of the canonists. In the hearts of these men Ignatius had written the principles and ideas which he would one day put on the printed pages of the Constitutions of the Society of Jesus, and on this day he led them in the creation of a bond of unity which was never broken. In 1546 Father Rodrigues, acting as Superior of the Jesuits in Portugal, instructed the Rector of the community at Coimbra to promulgate on the 15th of August some rules he had drawn up, because it was the anniversary of the vows at Montmartre, "to which day in a certain sense the Society of Jesus can trace its origins." [33]

The day was drawing to a close when the seven students, their minds filled with thoughts of the Holy Land, took leave of Montmartre and made their way back to the Latin Quarter. A bit to the southeast on the Ile de la Cité could be seen, graceful and delicate in the last rays of the setting sun, Sainte-Chapelle, sanctuary for the treasures from the Holy Land, the Crown of Thorns, the Lance, the Nails of the Crucifixion, and place of prayer for the noblest of France's kings, who twice raised aloft the oriflamme and led his nation's knighthood off to rescue Jerusalem from the Turk. In God's Providence Saint Louis never reached Jerusalem; neither would Ignatius and his friends.

Much study now lay ahead of them. Several had yet to take their Master's degree, and all had at least some theology to do. James Laínez recalled how they burnished their ideals, so liable to be tarnished through the routine of study. "We held fast in our purpose through a number of different means: meditation on divine things, frequent Confession and Holy Communion, the pursuit of sacred science, and then the vow by which we bound ourselves. . . ." [34] They maintained a semblance of common life by occasionally eating together, first at the residence of one of their group, and then at another's, bringing whatever food they might happen to have at the time. In these reunions they found strength and mutual encouragement. In their theological studies they scattered among the four places at Paris where lectures in theology were given, the Convent of the Dominicans, the Convent of the Franciscans, the Sorbonne and the Collège Navarre. The problem of keeping their unity was accentuated in March of 1535 when Ignatius, broken in health and acting on the advice of his doctors, left for an extended visit to Spain. At his departure Ignatius entrusted Peter, "the elder brother of us all," as Laínez remarked, with the responsibility of caring for the others.[35]

Over and above his care for his friends Peter scored two notable victories, one in the academic and the other in the apostolic field. By the spring of 1536 he had managed to put aside enough money to take his Master's biretta and in April he became Master Peter. But more precious than the Master's title were the three young men whom he received into the company of his little circle: Claude Jay, Paschase Broet and John Codure. They were the first fruits from among the many young men whom Peter in the course of his life was to win to the standard of Ignatius and the first evidence of his exceptional versatility in guiding others through the *Spiritual Exercises.*

Ignatius once made the observation that, of all the men he knew in the Society of Jesus, Peter was unmatched in giving the *Exercises.*[36] Father Jerome Nadal in an exhortation on the "Ministry of Preaching the Word of God" once took as an example Favre's ability to speak in a winning way on spiritual things. So striking was this power, observed Nadal, that the most prejudiced would capitulate to Peter, and Ignatius used to say, "Peter has the power of drawing water from a rock." But Jerome had pushed his praise just a bit too far, for there was at least one rock that would not respond to Peter's touch. And that rock was none other than Jerome himself. One year younger than Peter, this Majorcan of marked ability had come to Paris for his studies and had caught Ignatius' eye as a good prospect for his group. But Jerome kept Ignatius at a distance. Peter approached him, and Jerome's wry commentary on that meeting was: "He got nowhere." Neither did Ignatius until ten years later when, in Rome, Nadal at last found his vocation in the

Society of Jesus and became Ignatius' *alter ego* in the promulgation of the Constitutions of the Society.[37]

The first of Peter's retreatants to join the group was Claude Jay, his fellow countryman. Claude finally acted on Peter's suggestion that he give the Parisian touch to his intellectual formation, and was at the University by the beginning of the school year of 1534. Not long afterward he made the *Spiritual Exercises* under Peter's direction. Of medium height and with blond hair and gray eyes, Claude had a natural modesty and shyness as well as an amiability very much like that of his fellow Savoyard. A three-day abstinence from all food was an indication of the generous way in which he entered into the *Exercises*. On August 15, 1535, when Peter and the others returned to Montmartre to renew their vows, Claude joined them.

The second new member of the group was a thirty-five-year-old priest from Picardy, Paschase Broet. The son of prosperous farmer folk of Bertrancourt, halfway between Amiens and Arras, Paschase's stately bearing, finely proportioned face and beautiful red beard gave him the appearance of a ruler of castles and wide domains. He had begun his studies in his native village, continued them at Amiens, decided to be a priest and received Holy Orders in 1524. After ten years of priestly work in Picardy he came to Paris to round off his studies and took up residence in Collège Calvin where Bobadilla was living. He met Peter, probably through Bobadilla, and made the *Exercises* under his direction.

The third new member of the group was John Codure, a native of the tiny town of Seyne, high in the Alps and in the shadow of towering Mt. Blanc. John had already done some theology before he came to Paris, and matriculated at Collège Lisieux at the close of 1534. Innocent, intensely desirous

40

for a life of holiness, he made the *Exercises* under Peter. And on August 15, 1536, he and Broet went with Peter and his charges to Montmartre to join them in their vows which were renewed that day.

Meanwhile, war had again come to Europe. Saint Thomas More once told his son-in-law Roper that he would willingly be put into a sack and dropped into the Thames if three things that troubled Christendom could be settled. One of these three things was the chronic warfare among Christian princes. To the sorrow of men who still cherished the idea of a united Christendom, Francis and Charles were again at war in 1536. That year the *Paix des Dames* of 1529 broke down over the question of the succession to the duchy of Milan, a problem created by the death of the childless Francesco Sforza. The French troops moved into Provence as far as Fréjus. The shadow of this conflict fell over the University of Paris and made it imperative for the subjects of the Emperor to think of withdrawing from France. It was essential, therefore, to push on as fast as they could with their studies. This they promptly did, and by the fall all could take glory in the celebrated title, Master of Arts of the University of Paris.

In southern France the armies maneuvered, fought, and maneuvered again. One of the battlefield stories that very probably reached Paris was that of the gallantry of two Spanish officers at the assault on the French fortification of Muy near Fréjus. Garcilaso de la Vega, the most renowned of Castile's lyric poets, at the head of an attack was trying to scale the walls when the French hurled him from the ladder into the moat below. Another officer, the twenty-six-year-old Marquis of Lombay, Francis Borgia, jumped into the moat and carried de la Vega to safety.[38] Six years later the paths of Borgia and Favre would cross at Barcelona, and Borgia

41

would hear from Peter about the new Society of Jesus and its ideals to which, in time, he would give himself with all the gallantry and devotion that distinguished his action at the fortress of Muy. The rumblings of war in Paris became louder. In October a letter was received from the King, followed by still another from du Bellay, urging the people to carry on the work of fortification and to make the city secure against attack. On November 3rd, a procession went to Sainte-Chapelle to pray for the success of the French troops. The original plan that Ignatius drew up with his friends before he started for Spain in the spring of 1535 called for their departure from Paris on January 25, 1537. They chose Venice, port of embarkation of pilgrims to the Holy Land, as the rendezvous where Ignatius would again join them. But the war had changed the entire complexion of things. Peter and the others decided that it was imperative to delay their journey no longer if they were to have any hope of meeting Ignatius in the near future. They therefore determined to leave in mid-November.

But a journey to Venice was easier said than done. The ordinary routes into Italy from France were closed by the warring armies. They sought the advice of two of the University Doctors, who approved their plan, but made it clear that in giving approval they were not minimizing the difficulties that it involved. A third Doctor who had heard of the plan stopped Peter one day, spoke with a severe bluntness and hammered at the idea that he had no business leaving the city. "Is it true what I have been hearing about you, Favre? You are not leaving Paris, are you? It is my decided opinion that you cannot leave here without committing serious sin." The point of the Doctor's argument was that the good Peter was certainly doing in Paris was worth more than the good he might possibly do elsewhere. "Do not

42

think," he continued, "that I am speaking lightly. If you wish I shall, in a convocation of all the Doctors of the Theological Faculty of Paris, back up what I have said with the very strongest of reasons." Father Rodrigues, to whom we owe the recording of this incident, did not put down just how Peter phrased his reply to the Doctor, but simply closed the story with the abrupt remark: "Divine Providence, however, had for a long time decided otherwise." [39]

The nine friends left Paris in two groups with an interval of five or six days between them. While the first group waited at Meaux, the others distributed their possessions to the poor, save for some writing paper, books and necessary travelling money. The second group left on the 15th of November. The days of mid-November were dull, grey and rainy. But all the mists and dampness that could gather on the road through Belleville, Pantin, Bondy and Meaux could never becloud the luminous possessions they carried in their minds and hearts. Paris had given them much—contact with a rich cultural tradition, intellectual enlargement, a bond of friendship, the experience of the *Spiritual Exercises,* their common purpose and ideals, their vows. Small wonder that, as Simon Rodrigues remembered, their feet hardly touched the ground, so intense was their inner joy.[40]

III. Decisions in Italy

TO ONE who has read several of the biographies of these first disciples of Ignatius, the route they followed from Paris to Venice must be as familiar as a parade ground to a drillmaster. For the story of Laínez or Xavier or Salmerón or any one of the others on the road from Paris to Lorraine, from Lorraine to Germany, from Germany to Italy, is essentially the same. Their experiences were almost identical, and very seldom does Simon Rodrigues, to whom credit is due for gathering most of the details, turn the spotlight on any one individual. So it is that Peter's story, for the time being, becomes the story of this phalanx of students from Paris in their long, threadbare scholars' cassocks, with their broad-brimmed hats, staffs in hand, their Breviaries and notes in leather knapsacks slung across their shoulders, rosaries hung about their necks.[1] The serious possibility of meeting the warring armies in southeastern France forced them to decide on a less direct route eastward through Champagne, then southward through Lorraine and Germany into Italy.

The first group to leave Paris waited at Meaux and assisted at daily Mass at the Chapel of Saint-Fiacre two miles outside the town. When all were together again, after some deliberation, they decided to travel together rather than break up into smaller groups. They moved eastward, along the mired highways and under gray November skies, through the hilly countryside washed by the Marne, past the meadows, fields, orchards that stretched between Château-Thierry, Dormans and Épernay. At Épernay they left the Marne and travelled through the lonely tableland of Champagne to Sainte-Menhould at the border of Lorraine. It rained continuously all the time they were in France; their meals were decidedly on the lean side. Despite their precautions to take a longer route, they nevertheless ran into French soldiers who demanded that they identify themselves. The Spaniards in the group demurely kept their silence while the Frenchmen spoke up for all: "We are students of Paris." In Lorraine they turned southward through the Argonne forest and followed the route through Metz, the windswept plain of the Moselle into the valley of the Meurthe. At the end of November they arrived at the great center of pilgrimage near Nancy, Saint Nicholas-du-Port. Each day the three priests offered the Holy Sacrifice of the Mass and the non-priests received Holy Communion. One of the things Peter carried with him was his little Roman Missal, printed in Gothic type, which was lost in the destruction of the Jesuit Professed House in Madrid by the revolutionaries in 1931.[2]

A three days' walk from Saint Nicholas-du-Port brought them to Strasbourg, an important center in the Holy Roman Empire and theological citadel of the ex-Dominican Martin Bucer. Now that they were within the boundaries of the Empire it was the turn of the Spaniards, as subjects of the Emperor, to take over the office of spokesmen from their French brethren. It was now early December and that year the winter was particularly severe. Wine that was not specially protected froze in the casks.[3] The roads were covered with snow. After three days of trudging across the Alsatian plains they entered the city of Bâle, now made over to the image of Ulrich Zwingli. They were taking their lives in their hands because feeling was running high against Catholics, and more than once they had to break lances in disputation with Protestants who had challenged them.

45

Freezing cold, discomfort, danger to life and limb could not dampen the spirits of these men who in Rodrigues' words "desired with the greatest eagerness to suffer such things for God's sake." They pushed on to Constance, through the Alps, often losing their way in the high mountains and deep valleys with snow over their knees, through Trent, Bassano, Castelfranco, Mestre to the beautiful city of the lagoons where they arrived on January 8, 1537, "safe in body and joyful in spirit," as Peter observed.[4]

Ignatius had finished his sojourn at Azpeitia about the end of July, 1535, and had been at Venice since the end of December of the same year. There he continued his theological studies and gave the *Spiritual Exercises* to a considerable number of persons, several of whom were men of high position. To match the three Paris reinforcements, Jay, Broet and Codure, Ignatius was able to produce three fish of his own catching. They were Diego Hoses, a priest from Malaga in Andalusia, and two cousins of Francis Xavier from Estelle in Navarre, the brothers Estaban and Diego de Eguia. The two de Eguias had met Ignatius at Venice on their return from Jerusalem, made the *Exercises,* decided to leave the world once they had returned to Navarre to set their affairs in order, a resolve which in time brought them to Rome and Ignatius.[5]

January and the next few months of winter were no time to be out on the Mediterranean. Ignatius, therefore, found work for his ten companions while they waited the reopening of the shipping season to the Holy Land. He sent Hoses, Rodrigues and three others to the Hospital of Saints John and Paul in the Northern sector of the city, and Favre, Xavier, Laínez and two others to the Hospital of the Incurables on the Giudecca Canal, south of the Grand Canal. To the wonder of the Venetians, who came to the hospitals to

46

confirm for themselves the stories they had heard, these men, all foreigners to them, swept the buildings, made the beds, washed the sick, dug graves. Hoses heard confessions at Saints John and Paul, and Peter, whose Spanish, learned during his long years at Sainte-Barbe, seemed to give him a fair enough understanding of Italian, did the same at the Incurables. This was their regular program of mercy until the middle of Lent when Ignatius decided that it was time to go to Rome, present themselves to the Pope, explain their hopes for laboring in the Holy Land and request permission for the ordination of the non-priests. He decided to remain in Venice himself because he had good reason to believe that he was *persona non grata* to two men of influence at the Vatican, Doctor Pedro Ortiz and Cardinal Gian Pietro Caraffa. Doctor Ortiz, personal representative of Charles V at the Papal Court, had occasion to observe Ignatius' activities at Paris and was not at all kindly disposed. Caraffa, co-founder of the Theatines, would find it hard to forget that Ignatius had in no uncertain terms told him that he thought the Theatines' organizational plan left much to be desired.

On March 16th the ten disciples of Ignatius, plus two others who wanted to go to Rome and Jerusalem with them, a priest named Miguel Arias and Xavier's former servant, Miguel Landivar, started for Rome. This journey from Venice to Rome was probably the equal in hardship of the earlier journey from Paris to Venice. Peter and his friends seemed to have a bent for being on the road when traveling conditions were at the worst. They had come from Paris through winter's snow; now with the heavy spring rains they met swollen streams and flooded countryside. Faithful to the Lenten fast all the way and not always enjoying the best of success in begging, there were times when they almost starved. Simon Rodrigues recalled that often enough

47

it looked as though they could not go a step further, so exhausted were they from hunger and fatigue. But each one diverted his attention from his own discomfort by an outpouring of sympathy and concern for the sufferings of others. On Passion Sunday, when they had but two small loaves of bread among them, they came to the River Po, heavily swollen and overflowing its banks. They persuaded a reluctant boatman to ferry them across to the other bank, but that did not save them from the need of walking through the overflow that was sometimes up to their chests. They then came upon a pine tree grove which provided them with a welcome supplement to the two loaves of bread. So acute was their hunger that they took to breaking and eating the pine cones they found there. At Ancona one of the travelers, whom Rodrigues singled out for his exceptional talents and learning, walked among the market women begging some food and receiving from one a radish, from another some fruit, from the others a like contribution. Rodrigues too obtained some fruit, as he said, on this occasion, namely, the conviction of his own unworthiness to be in the company of men of such holiness.[6] They broke their journey by a three-day visit at the Shrine of the Holy House of Loretto and on Palm Sunday, March 25, 1537, they walked through the Porta del Popolo into the Eternal City.

The group first lodged in the hospitals of their respective nationalities. Soon the impoverished state of the new arrivals came to the notice of some Spaniards who, impressed by their evident selflessness and touched by a sense of national pride, saw to it that all, including even the French, were taken care of at the Hospital of St. James where they received simple but sufficient food.[7] On Tuesday of Easter Week they had an audience with the Holy Father. Strangely enough, this privilege was obtained through the kind favor

48

of none other than one of the two men whom Ignatius preferred not to meet, Doctor Ortiz. This rather corpulent and rotund Spanish priest, high in the esteem of such men as Cardinals Contarini and Aleander, did a sudden about-face in his attitude toward Ignatius' activities and became one of his most energetic supporters.[8] Pope Paul III could not but give a gracious reception to men so obviously devoted to poverty and with a background of theological training at Paris. Elected just less than two months after their vows at Montmartre in 1534, this man of intense intellectual power and broad diplomatic experience realized that a break had to be made with the Papal system of the Borgia, the Rovere and the de Medici clans. Yet Paul did not go the whole way in his dedication to the cause of Catholic reform and often enough he sacrificed the interests of the Church to those of the Farnese family. To his contemporaries, Alessandro Farnese was somewhat of an enigma, pressing for the spiritual revitalization of the Church even while he remained in some ways a child of the Renaissance. "Things new and old contended within him." [9]

The audience which Paul III granted these new arrivals in Rome was of a rather odd sort and definitely put them on their mettle. It was a combination meal and intellectual discussion. While Paul dined, the men from Venice carried on an oral review of things theological. The Pope was delighted with their performance, especially because they carried their learning with an attractive modesty and humility. He rose from table, held his arms outstretched as though he would embrace them all, told them that if there was anything he could do for them he would be glad to do it. They knelt at his feet and told him of their hopes. Their request for permission to go to Jerusalem he gladly granted, but his awareness that once more the war clouds were forming over the Mediterranean area prompted him to add, "I think it hardly likely that you will get there." [10] This first meeting of Alessandro Farnese, Pope of an era of papal change, with his arms outstretched, and Favre, Laínez, Bobadilla, Salmerón, men identified with the flood tide of Catholic reform, kneeling at the feet of the Supreme Pontiff, had a significance and meaning for the future hardly guessed by those who looked on.

Although the audience had taken place on April 3rd, their return to the Republic of Saint Mark was held up until the beginning of May. The Pope's permissions, expansively and spontaneously given, were nevertheless quite informal, and it was still necessary to place all in order according to the protocol at the Vatican Chancery. They received a taste of how terribly time-consuming official procedure can be and how formal a process it was to draw up the necessary documents and send them through the proper channels. Peter as spokesman for his friends took care of the written petition to the Holy Father for permission to go to the Holy Land. It was April 27th before Cardinal Pucci set his stamp of approval on the request. On the same day the Cardinal also gave them the official document conveying the approval of the ordination of the non-priests. Three days later Cardinal Ghinnuci issued the document with papal permission for Favre, Arias and Hoses to hear confessions and absolve from cases reserved to the bishops. [11]

It was, therefore, a story of a successful mission to Rome that they could give Ignatius on their return to Venice in early May. Their hopes of sailing to the Holy Land that summer, however, gradually diminished in an atmosphere of persistent rumor that Venice, the Emperor and the Papacy were forming an alliance against the Moslems. Relations between the Venetian Republic and the Ottoman Empire had become strained, and as early as the previous year reports were in the air that the Sultan was readying an expedition against Italy. Venice was playing a game of waiting, but this strategy collapsed in the face of the Sultan's declaration of war against her and his attack on Corfu. Despite misgivings, the first seapower of Europe was forced into an alliance with the Papacy and the Empire. There was no point in drafting plans for a pilgrimage across the Mediterranean that summer.

On the feast of Saint John the Baptist, June 24, 1537, six were ordained to the priesthood by the Bishop of Arbe, Vincenzo Nigusanti. Because he had not yet reached the minimum canonical age, Salmerón had to postpone his reception of Orders. The newly ordained did not say their first Masses immediately but went back to the hospitals to care for the sick as they had done a few months before. By the end of July, however, they realized that this work was not allowing them the recollection that they would like to have as preparation for their first Masses. They decided, therefore, to scatter to various parts of the Venetian territory in groups of two or three and devote themselves to prayer and meditation. On July 25th, Peter accompanied Ignatius and Laínez to Vicenza, Xavier and Salmerón went to Montelice, Jay and Rodrigues to Bassano, Broet and Bobadilla to Verona, Hoses and Codure to Treviso.

Ignatius, Peter and James Laínez found an abandoned convent of the Hieronymites of Fiesole standing in an open field a short distance outside the Porta di Santa Croce of Vicenza. The convent had been a war casualty with doors and windows ripped away. Here the three stayed alone for forty days. They slept on a bit of straw which they had brought with them. Ignatius took over the work of cooking whatever Favre and Laínez were able to beg in the city. He was never overburdened with labor, but his ingenuity was certainly taxed, because frequently all his friends brought back from their begging tour was a little bread. The monotony of the diet was occasionally broken by a little oil or butter, and it is small wonder that Ignatius and Laínez both became ill and ran a fever.[12] While Ignatius was recuperating, but still a rather weak man, word came that Simon Rodrigues was extremely ill at Bassano. Disregarding his own condition Ignatius left Laínez in the hospital at Vicenza, took Peter with him and headed for Bassano. Ignatius moved along with the speed of an army on a forced march, and Peter had all he could do to keep up with him. On the road, with the assurance he received in prayer, Ignatius told Peter that their Portuguese friend would not die. They found Simon in a hermitage outside the town and, despite his condition, lying on some planks. Ignatius embraced Simon "*in Domino*," and immediately Rodrigues felt his strength begin to return, a grace which both he and Favre were convinced was an answer to the prayer of Ignatius. But Ignatius' concern did not stop with prayer, for he insisted that Rodrigues be properly cared for and that the planks be replaced by a bed.[13] Simon was soon on the way to recovery and Ignatius and Peter started back for Vicenza on September 1st.

After forty days at Treviso, Codure rejoined Ignatius, Peter and Laínez, apparently the first to do so. Swallowing whatever promptings of human respect might have deterred them because of their poor command of Italian, they decided to launch a program of preaching in the town. It was a well-synchronized venture, for on the same day the four took up positions on four different streets of the town, and at the very same hour. To gather an audience they first shouted and waved their hats. In a way Ignatius set the literary tone of the sermons by the very first word out of his mouth. He

wanted to say in Italian: "Today Holy Mother Church, etc."
The French *aujourd'hui* became mixed up with the Italian
oggi and fell from his lips as *hojuordi*. Results at first were
what might be expected from such a babel of tongues. In
time, however, the fire of charity that inspired the garbled
words of these four men touched the souls of Vicenza's
citizens, who rallied to their visiting preachers and saw to it
that they no longer lived in such extreme want.[14]

With the conclusion of the rigorous preparation for their
first Masses, the others returned during September to
Vicenza from the different corners of the Venetian Republic.
About this great event of their lives, the first time they
offered the Eucharistic Sacrifice, they have written hardly a
word. Rodrigues deferred his for a while and said it at
Ferrara. Ignatius, possibly with the hope of saying his at
Bethlehem, waited a year and then said it on Christmas
day, 1538, at the altar of the Crib of the Saviour in the
Basilica of Saint Mary Major in Rome. Summer was over and
with it passed the hope of sailing to the Holy Land in the
immediate future. By the terms of their vow, January 8,
1538, the anniversary of their arrival at Venice from Paris
would be the date on which their obligation to go to the
Holy Land would cease. After this they were to place themselves at the disposal of the Holy Father.[15] In October they
decided on another temporary dispersion, this time to the
universities in the northern and central parts of Italy with
the hope of interesting other young men in their ideals. Jay
and Rodrigues were to go to Ferrara, Xavier and Bobadilla
to Bologna, Broet and Salmerón to Siena, Codure and Hoses
to Padua. Doctor Ortiz' cordiality of the previous spring had
apparently removed Ignatius' reluctance to go to the Eternal
City, and so it was there that he went, accompanied by
Favre and Laínez.

Three years had elapsed since the first time they pronounced their vows at Montmartre. In the oneness of their ideals and aspirations they had become more and more identified with each other in a unity that was easily discernible by others and which naturally provoked questioning. They felt it was time to decide just what they should call themselves. The group therefore prayed and pondered over the question. The only leader they had was Christ Jesus. Him alone it was their desire to serve. It was only proper, then, that they should call themselves the Company of Jesus, *Compañía de Jesús*. And so it was decided.[16] Ignatius, Favre and Laínez started for Rome about the 15th of October.

Nine miles from Rome at La Storta the three travelers entered the chapel located at the cross of the old Claudian and Cassian ways. There Ignatius received a vision of God the Father and Christ Our Lord with His Cross, the Father placing Ignatius near to Christ and Christ saying, "I shall be with you." [17] This vision confirmed Ignatius in his conviction that *Company of Jesus* was the proper name for his little group. But the words that were spoken, as he told Favre and Laínez, were a portent of difficulties ahead, for at the time he heard them he also saw in a storm of tribulation all the doors of Rome closed to them. "I am not sure," he said, "but that they may crucify us in Rome. But one thing I am certain of, Christ Jesus will be favorable to us." With this assurance that their Divine Leader would be caring for them in the Eternal City, come what may, they passed through the Flaminian Gate toward the end of October.[18]

* * *

Months of trial and distress at Rome Ignatius and his friends were most certainly to have, in full measure and flowing over. In the beginning, however, their initial experiences could not have been more encouraging. Doctor Ortiz gave them a most cordial welcome. A gentleman named Quirino Garzonio, son of the fashionable and wealthy Roman patrician, Gasparo Garzonio, extended to them the use of his country home situated on a hill crowned by the Convent of Trinita de' Monti. Small wonder that Ignatius referred to his benefactor as "*molto magnifico Signore*." [19] Pope Paul manifested his confidence by his assignment of Favre and Laínez, probably at the recommendation of Ortiz, to professorial positions at Rome's university, the Sapienza—the former as lecturer on Holy Scripture and Positive Theology, and the latter as lecturer on Scholastic Theology. The Sapienza had been a victim in the devastating sack of Rome in 1527 and had been closed by Clement VII. Paul was anxious to recreate the brilliance it enjoyed in the days of Leo X and was therefore on the watch for professors who would accomplish this for him. Favre and Laínez joined the faculty in November, 1537, and in all likelihood held their positions until May of 1539.[20] They also joined the ranks of those theologians who went regularly to the Papal Palace to provide the Holy Father with the theological discussion he desired as part of the atmosphere at dinner.

Meanwhile, Ignatius busied himself in giving the *Spiritual Exercises*. Among his retreatants could be numbered such important personages as Doctor Ortiz and the refined and noble-minded Gaspar Contarini, elevated to the Cardinalate in 1535 and generally respected for his intelligent approach to the problems of ecclesiastical reform. The completeness of Ortiz' devotion to Ignatius was shown in the way he extended his retreat, normally a month, to forty days. He would gladly have joined Ignatius' group but for his excessive weight which, so it was judged, rendered him unfit

55

for the kind of work contemplated by Ignatius.[21] Through the good will of such retreatants and the scholarly work of Favre and Laínez at the Sapienza, a certain permanence was attained, and Ignatius felt it was time for others to come to Rome from northern and central Italy. By the latter part of April, shortly after Easter, all had arrived at the Eternal City and joined Ignatius, Favre and Laínez at the house under the Trinita de' Monti.

On May 5th Cardinal Vincenzo Caraffa gave all of them faculties to preach, hear confessions, absolve from certain reserved cases. They fanned out through the city and preached in several different churches, including San Salvatore in Lauro, San Luigi di' Francesi, San Angelo in Pescheria. Peter and Francis Xavier worked together at the church of San Lorenzo in Damaso. It was more than just their labored Italian that caused something of a sensation in the city. Lent and Advent were the time-honored seasons for preaching at Rome. And this the monks had kept as their own special preserve. When, therefore, these newcomers to Rome stepped into the pulpits during the Paschal season, people gaped in amazement and commented, "We thought that only monks did preaching." [22]

There seemed to be no limit to the good will that Ignatius and his followers found in Rome. But all was not as well as appeared on the surface. Ever since the previous Lent, when Ignatius, Favre and Laínez were alone, a storm had been in the making. The troublemaker was an Augustinian Friar named Fra Agostino de Piemonte. Fra Agostino was the Lenten preacher at the church of his Order near the Piazza Novara. Favre and Laínez dropped in to hear the friar, and on their astonished ears, attuned somewhat to the sound of heterodoxy from their experiences with Protestants in Germany and Switzerland, there fell the familiar theses of

Lutheranism. They approached Fra Agostino privately and in a spirit of charity tried to point out to him his errors. Their admonition was ignored. Their next step was to take to the pulpit themselves and smash what Rodrigues called "the cup of heresy" that was being offered to the Roman people.[23] It was an audacious move because in crossing swords with Fra Agostino they were combatting no mere theological pygmy. He was a "name" preacher; he was Prior of San Agostino in Pavia; he was a spellbinder in the pulpit. His majestic appearance and his stirring eloquence won for him a great following, including some of the people in the Spanish curia at Rome. It was in fact three of these Spaniards who jumped to the defense of the friar and, being of the mentality that believes name-calling is the best answer to an argument, set up a nasty smear campaign against the admonitors of their hero. Charges ran from the ridiculous to the serious. Ignatius was supposed to have said that he hoped to receive just as much heavenly glory as the Apostle Paul, if not more than he; Ignatius and his friends were wanted by authorities in Spain, Paris, Venice and other Italian states on charges of heresy. These stories spread through the city. The chief calumniators, Francisco de Mudarra, Pedro de Castilla and an accomplice named Barrera, found a very accommodatingly spiteful witness for their stories in Miguel Landivar, who was once Xavier's servant. Miguel kept bobbing up now and again in the alternate role of sinister adversary or repentant sinner. At Paris he had threatened to kill Ignatius for winning Xavier to his ideals; at Venice he wanted to join Ignatius on his enterprise to the Holy Land; at Rome he was faithless to his resolution and disappeared with Antonio Arias; later at Rome he returned to the fold with many protestations of sorrow for his fickleness and threw all the blame on Arias; now he was star witness against his former friends as one who knew from personal experience the inner workings of this infamous group of men. Fra Agostino's champions were not exactly agreed on what precise punishment should be meted out to the men of the "Company of Jesus," but all their recommendations, diverse as they were, were drastic enough. Some would have them burned to death; others would send them into exile; others would condemn them to the galleys. Ignatius' anticipation of serious trials was being realized. The storm was serious enough to shake the confidence of a certain priest named Lawrence García, who had recently joined Ignatius. For García, prudence was the better part of valor; so he left Rome in a hurry and headed for Paris.

Ignatius reacted to the whole situation with sureness and precision. His objective was the complete exoneration of himself and his friends and he persevered, even though it took eight months, until he attained it. Landivar was convicted of lying and exiled from the city. Mudarra and Barrera retracted in the presence of Benedetto Conversini, the governor of Rome. This brought the campaign of slander to a close, but Ignatius wanted more than just the silencing of the liars. A great deal of damage had been done and he felt that the only way it could be repaired was by an official declaration of innocence. Doctor Ortiz and other friends, even his companions, urged him to leave well enough alone. Ignatius, however, would not be dissuaded and he took the matter personally to the Pope. He had his way, for on November 18th Benedetto Conversini placed his signature to a document vindicating the life and teaching of Ignatius of Loyola and his companions. Polanco closed his description of the affair as follows: "What Satan cooked up to bring down the Society at its very beginning, God turned to the increase of its good odor and reputation." [24]

58

Twice during these stormy months they changed their residence. The home of Quirino Garzonio at Trinita de' Monti could not conveniently house the increased number when all had assembled in Rome in April. To find suitable lodgings for the summer months some friends rented a house for them near to the residence of Doctor Ortiz at Ponte Sisto. They moved in on June 1st and stayed until the lease expired on September 30th. Friends again anticipated their needs and arranged the rental of a house from a gentleman named Antonio Frangipani, situated not far from Aracoeli church near the Torre del Melangolo.

Within a week after Conversini's decree of innocence of November 18th, Ignatius and his companions found themselves in a situation which prompted them to make a decision of major importance. It all started with a chance remark by the Pope. One day some of the Fathers were at the Papal Palace carrying on one of their mealtime theological discussions. Paul threw the question to them: "Why are you men so set on going to Jerusalem? You have a truly genuine Jerusalem here in Italy if you are anxious to accomplish some good in God's Church." The disputants brought what the Pope said back to their companions. This started them on a new line of thought. Almost a year had passed since the obligation of their vow to go to Jerusalem had lapsed. Despite this fact, they remained reluctant to give up hope of eventually getting to Palestine. They had said nothing to the Pope about the alternate part of their vow by which they were to place themselves at his disposal in lieu of the pilgrimage. But now the time for this was clearly at hand. They sought an audience with Paul III, and in a spirit of sacrifice they presented themselves to him as ready to go to any part of the world, even the Indies, should he so desire. The Pope accepted their offer which, in the words of Favre, was "a

memorable blessing and the quasi-foundation of the whole
Society. . . . Therefore I shall ever feel, as indeed does
each of the others, the obligation of giving thanks to Christ
Jesus, Head of the Universal and Catholic Church, Who
through the voice of His Vicar on earth has deigned to
show His pleasure in our serving Him and His wish to use us
in aeternum." [25]

The norm for their future apostolate was now publicly
ratified: the good pleasure of the Supreme Pontiff. In a day
or two after their audience with Paul III, Peter had occasion
to appeal to this norm in a letter to an old friend at Paris, the
President of Sainte-Barbe, Dr. Gouveia. Gouveia had received a letter from a former student of his, Jeronimo Osorio,
with news that would quicken any apostolic heart, the story
of the conversion of 60,000 Malabarese in India. The news
from Osorio set him to writing, first, to King John of Portugal
to tell him about Ignatius' group, who by their piety and
learning were just the men for the missions in the Portuguese
Indies, and then to Simon Rodrigues to spread before him
and his companions the panorama of a tremendous apostolic
opportunity. Gouveia, of course, knew that Simon and his
friends were especially taken up with the idea of a mission
among the Moslems in the Holy Land. But he had his special
bait to draw them away from that plan. "The language of
India," wrote the good Doctor, "is much easier to learn than
the Moslem tongue, and the hearts of their people are more
receptive and less obdurate than those of the Moors." [26] In
the name of Simon and all of their group, Peter answered
Gouveia's letter. Much as they appreciated the good Doctor's
interest in the Indies, it was not for them to decide whether
or not they should go there. They had surrendered their
freedom of movement to the Pope, who, as Universal Pastor,
knew better than anyone else the varying needs of the dif-

ferent parts of the Church. "If the Pope will send us where you speak of," wrote Peter, "we shall go, and with joy in our hearts. . . . Distance indeed has no fears for us. Nor does the labor of learning another language. Only let that be done which is most pleasing to Christ." [27]

At Christmas 1538, winter took hold of Rome with a ruthless, relentless grip and did not let loose until the end of May. Bitter cold, endless rain and sleet forged a season that few could ever forget, the worst Rome had experienced in forty years. The crops in the neighboring farmlands had been poor. The prices of corn, oil, cheese, wheat spiraled to unheard-of heights. Cattle, sheep, goats, cows died of the cold. Famine swept the countryside and droves of people from the Campagna and the towns in the mountains poured into Rome for food and shelter. The city was not prepared for this flood of humanity who met closed doors on all sides. They roamed through the streets that in the mornings were dotted with the stiff corpses of those who had frozen to death during the night. "No one," recorded Simon Rodrigues in one melancholy sentence, "took care of these poor people, no one showed any friendliness. Nor was any to be found who was touched by the calamities of these miserable wretches." [28] Into this scene of desolation the men of the "Company of Jesus" stepped with a radiant charity that carried into the narrow alleys of sixteenth-century Rome the compassion of Christ for the multitude on Galilee's hillside. By night they went through the streets and brought back to their house the poor they had found. At the house they washed their feet, gave them the bread they had themselves begged. They warmed them at the fire kept alive by the wood they themselves had collected. They put them to bed on straw they themselves had gathered. These corporal works of mercy were supplemented by instruction in the

61

catechism and in prayer. Some way or other they were able to put three to four hundred under their roof. Over and beyond these, the Fathers were able to care for about two thousand others in other parts of the city.

But all this suffering did not dim the grandeur of the gaudy and showy events of the Carnival Days of 1539. Large amounts of money, including papal funds, were wasted on this annual extravaganza. Sports events, normally held at Monte Testacio, were run off on the Piazza San Pietro. From the Castel San Angelo, Paul III, still under the spell of the Renaissance, reviewed the procession with its mighty carriages and with its line-up of city officials all decked out in costumes of the ancient world. It was a pagan show, and men of the courage of Caraffa and Contarini let it be known, the Pope notwithstanding, that they thought it an unbecoming and shameful performance.[29] In time, the exquisite charity of Ignatius and his disciples shattered the complacency of the well-to-do at Rome. Men of distinguished position, even Cardinals, confessed their shame at the sight of poor men, themselves without necessary food, carrying on a charitable work of such proportions while they, blessed with wealth, were doing nothing.[30] Feeling now the warmth of fire, savouring the pith of bread, sensing the tenderness of compassionate love, the poor of Rome looked into the faces of Ignatius, Peter, Francis, Claude and the others to discover gazing upon them the eyes of Christ, for the life with which these men were fired was the very life of Christ, and the desire they shared in common was that of knowing Christ more intimately, loving Him more ardently, following Him more closely. These were the things the Romans saw; and they were great things. But what they did not see was something Ignatius and his little circle were putting together by night when the day's work was done, something destined

62

to endure for centuries. During the Lent of 1539 they drew up with clear, bold lines the plans for a new religious order.

* * *

On March 19, Gian Pietro Caraffa put his name to a document by virtue of which Father Paschase Broet was ordered to take a companion from among the "Company of Jesus" and proceed "in virtue of holy obedience" to Siena and there to undertake the reform of the Monasteries of San Prospero and Sant' Agnese.[31] This order was the first wedge that threatened to break apart the unity of the men of the "Company of Jesus." That others would follow was inevitable since, as Ignatius observed, they had been *"infestados"* by requests from different prelates to work within their jurisdictions. Face to face with the prospect of never being together again after so many years of close companionship, they decided to talk over among themselves their future manner of life and the precise nature of their vocation. Their considerations were conducted in a most systematic way, particular *"dubia"* being discussed step by step and approached with singular detachment of spirit. By day, when they could find time, they prayed and reflected; at night each presented his own personal conclusion. It was either John Codure or Peter Favre who acted as secretary and wrote out the account of the proceedings. On every sentence of the account is the imprint of the earnestness, the sincerity, the simplicity with which these men wrestled with the problem of their future relationship.[32]

When Lent was almost over and the time was upon us when we must be divided and separated from one another, . . . we decided to meet for several days before our separation and discuss among ourselves the subject of our vocation and manner of life. After several meetings we discovered ourselves, some of us being

63

French, others Spaniards, others Savoyards, others Portuguese, to be split by differences of opinion on the question of our particular state in life. Yet in all of us there was one common mind and purpose, the seeking of God's good pleasure and His Perfect Will. . . . It was on the point of just what were the more expedient and fruitful means of achieving this Divine Will that our judgments were splintered. . . . Nor should anyone be surprised that this diversity should have existed among us, frail and weak as we are, when even the leaders and pillars of Holy Church, the Apostles, differed among themselves. . . . In view of this conflict of opinion that went nevertheless hand in hand with our intense desire of discovering some sort of *via media*, acceptable to all, we eventually reached the unanimous decision to give ourselves more fervently than usual to prayer, sacrifice and meditation. . . .

We therefore set to work and proposed to ourselves some *"dubia"* that merited carefully mature reflection and forethought. On these we thought, meditated, prayerfully pondered during the day. With a view to arriving at the truer judgment, tested and examined by the searching inquiries of several minds, at night each one presented to the group his personal opinion of what he judged the more expedient and proper.

On the first night that we met, this *"dubium"* was proposed: would it be better, now that we had offered and dedicated our life to Christ Our Lord and to His true and legitimate Vicar on earth to dispose of us as he willed, would it be better that we be so joined and bound into one body that no corporal division, no matter how great, would separate us one from another? That this point might be illustrated by an example: at this time the Pontiff is sending two of us to the city of Siena. Should we be mindful of those two and they of us in a spirit of common understanding, or should we have no greater concern about them than we have for those who are not of the Society? At length we decided in the affirmative, that, inasmuch as the Most Clement and Loving Lord had deigned to unite us, weak as we are and from such a variety of countries and backgrounds, we ought not break the God-given bond of unity, but rather confirm and strengthen it with the passage of time. . . .[33]

So run the proceedings of these meetings for fourteen pages of the *Monumenta Historica Societatis Jesu*. With the basic decision of preserving their unity arrived at, they then spent nearly three months at the task of delineating the character, the functions, the spirit of their body. Nearly an entire month was devoted to the second *"dubium"* on the list, the question of whether they should add to their vows of poverty and chastity, pronounced at Montmartre, the vow of obedience to one of their number. To do so would be the equivalent of forming a religious order. They spent several days in prayer and reflection, but received no light. So intent were they on discovering God's Will that they contemplated retiring into solitude for thirty or forty days, and by prayer, fasting and penance move God to clear up their indecision. This suggestion was overruled on the ground that their absence from Rome would give occasion for all sorts of gossip and ridiculous rumors. Besides, they were most reluctant to give up, even for a short while, their fruitful ministry of preaching and hearing confessions.

They therefore pressed their deliberations at Rome. To guarantee that the opinion of each would be the fruit of his own personal prayer and reflection, and free from possible influence of another, they decided not to talk over the question with one another except at the actual gathering for that purpose. One day was set aside for the presentation of objections to the vow of obedience. One of the Fathers felt that their human failings and sins would lessen the esteem of the faithful for the idea of the religious life and obedience. Another feared the possibility that the Pope, once aware that they desired to live under obedience, would force them to join an already established order in which their desire to work for souls might be frustrated. A third thought that the vow of obedience would frighten away prospective fellow workers, of whom many were needed for labor in the vast vineyard of the Lord. On the next day arguments in favor of the vow of obedience were advanced. One Father argued very practically. To try to handle everyday affairs without the obligation of obedience is an impossibility; what everybody is supposed to do none will do; without clear-cut responsibility each one tends to let the onus fall on the shoulders of another, "as we ourselves have not infrequently found out," added the Father, driving his point home. A second member of the group argued that without obedience their body would not be able to persevere. A third pressed for obedience on ascetical grounds. Obedience brings forth heroic and persevering virtue, because the man bound by obedience is most prompt to do what he is told, no matter how difficult. Besides, nothing cuts down pride and arrogance so effectively as does obedience.

For nearly a month they wrestled with this question, and like Jacob with the angel they would not let go until it yielded its answer to them. Their conclusion read:

For us it is both more expedient and urgent that we give obedience to one of our number. And this for a number of reasons: first, that we might the better and more definitely attain our initial desire of doing in all things the Divine Will; second, that the Society might be more surely preserved; third, that the details of business, both spiritual and temporal, might be cared for in the manner that they should.[34]

The gravity with which they regarded their decision, already reflected in the length and carefulness of the debate, was registered in the ceremony reminiscent of the solemnity

66

of their day of vows at Montmartre. During the discussions Peter Favre acted as confessor for the others, and on April 15th he assumed a role very like the one he played in the Chapel of Saint Denis on August 15th, 1534. While his friends knelt in prayer he celebrated Mass. At the Communion he asked each one if it was his desire that they form a religious order, dependent of course on the pleasure of the Pope, and if he was willing to join this same religious order. Each answered Peter in the affirmative and then received from him Holy Communion. After Mass each put his name to a document which read:

I . . . the undersigned state in the presence of Almighty God and the Most Blessed Virgin Mary and the entire heavenly court that, after prayer to God and after mature thought, I have freely arrived at the decision that it is more to God's praise and the Society's preservation that the vow of obedience be pronounced. Further, that I have deliberately offered myself, aside from any vow or other obligation, to enter the same Society, if the Pope *Domino concedente* should grant his confirmation. To the keeping of the memory of this decision, which I acknowledge is a gift of God, I now, with the same deliberation and despite my unworthiness, approach Holy Communion. The 15th of April, 1539.[35]

They acted with a sense of finality. The group had started a furrow in which was planted the seed of God's grace and which is still being traced across the field of the world's history.

Further discussions on the character of their organization moved along much more rapidly than those on the vow of obedience. Peter, acting as secretary, recorded their conclusions through May and part of June on such points as the teaching of catechism, the training of novices, the lifelong term of the general superior. At the beginning of May, Broet, accompanied by Rodrigues, set out for his mission to Siena. Bobadilla meanwhile had been designated for work in the Kingdom of Naples. This was the beginning of the diaspora they anticipated. It was next the turn of Peter and James Laínez. Cardinal Ennio Filonardi, recently assigned to the Legation of Parma, wanted two of the men of the "Company of Jesus," and the lot fell to them. Even before they could conclude the debates on the structure of their Company, they were on the road to Parma. That June 20th was a day of deeper separation than Peter could have imagined, for it was the last time that he saw John Codure, Paschase Broet, Alfonso Salmerón, Claude Jay, Francis Xavier. And it would be seven years before he would again see Ignatius, for it was to be that long before he would return to Rome.

IV. *Parma Dons an Aureole*

IN THE age of Frederick Barbarossa the cities of northern Italy, united by the ties of the Lombard League, formed a band across the top of the Italian peninsula that gave the Pope his first line of defense against the Hohenstaufen. On that vigorous ring of towns that stretched from the Genoan Gulf to the Adriatic Sea, Alexander III had staked his hopes in his struggle with the Emperor. This twelfth-century alliance of Papacy and Lombard League was in a sense re-created in the sixteenth century when Paul III, pushing his program of church reform, found in a number of these same Italian cities valuable allies against another enemy from north of the Alps, Lutheranism. The Popes would have been powerless in their determination to revitalize the Church were it not for the extraordinary number of devoted Bishops throughout the different parts of Christendom. And some of the staunchest Papal supporters were in the cities of northern Italy. The most illustrious was Gian Matteo Giberti of Verona whose legislation was adopted in several instances almost word for word by the Council of Trent. It was the spirit of Giberti that influenced the energetic and severe Cardinal Ercole Gonzaga of Mantua. Bernhard von Cles labored for reform in Trent, Francesco Cornaro in Brescia, Francesco Pisani in Padua and Treviso. The prestige of the Bishop of Modena, Giovanni Morone, spread far beyond his own diocese when he became one of the leading representatives of the Papacy in the work of reform in Germany.[1] These cities became islands of spiritual energy in the area of the Po, the Adige and the Miacio, and from them, through the initiative of the Bishops and the devoted lives of the newly founded Theatines, Barnabites and Ursulines, there radiated an idealism and a love for the Church that gradually cut into the gains made by ignorance, infidelity and secularism. It was the task of Favre and Laínez to lift Parma to a spiritual awareness that would enable that city to take its place with Verona, Padua, Mantua, Brescia in this sixteenth-century spiritualized Lombard League.

The Legation of Parma, including the two principal cities of Parma and Piacenza, came within the orbit of Papal government in 1512 when it was united to the States of the Church and was formed into the Province of Gallia Cispadana under the jurisdiction of a Papal Legate. One of those small fragments of territory north of Tuscany caught in the political cross currents of Renaissance Italy, Parma was in 1539 midway between a past of medieval Guelf loyalties and a future linked with the fortunes of the Farnese family. The Papal Legate in 1539 was the future Pope Julius III, Cardinal Giovanni Maria Ciocchi del Monte, who had received his assignment to Parma in October of 1537. Del Monte faced a nasty situation in his new jurisdiction, particularly because of the corruption among the priests, some of whom had put aside their cassocks, sported firearms and acted no better than street ruffians. War with its endless maneuvering of armed forces took its toll on the morals of the people; and this spiritual chaos was the right kind of soil for the doctrines of Lutheranism transplanted into northern Italy from Germany.[2] Cardinal Ennio Filonardi, appointed to succeed Del Monte in April of 1539 before the latter completed the customary biennium as Legate, was not blind to the situation he had to face and asked the Pope for two of the men from the "Company of Jesus" to assist him. Paul III left it up to the Fathers to decide which two should go.

70

Favre and Laínez were chosen. After almost two weeks on the road with Cardinal Filonardi, they entered Parma on July 1st.

The Cardinal invited his two yeomen to reside at the Legate's palace, but they chose to stay at the hospital of the Compagnia della Disciplina. The beginnings of their apostolic work were modest enough, limited as they were to the public exposition of Holy Scripture. Laínez spoke in the Cathedral, and Favre in the Church of San Gervasio e Protasio, recently committed to the care of the Friars of the Strict Observance. But it was not long before the citizens of Parma were aware of a new force in their city. In an age when preaching was almost unheard of, the talks by Favre and Laínez were draughts of clear cool water to parched throats. The widespread ignorance and superstition that prompted some one to call Abruzzi and Calabria an *India Italica* had its counterpart in northern Italy. In their program for church reform Cardinals Contarini, Pole, Caraffa and Cervini stressed the need of a rebirth of sacred eloquence. When, therefore, they found their city visited by these apostles of the spoken word, a number of the educated and cultured class approached Favre and Laínez with the request that they expand the scope of their talks beyond exclusively scriptural topics to include problems of morality and Christian living. This Peter and James did each Sunday and feast-day.[3] Within a few months the results were noteworthy enough to prompt the City Council to write to their representatives at Rome about it. They reported that about a hundred persons, some of them not particularly distinguished for piety in the past, were now confessing and receiving Holy Communion each month, and that this was the fruit of the preaching by Favre and Laínez, done *"con tanto fervore e bonissimo modo."* [4]

71

In itself the number one hundred does not seem particularly remarkable, but the fact that it was deemed a matter sufficiently important to be included in the report by the City Council points to the low ebb of sacramental life among the people in early sixteenth-century Italy. The sacrament of Penance had fallen into desuetude. There were priests who said Mass, chanted the Office, received income from their benefices, but to whom the hearing of confessions was a repugnant burden. In this wasteland of spiritual apathy, however, hope for a religious awakening was not completely dead, a hope nourished by a rich stream of Eucharistic devotion flowing through the centuries from its fountainhead in medieval Liége. Started by Saint Mary d'Aignies, it was carried into the Renaissance by the Brothers of the Common Life. Then Saint Ignatius and his men of the "Company of Jesus" joined the Theatines and Barnabites and channeled the waters of supernatural life to the towns and regions where they taught and preached.[5] This was the objective for which Favre and Laínez labored at Parma in their stress, day in and day out, on the need for the sacraments of Penance and Holy Eucharist in a vigorous Catholic life.

But what distinguished their work from that of other apostles working for the same renewal of sacramental life was the stamp that it bore of the *Spiritual Exercises*. For the most part Favre and Laínez taught within the framework of the *Exercises,* and it was this that gave their mission to Parma its unique character. They gave the *Exercises* to individuals or to small groups. These retreatants themselves became directors for many others. In this way the purifying power of the meditations on sin and the inspirational force of the contemplations on the Person of Christ radiated throughout the city. In March of 1540, nine months after their arrival, Peter wrote to Ignatius that he was unable to estimate the

72

number of retreatants, so many people were there who were giving the *Exercises*. Three months later Laínez sent a like report to Ignatius, recounting how recent exercitants were themselves guiding groups of ten to fourteen through the meditations. Parma so felt the change in the temper of its life as these little nodes of spiritual force increased that the Council of the city could write to Costanza Farnese, niece of Paul III, in March 1540 that "the greater part of the people of Parma are changed in their manner of life to the extent that they go to Confession and Holy Communion much more frequently than has been their habit. . . . The entire city is converted to a religious fidelity more intense than at any time in her past." [6]

In these personal contacts, made in the confessional and in retreats, Peter's penitents felt the power of his natural and supernatural gifts and his sure mastery of the principles of the spiritual life. One of the first from the Netherlands to enter the Society of Jesus, Jean Couvillon, delineated from personal experience some of the features of Favre as a spiritual director: his heart was a heart of mercy and understanding for others, made tender and sympathetic in the sufferings he himself endured; in him the scrupulous found comfort, the tempted found strength; with an ability to discern in a soul the promptings of either grace or the evil spirit, and with a countenance joyful and serene, his words of advice had a peculiar aptness for everyone who came to him.[7] Peter had a lofty concept of the office of confessor, and his personal ideal was to be to the penitent sinner the merciful vicar of the merciful Christ. This he translated into some instructions he left his friends a few years later:

The Holy Spirit will be given you if in the hearing of confessions you are gentle and mild, keeping yourself in a spirit of forbearance and not allowing yourself to be touched by an attitude of harshness or disgust that might possibly be occasioned by a penitent's crudeness. We must be on our guard lest we acquire a loathing for so important and holy a work. We are in the place of Christ, Who bears the sins of the world. . . . We must beware lest any sinner suffer chagrin in his approach to the representatives of the gentle Christ. . . . Let us avoid pharisaical sternness and that legalism that irritates no end; let us send away no one who would not gladly return to us. . . .[8]

A sensitive charity for others in their needs, a moving compassion for them in their suffering, a delicate sympathy for them in their weaknesses, these were the external manifestations of a heart moulded according to the Heart of the Merciful Christ. And how much the Merciful Christ meant to Peter he made clear in his *Memorial*:

On the feast of Saint Evaristus, Pope and Martyr, I rose at three in the morning and found great consolation in the many interior promptings and pious desires that came to me to pray for my neighbors in their needs, for Christians, Jews, Turks, heretics, as well as for the souls of the deceased. There passed before my mind's eye the different kinds of human suffering, men's weaknesses, sins, obstinacy, despair, sorrow, death, as well as the famines, the plagues, the other burdens they endure. Then there came to me the thought of Christ the Redeemer, Christ the Consoler, Christ the Lord God. I prayed to Him by the power of all these titles of His that He deign to give help and succor to all men. I also felt the desire and prayed with intense and unwonted feeling that I be given the grace to be the servant of Christ the Consoler, Christ the Helper, Christ the Rescuer, the Liberator, the Enricher, the Strengthener, and that through Him I might be able to give aid, to console, rescue from all sorts of danger, strengthen the many who are in need. . . .[9]

* * *

The Legation of Parma was the first great recruiting area for gaining new members for the "Company of Jesus." In compensation for what Favre and Laínez were giving to Parma, the people of that Province made a return offering of some of their most promising sons. Paul d'Achille was about twenty-seven years old, gentle and suave in manner, experienced as a private tutor. He was the second Italian to enlist under the Ignatian standard, the first having been Ignatius' Roman friend, Pietro Codazzo. Recognizing in him qualities that fitted him to become an unusually competent spiritual director, Favre and Laínez trained him in the art of giving the *Spiritual Exercises*. Elpidio Ugoleti, twenty-three years old, educated in music as well as *belles-lettres*, son of the famous librarian of Matthias Corvinus, enjoyed the reputation of being one of the best singers in Parma. It was more than just his beautiful voice that influenced Favre and Laínez to accept him into their group; the wisdom of their judgment was borne out by the more than ordinary prudence with which he governed Jesuit houses in Padua, Venice, Sicily, where, at Palermo, he was appointed Master of Novices. Giovanni Battista Viola, twenty-three years old, was to become identified with the city of Paris and the heroic story of trying to keep the Jesuit Collège de Clermont open in the face of a Gallican-spirited Parlement. Francesco and Benedetto Palmio, two of the five sons of the strong-souled and pious noblewoman Chiara Palmio, contributed greatly to the apostolic success of the early Jesuits in Italy, Francesco in the foundation of the Society of Jesus in Bologna and Benedetto by his energetic eloquence known up and down the entire Italian peninsula. Most famous of all whom Favre and Laínez inspired was the young man who was to be the first to have his name inscribed on the Jesuit Martyrology. Antonio Criminali, from the little town of Sissa about nine miles from Parma, did not act immediately, but in 1542 he made the decisive step, went to Rome and placed himself under the guidance of Ignatius. His strong inclination toward contemplation did not curtail a life of the most intense apostolic labor which took him to the East Indies, where he was cruelly killed in May of 1549; his death started the long procession of Jesuits who carry the palm of martrydom: John de Britto, Edmund Campion, Isaac Jogues, Anthony Azevedo, and many others.[10]

Jerome Doménech, a Spaniard, found his vocation to the "Company of Jesus" at Parma. Doménech was twenty-four years old in 1539. A canon of Valencia, his path happened to cross that of Xavier in Bologna when Francis was there in 1538. The friendship they formed was strengthened when they both eventually met again in Rome. Jerome had with the help of his uncle obtained a position as Scriptor in the Papal Curia, but in the summer of 1539 he decided to go to Paris to further his studies. Xavier gave him a letter to Favre and Laínez in which he expressed the hope that his Valencian friend would tarry a few days at Parma, make the *Spiritual Exercises* and elect to join their group. All worked out just as Xavier hoped. Jerome decided then and there to leave his uncle and his other traveling companions and to join Favre and Laínez in their work. On September 24th he wrote out in Catalan, his mother tongue, a vow to follow Christ in poverty. Jerome's uncle did not see things quite that way and took his protest to the Cardinal Legate. Filonardi received the distressed relative very sympathetically, but made it clear that no other group ranked as high in his estimation as the group to which Peter Favre and James Laínez belonged. Peter wrote to Xavier about the incident and related how the Cardinal impressed on the elder Doménech that if he sincerely desired the good of his nephew he would go out of his way to see him associated "with us rather than with anyone else." [11]

On this impressive list of recruits should be included the name of Angelo Paradisi of Brescia. In the spring of 1540, Brescia, about fifty miles north of Parma, was being turned inside out spiritually by a young follower of Ignatius, a Spaniard not yet ordained to the priesthood. Francis Strada, about twenty years old, endowed with exceptional oratorical gifts, was well on his way to meriting Ignatius' encomium that he was superior to all in preaching the meditations of the First Week of the *Exercises*. Sent to Brescia from Montepulciano in 1540, his eloquence stirred over a hundred young men to the resolution of consecrating themselves to God's service. Among them was Angelo Paradisi. Angelo not only wanted to serve Christ, but was determined to do so in the "Company of Jesus." Unwittingly he was the reason why Favre and Xavier missed the last opportunity they had to see each other in this life. On April 1st, 1540, Peter received word that Paradisi was seriously ill. He left for Brescia the next morning, the very day that Francis arrived at Parma en route to Lisbon and the Indies. Francis debated whether he ought to await Peter's return, but submitting to the judgment of the Portuguese Ambassador, Pedro Mascarenhas, and his other fellow travelers, he moved on without delay. When Peter heard that he missed Francis he wrote to Ignatius, "May the Lord by His grace bring it about that if we do not see each other in this world, we may be able to rejoice together in the next over both the separations and the reunions that we experienced here below for Christ alone." [12] In Brescia Peter found Angelo a bit better, but still too sick to talk at length about the tension that had developed between himself and his relatives who were set in their opposition to his joining Strada. Peter heard about the "large-scale battles" over the issue and wrote to Ignatius, "Without question I have great reason for giving praise to God Our Saviour because of Angelo's great constancy in a contest that is in many ways so cruel." [13]

Paradisi recovered, ironed out the difficulties with such amazing success that his relatives put him on the road to Rome with the assurance that they would take care of his needs during the entire period of his studies. Some of the Brescians tried to keep Peter with them, but he had strict orders from Cardinal Filonardi, who probably sensed the likelihood of this eventuality, that he should not allow himself to be delayed at Brescia. He arrived back at Parma on April 16th. Nine days later he himself fell ill, and for three months, until the middle of July, was confined to the home of some friends. A serious restraint on his activity though this sickness was, Peter interpreted it as another means sent by God for his personal spiritual growth. "Recall, O my soul," he wrote in his *Memorial*, "the three months' illness during which you were able to gain an unforgettably great spiritual harvest according to the light given you by the Lord, Whose purpose was your growth in spiritual perfection." [14]

There was at least one admirer of Peter whose ambition to join Ignatius' group met with rebuff. Giacoma Pallavicino, widow of the Marquis Girolamo Pallavicino, was a good woman who placed herself entirely under Peter's direction in the disposal of her extensive possessions. Years later she wanted to found a college of the Society of Jesus, but since her offer involved the care of a convent of nuns, Ignatius, with all due thanks to Giacoma, declined. She then asked that she be admitted into the Society of Jesus and signed her letter, in evident anticipation of Ignatius' acquiescence, "*Jacoppa dela Compagnia dai Jesus.*" She argued her case on the grounds that "she had been called by God through the voices of Master Peter and Master James of your holy Company" when they had been in Parma years before. Giacoma's request was doomed to failure because Ignatius by this time had had his memorable experience with the Spanish lady, Isabelle Roser, and had determined that his Society would not undertake the spiritual direction of women. But Giacoma had a mind of her own. If Ignatius was unbending, she too would not yield and continued to sign her name "Giacoma of the Society of Jesus." [15]

Another woman became one of the chief focal points in the reform of Parma. Giulia Zerbini was an invalid who made the *Spiritual Exercises* under a Father Giovanni Battista Pezzana, one of Peter's more prominent disciples. She turned her sickroom into a sort of classroom in which she explained to her visitors the methods of meditation as expounded in the *Spiritual Exercises*.[16]

On July 16, 1540, by order of Cardinal Filonardi, Laínez, accompanied by the versatile Paolo D'Achille, went to Piacenza, the other important urban center of the Parma Legation.[17] About the 20th of August two rumors were abroad, the first, without foundation, that the Pope had ordered Father Laínez to France, and the second, much more accurate, that Father Favre had received orders to go to Spain. Peter's name became associated with a mission to Spain through the devoted friend of the men of the "Company of Jesus," Doctor Pedro Ortiz. Ortiz had completed his business at the Vatican and was making ready to return to Spain. His imagination afire with a plan to establish a community of Loyola's men in his native land, he was able to convince Paul III to concur in the project. Orders were forthwith issued for Peter to accompany Ortiz to Spain. The reaction of the people of Parma was instantaneous. The City Council dispatched a message to their ambassadors in Rome,

79

Frederico del Prato and Angelo Cantelli, with instructions to approach the Holy See and to try to keep at least one of the Fathers at Parma. Giacoma Pallavacino acted even more rapidly. Taking matters into her own hands, she contacted Laura Pallavicino, a woman accustomed to getting her own way, besides enjoying the special advantage of being a relative of Paul III. Giacoma urged Laura to ask the Cardinal di Santa Fiore to petition the Pope that Father Favre be left at Parma. But all the pressure of the City Fathers and all the pious diplomacy of Giacoma were to no avail. Peter's orders to move on to Spain stood unchanged.

* * *

Faced with the prospect of losing the men who had meant so much to them in the spiritual rebirth of their city, the friends of Fathers Favre and Laínez requested some instructions by which they might be guided once the Fathers had withdrawn. Accordingly, in early September Peter put down on paper a few suggestions under the title, "A Directive and Aid for the Preservation of a Truly Christian and Spiritual Life." [18] A simple document, concise, without rhetorical flourish, it gives, nevertheless, a good insight into some of the principles that both priests stressed in their direction of souls. The core of their teaching was the basic need of frequent reception of Holy Communion. A few selections from the *Ordine et Aiuto* follow.

Since I must take leave of Parma for Spain, I wish to satisfy your pious desire as well as that of many others who like yourselves will not rest content unless I leave some sort of memorial. I do not mean a memorial of myself. Rather, I speak of a suggested regime to be followed in a life that is led for God and at a time when no other teacher is at hand.

First of all, I would wish that you be not deceived by the

80

thought that I have food to offer you as a guarantee of your perseverance in holiness other than the food you have already received. Aristotle would tell you the very same thing. When he speaks of bodily nourishment, he says that the foods which contribute to a person's basic nourishment the same contribute to his growth. You must therefore be unmoved in your conviction that the very same spiritual exercises in which your spirit has hitherto found nourishment continue to be just as necessary for you. This is especially true since your food is fundamentally that Heavenly Bread in Which the Angels and all the saints now find and will ever find their nourishment. This Heavenly Bread is much more essential for the spiritual life than material bread is for temporal life. . . .

Directions then follow for night prayer. They include a brief reflection on the four last things, an examination of conscience, a purpose to go to confession at a determined time. "With this done, pray to Our Lord to give you and all the living a peaceful night and eternal rest to the deceased, saying for this intention three *Our Fathers* and three *Hail Marys*." Peter's next item was direction for morning prayer in which he included a meditation either before a Crucifix or during Mass. "Listen to some particular word of Christ or think of some particular action of His. In the course of this prayer you can examine yourselves and excite yourselves to a holy life, not for the day only but for all the days that remain to you. . . ."

Peter followed this with a return to the subject of Holy Communion. He suggested that the Consecration of the Mass be the occasion for an act of spiritual Communion in preparation for the actual reception of the Body of Christ.

When the Consecration is finished, or at the moment the Sacred Host is elevated, you may begin to ask for remedies for your evil ways and for the graces that you lack, such as fortitude, knowledge, peace, and finally that crowning grace of a hunger and thirst for true justice. You may ask Christ, truly present before you, that He come spiritually to your souls. After this spiritual communion, arouse the desire for sacramental Communion, keeping in mind when it was that you last received and when it will be that you have decided to receive in the future.

This daily spiritual Communion will be an efficacious preparation for sacramental Communion just as daily spiritual Confession is an efficacious preparation for a fruitful sacramental Confession at a determined time and to a fixed confessor. For this reason I would like to see each Christian decide on and arrange for himself the days he is to confess and receive Holy Communion. In order that each one might the more easily do this I would like him to say to himself each morning: "On such and such a day I shall go to Confession and receive Holy Communion." I would like to see this done even though the day selected be two months away. Therefore, call to mind each morning the last Holy Communion and the next one. By this practice you will be showing your reverence for Communion. Otherwise there would be danger that you would not benefit to the full from this Food nor have a perfect longing for It. Aim even at not missing Confession and Holy Communion at least once a week.

Peter's next point of advice is a suggestion that each one be sure that his daily prayer and meditation be ordained to one or all of three purposes: the honor of God and His saints, one's personal salvation, the salvation of one's neighbor. The practice of the devotions recommended would be stepping-stones to that increase of virtue synonymous with a holier life. Peter's final paragraph is a lengthy one in which he distinguished the order of one's obligations in regard to one's own soul and body and the body and soul of one's neighbor. In this entire outline of obligations he kept his sight fixed on the supernatural purpose of all human activity. This simple,

82

unembellished *Ordine* concludes with Peter's request for prayer for himself and all his brothers in Christ. It was a beautiful *a rivedérci* to his friends of Parma, a guarantee that his teaching would live when his voice would no longer be heard among them.

* * *

The Sodality of the Blessed Virgin Mary, started by the Belgian Scholastic John Leunis at Rome in 1563, has become identified with the Jesuit apostolate of bringing to the laity a high level of Christian living. In the mid-sixteenth century, however, this Sodality of the Blessed Virgin was but one of several organizations set up by Jesuits as a means to a richer interior and apostolic life for the layman. Like trees breaking out in blossoms with the approach of May, the towns of Italy seemed to burgeon forth Sodalities at the coming of the Jesuits. Ignatius himself set up at Rome the *Confraternity of the Holy Twelve Apostles*. Father Jerome Nadal founded congregations at Trappani, Padua, and Messina. At Florence Father Louis du Coudret, Rector of the Jesuit College, founded a *Compagnia di Communicanti* in imitation of like groups at Venice, Genoa, Naples. And all of these predated the enterprise of John Leunis. At Parma there was an unusually successful organization called the *Compagnia del Nome Santissimo di Gesù*, and it has become the accepted thing, because of the writings of Fathers Orlandini, Boero and Cornely, to think of Peter Favre as the founder of this particular sodality. Peter would be the first to want to see the mantle of glory rest where it ought, and in this case it belongs on the shoulders of a Milanese layman named Rinaldo. The place reserved for Peter by his admirers in the group of Ignatius, Nadal, du Coudret, Leunis, as a founder of a Sodality must be denied him.[19]

Rinaldo happened to be in Parma for some reason or other and obtained from Nicolo Bozzalli, the Vicar of the diocese, authorization to preach the word of God, a permission not too unusually given to laymen in those days. Rinaldo used this faculty for the first time on January 1, 1541, in the oratory of the Disciplina di San Paolo. His sermon was on the need of teaching Christian Doctrine to the children, and so effective was it that a hundred of his listeners decided to take up this apostolate. A few days later, on the feast of the Epiphany, the *Compagnia di Gesù*, later known as the *Compagnia del Nome Santissimo di Gesù*, was formed. This was three months after Peter had taken his leave of Parma. Many of those, however, whom Rinaldo moved to action had been trained by Favre and Laínez, and the statutes of the *Compagnia*, the practical instructions for leading a soul to perfection, the emphasis on frequent Holy Communion, breathing as they do the spirit of Peter and James, were certainly drawn up by someone trained by them. Although neither Favre nor Laínez set up the actual structure of the *Compagnia del Nome Santissimo di Gesù*, they had certainly gathered together the beams, forms, joists, posts, traves that made its erection a possibility.

At the very time that Peter was preparing to leave Parma, Ignatius at Rome was bringing to a happy conclusion that for which he had been working and praying for months on end. September 27, 1540, was the memorable day when in the Palace of Saint Mark Pope Paul III signed the Bull *Regimini Militantis Ecclesiae* confirming the Company of Jesus as a religious order. It was a hard-won victory. Difficulties had been many and at times it seemed that Ignatius' hopes would be denied. But his friends at the Papal Court also were many, among them being Frederico del Prato, ambassador from Parma, with his instructions to try to change the mind of Cardinal Bartolomeo Guidiccioni, vigorous opponent of the creation of new religious orders. It was one way the people of Parma had of showing their gratitude for what Favre and Laínez had given them.[20]

Doctor Ortiz was making his way northward from Rome to Parma when he received a change of orders from the Emperor Charles V. That fall, in the city of Worms, a religious colloquy between the Catholics and Protestants was to be held, and the Emperor wanted Ortiz to be there. Peter, with every expectation of starting for Spain with the Doctor, had to change his plans accordingly. His entry into the Holy Roman Empire that October of 1540 was the epiphany of the recently approved Society of Jesus in Germany.[21]

V. The Voices of the Two Germanies

WITHIN a short time after the men of the "Company of Jesus" began to leave Rome for their different assignments, the house *"appreso La Torre Marangula"* became more and more like to a watchtower from which Ignatius could scan the length and breadth of Europe. As letters multiplied and came in from places as near as Montepulciano and as far distant as Paris and Lisbon, Ignatius' horizon widened, and he could not but feel that the problems of these places were personally his own, so intimately were they touching the lives of his sons. Peter's first message from Worms added the vast area of Germany to the growing list of nations that Ignatius was taking to his heart. For Ignatius, Peter's letters were a gold mine of firsthand information about the melancholy state of that *"pobre nación,"* and especially about the ups and downs of the momentous religious debates at Worms and Regensburg. Page after page was filled with the names of the great, men like Charles V, Melanchthon, Granvelle, Eck, of whom Ignatius must certainly have heard, as well as the names of the lesser lights, Phlug, Gropper, Cochlaeus, of whom he was possibly learning now for the first time.

Peter could not have arrived at a more opportune time to take in at one glance the thoroughly confused state Germany was then in. From November of 1540 until July of the following year the two venerable cities of Worms and Regensburg were the setting for a dramatic demonstration of the involved and complex situation within the Empire. The Emperor was pushing hard for a *rapprochement* between Catholics and

86

Protestants and pinned high hopes on the religious Colloquy that he arranged to be held at Worms, to be followed by an imperial Diet at Regensburg. In these two cities were massed face to face the forces that were dividing Germany, and here were expressed the ideas, the emotions, the prejudices that made reflective men realize that they were eyewitnesses to the end of the religious unity of Europe. The Protestant theologians, Bucer and Melanchthon, were there, unmoved in their basic denial of papal claims to supremacy in things doctrinal; the two Dukes of Bavaria were in attendance, sincere Catholics but determined that no union be effected because unity would make the Emperor strong, a result that to them would be intolerable; representatives of the French king were there, fishing in troubled waters and urging both Catholics and Protestants to refuse agreement because a divided Germany was a major "must" on France's eastern frontier; debates on the nature of justification exposed the want of clarity among the Catholics themselves on this key theological problem. The year 1540 was a particularly bleak time for the Catholic cause since just the year before two important states, the duchy of Saxony and the electorate of Brandenburg, went over to Lutheranism. Cardinal Morone believed that within thirty years, if the trend of events remained unchecked, Germany would have completely apostatized. So many were the Catholic Estates which were ready to effect unity with the Lutherans by making concessions, that the prelate judged that the way was indeed open to the achievement of unity, but it would be a Lutheran unity.[1]

The Colloquy of Worms opened on November 25, 1540, and dragged on until January 18th of the following year. It was arranged that each side in the discussions would have eleven votes. The Protestants presented a united front on the basis of the Augsburg Confession. The Catholics were

87

split wide open. In the event of a vote, from among the Catholic representatives chosen by King Ferdinand, three— the Elector of Brandenburg, the Elector Palatine and the Duke of Jülich—could safely be included on the Protestant side. Three of the remaining eight were none too loyal. In this situation the Catholic hero was Cardinal Morone, who made it his objective to keep the Colloquy from turning into an open debate with the awful prospect of three supposedly Catholic spokesmen openly admitting Lutheran doctrine. He warded off this eventuality, for a time at least, by arranging that each side present its arguments in the form of written memoranda. For nearly two months he conducted a running battle with Granvelle, the Emperor's representative, and by protest and counter suggestion he held off any balloting on religious questions.

Much as Peter desired to assist in the business of the Colloquy, he was forced into the position of a mere by- stander. A prearranged disposition, the purpose of which was to exclude all possible irritation and annoyance to the Protes- tants, sealed off the Lutheran disputants from any contact with private Catholic theologians. Peter watched develop- ments for a month before he sent his first report to Rome. His eyes had been opened to the harsh realities at Worms and he could not help but paint a grim picture for Ignatius.

I am convinced that not a single Lutheran from Worms or any place else has been converted from his errors through the efforts of those who are gathered here for that precise purpose. In other words, I see no fruit that has been gained so far as the conversion of the Lutherans is concerned. In fact, it is clear that they are the ones who are gaining ground, even over those who have come here as professed Catholics. . . . I have not spoken with Melanchthon or any of the other Lutherans. Many of the doctors would like me to have a talk with him, and I certainly have had many holy desires to do so. However, I want to do nothing that is at variance with the judgment of those who shoulder the responsibility of this Colloquy: and their mind is that no one should treat with the Lutherans for fear an obstruction be created to the smooth running of the meeting. For the same reason Doctor Ortiz has restrained me, although he personally would like to see me in touch with the Lutherans, realizing as he does that, with the help of God Our Lord, I would not debate with them in a contentious spirit, nor would I by nettling them block the hoped for good. . . .[2]

So careful was Granvelle that nothing be done to annoy the Protestants that he would not even allow Peter to teach catechism to some children. Eventually, however, he did find something for him to do that would apparently attract less attention. "In place of the children I have two Turks whom Granvelle recommended to me for the instruction required before they embrace Christianity. They are very well disposed." [3]

Peter's letters to Rome were not as frequent as Ignatius would have liked. Ignatius insisted that he wanted to be kept abreast of the religious situation in Germany. Peter had to admit his negligence but pleaded his reluctance to write about the colloquy and the gloomy prospects for its success.[4]

The Protestants tell us that their purpose is simply the reformation of the Church, and they make this assertion in such a convincing way that ignorant and stupid people believe them even when they see them desecrating statues, overturning altars —save one in each church—blaspheming those who hear private Masses or pray to the saints. And all the while they want it understood that they seek naught but reformation. To see the blindness that has befallen this nation is something to arouse the fear of Christ Our Lord. I have made these few observations so that you might realize that it would be misleading to describe the situation here as a mere disagreement over a few minor issues. The aim of the Protestants is to leave not a stone upon a stone. This they work at with the most obstinate stubbornness, their supreme desire being, as I have pointed out, to cause an irreparable cleavage in Holy Mother the Church, against which, however, not even the gates of hell will ever prevail.[5]

Peter learned quickly at Worms. Whatever the way to religious peace might be, it certainly was not down the road of conferences such as he was witnessing with all their over-tones of power politics, avarice and secularism. Peter's ideas were not original. Others had arrived at the same viewpoint before he did. John Cochlaeus argued against the suggestion of a national German Council, about which there were rumors at that time. "With the conference as a pretext the Protestants aim at dragging out the business so that in the meantime they might spread their beliefs into other parts of Germany."[6]

In the Empire at this time was the enterprising Scot and Primate of Armagh, Robert Wauchope. He sounded the same idea. "It is now clearer than day that the Protestants . . . have been pressing for councils, both private and na-tional, with the purpose of causing a large scale defection from the Church. . . ."[7] Merely to lament the ineptitude of diets and colloquies would have been negative indeed. Peter recognized that Germany's religious problem was more than just a clash of theological propositions. Not that he ever minimized the need of a clear and intelligent grasp of the religious truths in question. But beyond the high-level dis-cussions of a few theologians lay the whole of Germany with its thousands of people deprived of the sacraments by faith-less priests and prey to superstition because of their ignorance. These were the conditions in which heresy was bred. Peter's mind took all this in and he came to the conclusion that Germany's hope was in a return to a life of prayer, of fidelity to the sacraments, of the practice of charity. For him the heresies of the day were nothing more than "a dearth of piety, of humility, patience, chastity and charity." [8] It was not so much the doctrines of Luther as the bad example of the priests that was causing the defection of so many people. "Would to God," wrote Peter,

that there were in each city two or three priests who, not living in concubinage nor guilty of other public sins, were filled with zeal for souls. I have no doubt that then with the Lord's help these ordinary and simple people would be brought back. . . . They are led astray not so much by the teaching and seeming good of the Lutherans as by the wickedness of those very ones who should be examples of zeal. . . .[9]

He felt sure that if the German people could be brought back to the peace of Christ found in the sacrament of Penance and to the love of Christ fed by the Holy Eucharist, if they could be drawn once again to an appreciation of the Communion of Saints, then indeed would a great part of the problem disappear. "What would the heretics of this present extremely dispirited age do," he asked,

if they should behold any one city determined to grow in the understanding and in the practice of some particular article of the faith in which they differ from us? If they should see confession esteemed more than heretofore, the laity flocking to the confessional, being cleansed of their sins and with increasing joy repeatedly returning to this Sacrament, they would not dare to promise themselves any success in that particular region. If they should see the practice of frequent Communion in the churches, with people receiving their Strength and their Light every week, others every two weeks, not one of them would presume to preach the Zwinglian doctrine on Holy Communion. . . . For that man is quite a disconcerted man indeed who finds himself

91

made into a laughing stock, or even without an audience. What would the heretics do if no one listened to them or if everybody laughed at them? [10]

This remained Peter's unchanged conviction during the entirety of his apostolic labor in Germany. His analysis of the Germany he saw was not that of the diplomat who would tend to see merely a conflict of claims that had to be resolved; nor was it that of the legalist, prone to discover a solution in new laws and regulations. Peter looked at Germany through the eyes of the shepherd of souls. He thought in terms of souls to be freed from sin and opened to the cleansing and strengthening stream of divine grace.

After weeks of postponement of open debate, Granvelle finally called the session to order for face-to-face discussion on January 14, 1541. At the close of the fourth day of intense debate on the question of original sin, he terminated the meetings and announced their transfer to Regensburg, where the Emperor himself was expected to be present. The Worms phase of the Emperor's plans for achieving a religious peace was a failure. And in view of the basic principles of the disputants, by their very nature irreconcilable, it did not augur well for the Hapsburg hopes at Regensburg.

＊　＊　＊

It was fortunate that Peter did not become enmeshed in the business of the Colloquy, marked as it was for disintegration, because in standing aside from the central business at Worms he was free to make friends with several of the nobility and clergy who assisted the Catholic leaders of the conference. He was of course unknown when he came into Germany, but it was not long before his reputation spread. Two months after his arrival at Worms, he informed Ignatius that several of the households of Granvelle and the Bishop of Arras had become his "spiritual sons," and that the Legate to Germany, Cardinal Morone, was among those who had come to him for confession.[11] To know Peter was to discover the Society of Jesus. As the radius of his influence became more extended with the passing months, and as the confessions multiplied and those applying to make the *Spiritual Exercises* increased, the knowledge of and reverence for the new religious Order grew among the men from many different nations gathered at Worms—Germans, Italians, Spaniards and Portuguese.

Perhaps Peter's most important single achievement at Worms was the encouragement that he gave his host, the Vicar General and Inquisitor. Depressed at the sight of the serious losses to the Church, he was at the point of surrendering his double responsibility in the city. Lutheranism was being openly taught in the convent church of Saint Dominic; infidelity among the priests was appalling. The disheartened man made the *Spiritual Exercises* under Peter's direction, and so animated did he become with the conviction of their power and efficacy that he aroused in many who were *"duros como piedras"* a desire to make them.[12]

One of the more famous theologians whom Peter met at Worms was the tireless pamphleteer, John Cochlaeus, of the party of Ferdinand, King of the Romans. Cochlaeus became one of Peter's warmest admirers, and on one occasion, when he heard Peter speak of the difference between the knowledge of spiritual things and the taste for them, he remarked, "I am delighted that at last we have discovered a master of the affective life." He wanted to make the *Exercises* then and there. But Peter was due to leave Worms for Regensburg by way of Speyer, and he had to postpone his retreat until he would see Peter again at the forthcoming Diet.

Another friend Peter made just before leaving Worms was the Portuguese representative at the court of the Emperor, Francisco Lobo.[13]

With the closing down of the Colloquy, Peter took leave of his grateful host, the Vicar General, and turned south to the ancient city of Speyer. He did not arrive there unannounced, for the Vicar General had written ahead and several people were awaiting him with the hope of making the *Spiritual Exercises*. Peter also carried a letter from the Vicar General to the Bishop of Speyer, Philip II of Fleisheim, who received him most cordially and became quite interested in the Society of Jesus. Peter wrote to Ignatius on January 25, 1541:

> On three occasions I explained at length to him [the Bishop] the work of the Company and he showed that he was very impressed. He invited me to dinner last Thursday, the very day he invited the Duke of Bavaria, the brother of the Count Palatine and the Archbishop of Trier. I spoke to all of them about the work of the Company. Later on the Bishop sent his Vicar General to me, and for the past three days we discussed things of a spiritual nature. The outcome of it all is that he is very much inclined to make the *Exercises*. . . .[14]

The Vicar General, whose name was George Mussbach, followed up on his good dispositions and made the First Week of the *Exercises* with great generosity, while the Bishop promised to make a retreat after he had gone to Regensburg for the Diet.[15] Meanwhile, Doctor Ortiz was proving to be quite a publicity agent for Peter, telling the different courtiers he met that the thing they ought to do was to make the *Exercises* under Peter's direction and confess to him. One day when Peter was with Doctor Ortiz, they met Charles III of Savoy. Duke Charles was in exile because

94

of the French occupation of his country, and there was little that he could do in a practical way to help Peter, but he did assure him of the good will of the house of Savoy and of his desire to be of assistance.[16]

Peter remained at Speyer only about two weeks. He was happy about what he was accomplishing there and he could see a very promising harvest for the future, but, as he told Ignatius, "I would not give up the idea of going to Regensburg because of what remains yet to be done here, because my hope is that I shall accomplish incomparably more in the service of God Our Saviour at Regensburg." [17]

❀ ❀ ❀

After the Fourth Week of the *Spiritual Exercises,* Saint Ignatius introduces an exercise called *A Contemplation to Attain the Love of God* in which he bids the retreatant to cast his mind's eye over the blessings of creation and Redemption, to reflect on God's presence in creatures and to pray for such a sense of gratitude that he will give himself entirely to the love and service of His Divine Majesty. Ignatius' awareness of God's presence in the world was an abiding attitude which he wrote into the Constitutions of the Society of Jesus and made one of the norms of the interior life of the Jesuit. He called it the "seeking of God in all things." Peter learned this lesson personally from Ignatius, so well indeed that his life of labor and his life of prayer blended into one unified act of love and service of God. One admirer of Peter has called him *"un Chartreux itinérant—*a Carthusian of the Highway." [18] Of the journey from Speyer to Regensburg Peter wrote in his *Memorial*:

In January of 1541 we set out for Regensburg, the seat of the Imperial Diet. On the journey I enjoyed deep consolation in a variety of forms of prayer and contemplation. New subject

95

matter also came to mind, such as on approaching or beholding or hearing of any particular locality to ask God that the archangel guardians of that region and the angel guardians of the inhabitants be propitious to us; then to ask that Jesus Christ, present as the ever true Guardian and Pastor in the tabernacle of the neighborhood church, might assist us and be solicitous for all the needs of the inhabitants, those in sin and at the point of death, those tried by affliction, and then for the souls of the faithful departed.

While passing by mountains, fields or vineyards still other forms of prayer suggested themselves, such as to ask God for a greater abundance of blessings of this kind, or to thank Him for them in view of the failure of the owners to do so, or to beg the Divine Pardon for those who in their ignorance do not recognize these blessings for what they are nor Him from Whose hand they come. I likewise called upon the saints to whose protection these regions were committed and I asked them to do what the inhabitants did not know how to do, ask God's forgiveness, render thanks and petition for their needs.[19]

Years later Father Jerome Nadal gathered together some *dicta* of the first Fathers of the Society and among them he included a list of suggestions that Peter Favre had drawn up for one about to undertake a journey:

When we enter a city or town, we should invoke its angels, archangels and patron saints. In our greeting to them and in our request for their help, we should be as familiar with them as though we were paying a visit to our fellowmen. . . . We should give thanks for the blessings showered on that region, for the fruits of the earth, the streams and all such things, reflecting how great is the number who receive all these blessings and how few there are who give thanks to God. . . .

When we happen to meet unknown persons on the road, be they soldiers or others, we should close our minds to suspicious thoughts and think but good of them. In our heart we should

96

wish them well and think how we might be united with them in the bond of charity. . . . If something untoward should happen, we should receive it as coming not from man but from God without Whose providential guidance nothing can take place. . . .[20]

These passages form small windows that open into Peter's soul and disclose a life of mind and heart animated by an esteem for those interior things which Saint Ignatius described as the source of the Jesuit's ardor and tirelessness in labor.

*　*　*

If the saints of heaven were capable of showing bad humor, a frown of the deepest kind must have crossed the Irish face of good Saint Marianus of Tir Conaill as he looked down upon the sessions of the Diet of Regensburg. For Muiredach mac Robartaig—the Irish form of Saint Marianus' name—had in the eleventh century left his home beyond the seas, had settled at Regensburg, and had entered into the labor of those countless other Irish monks, exiles for Christ, in order to bring Central Europe into the Christian Church. In their honor the Schotten-Kirche had been built at Regensburg. But now, after all these centuries, Muiredach mac Robartaig of Tir Conaill beheld the spectacle of men disavowing in the very city of his labors the unity he had helped to create in Europe.

The Emperor arrived at Regensburg on February 21, 1541, and his presence announced to Europe his determination to heal the wound that had been opened over twenty years before and was becoming more festered each day. Charles was conscious of his broad inheritance, Burgundy and its colorful court life, the Netherlands and their spirit of daring, Spain and its crusading mood, the Empire and its concept of universal jurisdiction. But above all was he aware that all of these dominions, so diverse in custom, language and habit, were one in committing to him the tradition of European unity in the Catholic faith. At Worms in 1521, after he had met Luther face to face, he had shown that this was his understanding of his responsibility. Now he was throwing the full weight of his Hapsburg influence to bring about at Regensburg a religious peace.

When the Emperor arrived, the hopes of the imperial circle for the success of the negotiations were high. Charles himself, pleased with the appointment of Cardinal Contarini as *legatus a latere*, anticipated that the Protestants would be moved by the genuine sincerity and character of the Cardinal to make concessions. The sanguine atmosphere of the court was reflected by churchmen such as Campeggio and Poggio, but Cardinal Morone, who looked at Germany through experienced eyes, had no illusions about what to expect. At Worms in a discussion with Melanchthon, Capito and Sturm he was left without doubt about their aversion to any program of union.

Cardinal Contarini came through the Brenner Pass in early March, arrived at Innsbruck on the 11th and made his solemn entry into Regensburg on the 12th. In his optimism, springing partially from his crediting others with his own generous desires as well as from his inaccurate estimate of the Lutheran position, he refused to believe that the situation in Germany was beyond repair. He told Eck, who was convinced of the futility of the conferences: "Even in the most desperate circumstances the Christian ought not to abandon hope, since he must go on hoping even against hope. . . ." [21] He was the great figure of the Diet. In his courtesy, intelligence, nobility of mind he rose above all like the tall, graceful, cathedral spire that dominates the town below.

The Diet opened in early April. The Emperor's program called for the choice of the more moderate and restrained disputants from both the Catholic and Protestant groups. They were to report to him on the points of agreement, and he in turn would pass them on to the Legates for future action. Melanchthon, Bucer and Pistorius were the choices of the Protestant side; the Catholic designees were Gropper, Pflug and Eck. Granvelle and the Count Palatine were designated as Presidents of the sessions. The names of the Catholic representatives, especially that of Eck, did not sit well with at least some of the Protestants. On April 22nd Francis Burchardt wrote:

> What hope can one have of spreading the truth when that sotted quibbler Eck is being employed in affairs such as these? Julius Pflug cannot move without the Pope. And as for the third, Gropper, he is a good and moderate enough fellow but he is held down by the other two, the bellowing Eck and the crafty Pflug.[22]

In the beginning the results of the sessions seemed to bear out the optimism of the Imperialists, Poggio and Contarini. Contarini's greatness was so making itself felt that even the doubtful Morone could write:

> The Legate increases in favor every hour, and Granvelle as well as the other ministers say that God in His goodness has created him for this very purpose; for he displays the greatest gentleness, sagacity and learning, surpassing in the last respect all others here in the general opinion, so that even his opponents are beginning not only to love but to reverence him.[23]

The discussions on original sin, free will and the original state of man did not cause serious embarrassment, but they hit a snag on the question of justification until a formula postulating a *duplex justitia,* an odd combination of Catholic and Protestant views, was worked out. The early harmony in the Diet proved, however, to be but an Indian Summer, and when the question of the Holy Eucharist came up for discussion, stormy weather set in and ultimately the program of the Emperor was wrecked.

* * *

In the high-level discussions among the leading theologians Peter had no part, and there is no evidence that it was even suggested, as it had been at Worms, that he be allowed to speak to any of the Protestant party. The pattern of his five months in Regensburg was very much like that at Worms and Speyer, hearing confessions, giving the *Spiritual Exercises,* private conferences. By this time, however, the demands on his energies had increased to the point that he was unable to do all that was asked of him.

John Cochlaeus was finally able to make the *Exercises* and felt that he had received a sufficiently sure grasp of them to enable him to give them himself to the Bishop of Meissen, John III of Maltitz. Preaching was something that Cochlaeus had never before undertaken, and in fact had never contemplated doing, but now, as he told Peter, he felt that it was a work to which he should now give his attention.[24] The Portuguese Ambassador, Francisco Lobo, made the *Exercises* in a modified fashion by giving an hour or two each day to the meditations and reflections. There was a Benedictine Abbot from the Imperial Abbey of Kempten at the Diet and he, even before he completed the *Exercises,* considered himself richer and more blessed with what Peter had given and was yet to give him than with the twelve thousand ducats to which he was entitled by virtue of his office. He wrote to Rome and expressed his desire of becoming a Theatine.[25]

Most numerous of Peter's devotees were the Spanish noblemen in the entourage of the Emperor. Their graceful Latin names—Sancho, Rodriguez, de Figueroa, Manrique de Lara—seemed somewhat out of place in towns called Ingolstadt, Straubing, Eichstätt, Regensburg, but it was proof, for any who might doubt, that the Spanish sun was high over the lands of the German Empire. These men of Spain flocked to Peter for confession and spiritual counsel. Don Sancho de Castilla was called by Peter *"mi primogenito"* of those who made the *Exercises*.[26] There were the Marquis of Terranova and his two sons, one of whom was Bishop of Zergento, and later Cardinal; Peter Vaquar, Bishop of Alguer, one time Regent of the Council of Aragon and Inquisitor of Toledo for eighteen years, about whom Peter made the following observation to Ignatius: "You can be sure that if the Inquisition had any scruple, or if it had any unfavorable data about our men, this gentleman would not have chosen me for his confessor. . . ."[27] Another *hijo mio* was John Rodriguez de Figueroa before whom Ignatius had been accused in Alcalá and by whom he had been absolved. There was Don Juan de Granada, nephew of Babdal, last King of Granada, who came to Peter to make the *Exercises* and resolved to confess each week and receive Holy Communion every two weeks. Another was Don Hernando de la Cerda, second son of the Duke of Medinaceli. Don Francisco Manrique de Lara, future Bishop of Salamanca and brother of the Duke of Najera, was delighted with the way Peter explained the spiritual life and was won over to the idea of making a retreat. Without setting foot in Spain Peter was laying the foundations of the Society there. These men of distinction, whose spiritual endowments Peter singled out for special praise, were captivated by the force of Ignatius' teaching as it came to them in the person of Favre, and they carried back with them to their homes south of the Pyrenees the remembrance of a unique and blessed experience.[28] Another champion of the *Exercises* was Robert Wauchope, the Primate of Armagh. With a zeal worthy of a successor of Saint Patrick, he assumed the task of retreat master and guided others through the *Exercises*. There were Italians too, such as the Count of Mirandola and his two sons, who came within the scope of Peter's influence in Germany.[29]

So the work of retreats went on while Eck, Melanchthon and the other theologians wrangled among themselves. Like the peaceful and sweet refrain of a monks' choir that drifts from a distant church through the din and haggling of the marketplace, the soft voice of this Jesuit, repeating the phrases he learned from his spiritual father, floated through the dissonance and discord of the Regensburg Diet. "By this means to save his soul"; "Recall to mind the gravity and malice of sin against our Creator and Lord"; "I will consider who I am"; "Imagine Christ Our Lord present before you on the Cross"; "Here it will be to ask for an intimate knowledge of Our Lord"; "A colloquy should be addressed to our Lady, asking her to obtain for me from her Son and Lord to be received under His standard." These were the phrases that struck root in the souls of so many of the men at Regensburg. From them sprang the fruit of a positive and constructive personal holiness even while the news from the chambers of the Diet was foreboding and presaged failure of the Emperor's fondest hopes.

Peter did practically no preaching during the months of the Regensburg Diet. Recognizing that his unique gift was in the work of personal spiritual direction and retreats, Peter had a very low estimate of his oratorical ability. "I do no preaching," he told Ignatius, "lest my daily growing influence among the gentlemen here in the confessional and in private conversation suffer as a consequence. . . ."[30]

With the spread of Peter's reputation certain features of his spiritual direction became identified with him in the minds of the men at the Diet. One day an ecclesiastic of dignity was speaking to a certain gentleman and happened to mention the benefits of the particular examination of conscience. He was promptly told, "It is quite clear that you have learned this from Master Favre."[31] The work that began so modestly at Worms had increased to the degree that Peter was incapable of doing all that was asked of him. In the middle of March, 1541, he wrote to Ignatius:

May it please the Divine Mercy, Who has placed us here in these particular circumstances, to give us the grace, no matter what the situation may be, to go forth, bear fruit and that our fruit may remain. At present I am in great need of such help from God to take care of the incredible harvest that I behold here at the imperial court. There are so many who want to speak to me on spiritual matters and so many who desire to confess to me that I am afraid of being overwhelmed. I am alone, and these men are persons of prominence. Ask Our Lord to give me the grace to know how to handle myself in this work and to do always what is to His greater glory.[32]

Two weeks before Easter the confessions were so numerous that Peter could keep only three persons on retreat and was forced to postpone others until after Easter Sunday. At the end of May he again wrote to Ignatius,

I can say in all truth that if ten of the Company were here at this very moment we would have work for them to do conformed *á nuestra profesión.* Doctor Ortiz would have a hundred of us, convinced as he is that there is enough to do at the court to engage that number.[33]

103

Peter had learned two lessons from Ignatius about the *Exercises:* their flexibility and the intimate relationship that should exist between retreatant and director. There were no retreat houses with their special facilities for the preservation of a spirit of recollection. The best had to be made of what each locality had to offer, and it was the rare retreatant who made the *Exercises* through a full thirty-day period. Some retreatants, under pressure of business, could not give even a single day in its entirety. Each retreatant did not have the same endowments of nature and grace. Ignatius had given retreats in modified form at Manresa and Alcalá and he had written the principle of adaptation into the text of the *Exercises.* This principle Peter constantly employed. In most of his retreats at Parma, Worms and Regensburg, he emphasized the truths of the First Week, the general Confession, the examination of conscience and frequent Holy Communion. In Ignatius Peter also found his model of the director, alert to the movements of the Holy Spirit in the soul of the retreatant. Peter usually gave his retreats to individuals, and when he gave them to groups, as at Parma, the numbers were small. This made possible that intimate knowledge Ignatius desired the director to have of the spiritual state of his retreatant.[34]

While at Regensburg, Peter drew up a list of suggestions to help his friends in their desire to lead an ordered spiritual life. The relationship between this outline of practical suggestions and his retreat work was very close, and it seems that he gave a copy of the outline, either in whole or in part, to his retreatants during the *Exercises,* not only as an aid to the immediate task of the retreat, but also as a guidepost for the future. As might be expected, a number of the ideas are substantially the same as those he left with the people of Parma. A few of these suggestions follow:

Make a review of one's past life and a general confession. Make daily the vitally necessary examination of conscience. This examination is divided into five points: 1. Thanksgiving to God for His blessings; 2. Petition for the grace to recognize one's sins; 3. The searching into one's thoughts, words and actions; 4. A prayer for mercy; 5. A purpose of amendment and the confession of any serious sins. Have a fixed time to receive Holy Communion, at least every one or two weeks. Bring to mind certain principles, easily recallable in their terse and axiomatic form, such as *Conquer yourself, Remember the four last things, Carry your cross daily, Follow the Crucified Christ.*

Safeguard the time given to prayer by three simple precautions: 1. In anticipation of prayer, a consideration of what one is about to do; 2. During the prayer itself in order to keep attention, the recitation of the aspiration *Father, in the Name of Jesus, give me the Spirit;* 3. After the prayer, an examination of how the prayer went. If well, thanks should be given to God; if poorly, the fault should be acknowledged. Show these headings among your friends so that they may take up these practices. Hang them up on the wall of your own room.[35]

The text of the *Spiritual Exercises* and the suggestions he distributed among his friends, a number of them transplanted from the narrower context of a retreat into the broader field of daily life, traced the lineaments of Peter's work at Worms, Speyer and Regensburg, and gave it a character that made his status a unique one among the many theologians, diplomats and courtiers assembled around Charles V. He helped the men at the Imperial Diet discover the deep well of desire for God within their hearts, and they, in numbers that grew each day, beat a path to his door to listen and learn how this desire might be gratified. This particular mode of apostolic work sketched the pattern for most of Peter's future ministry which, be it in Germany, the Netherlands, Portugal or Spain, had its point of departure in the *Spiritual Exercises* and their great principles.

*   *   *

About two weeks after Peter had arrived at Regensburg, six other Jesuits gathered together at Rome for the important task of fixing more precisely and in greater detail the form of their religious life by drawing up Constitutions. In the latter part of September 1540, when the Bull *Regimini Militantis* was issued by the Holy Father, only three Jesuits were in Rome: Ignatius, Codure and Salmerón. The others were scattered to different parts of Europe, Xavier and Rodriguez to Portugal, Broet to Siena, Jay to Brescia, Laínez to Piacenza, Bobadilla to the Kingdom of Naples. The need for the presence of more men for this important work moved Ignatius, who canonically was not Superior but who in the words of Polanco was "the hand at the rudder of this ship," to ask the Pope to permit at least Laínez, Broet and Jay to return to Rome. The six Fathers met on March 4, 1541, on which day Ignatius and Codure were designated to deliberate on the different problems relative to the Constitutions and then to refer their conclusions to the Society as a whole. They began their task on the 10th. Toward the end of the month or at the beginning of April, the six at Rome placed their signatures at the end of the forty-nine points that were decided on by Ignatius and Codure. Factors essential to the intelligent and orderly running of a religious group, such as the understanding of poverty, the training of novices, the formation of members, the extent of the General's power, were covered by these points, and so was clarified the constitutional aspect of what a modern Benedictine scholar has so magnanimously called "perhaps the greatest single religious impulse since the preaching of the apostles, which spread over Europe from Manresa." [36]

The next item of importance in the history of the young Society was the election of its first General. Three days of prayer by the Fathers in Rome preceded the writing of the ballots, which, when sealed, were left in the ballot box for nine more days. Xavier and Rodriguez had anticipated this event and before leaving for Lisbon in March, 1540, had written out their choice. Favre also anticipated the election and sent three copies of his vote, one from Parma in August, 1540, one from Worms in December of the same year, and the last from Regensburg in January, 1541. As the others had done, Peter chose Ignatius. His ballot from Worms read:

> In regard to the first Superior to whom we are to make the vow of obedience, I give my vote to Ignatius, and in the case of his death (*id quod absit*) to Master Francis Xavier. I likewise offer myself from this time on as being under the obligation to obey whoever is elected by the Company or those who are assembled over it; also, any ordinations or Constitutions they in Rome have drawn up. I ask all for the service of Our God to keep me as one of their companions in all they undertake and as a sharer in all their works. In affirmation of this I here place my name written with my own hand, in the Year of Our Lord 1540, on the Feast of St. John the Evangelist. Peter Favre. [37]

The ballot of a month later is more brief but substantially the same: the vote for Ignatius, a second choice for Xavier in case of Ignatius' death, and his act of submission to what should be decided by the Company in his absence.

Besides Peter, three others expressed a second choice on their ballots. These three, Xavier, Rodriguez and Codure, were unanimous in their selection of Favre. Xavier indicated his choice of Ignatius and then added: "After his death—and I now voice the sentiments of my soul as though I had to

107

face death at this moment—let our General be Father Master Peter Favre." [38] Rodriguez wrote: "If he, Ignatius, should not be at hand because of death or some mishap, Peter Favre should be his successor." [39] Codure, expecting to leave for Ireland on a mission for the Holy Father, dated his ballot March 5th, 1540. The person of his choice was

he for whom I bear testimony that I have ever known him as zealous for God's honor and as most ardent for the salvation of souls, and so deserving to be placed in charge of others, seeing that he has ever made himself the least of all and the servant of all, reverend Father Ignatius of Loyola. After him, in my judgment, the one to be preferred is he endowed with equal virtue, Father Peter Favre. This is the truth before God the Father and Our Lord Jesus Christ. Nor would I think of speaking differently if I knew with certainty that this would be the last hour of my life.[40]

Ignatius accepted his election with reluctance and on April 22nd he and his companions at Rome pronounced their vows as members of the Society of Jesus in the Chapel of the Crucifix in the basilica of Saint Paul Outside-the-Walls.

❖　❖　❖

At Regensburg the Diet gradually deteriorated over the question of the Holy Eucharist, and Contarini's eyes were opened to the depth of the differences between the Catholics and the Protestants. The Protestants denied the doctrine of transubstantiation, and the Legate recognized the denial for what it was, the repudiation of a fundamental truth of Christ's teaching.

Outside the conference of the theologians, among the people, there was a widespread attitude of disrespect toward religious practice and the ceremonies of the Church. On Holy Thursday the populace jeered the Emperor as he took part in the ceremony of washing the feet.[41] Peter had little confidence in the power of disputation to change such an atmosphere of irreverence and disbelief, and he felt that the essential need was in the living examples of pure, charitable and devout lives among those who were known to be Catholics. He tried to meet this need in a partial sort of way by the use he made of the letters he received from his brother Jesuits in different parts of Europe, in which were recited their accomplishments for the glory of the Church. Peter showed these letters to his friends, and the *gesta Dei per Jesuitas* at Paris, Rome, Parma, Spain brought courage to souls who needed but a bit of inspiration. "Believe me," wrote Peter to Ignatius,

when I say that such deeds of our men are a source of greater edification than the frequent disputations on faith and works which daily occupy the doctors of Germany. It means a great deal to the Germans to know that the Roman Church is not reduced to such an extreme in its spiritual vitality that it is without members who actually embrace her way of life and her doctrine. I do not fail to encourage these people with news of this kind, just as there are those who weaken them by always writing of examples of wickedness, a factor which goes a long way in their justification of heresy and error. . . .[42]

The men at the court, accustomed to receiving news primarily of a secular nature, read the letters that came to Peter with a mixture of surprise and of respect, seeing the great preoccupation for the spread of the Faith that they expressed.

Some of these gentlemen wonder when they see letters in which is found nothing of worldly concern or interest and which do not rake over the faults of others. Others take hope, realizing that all is not lost, that even now souls are being converted to the Catholic faith, and that many sinners are returning to a life conformed to their beliefs. . . .[43]

On May 31st the conference was terminated by the drawing up of twenty-three articles into what became known as the *Book of Regensburg* and which was submitted to the Estates on June 8th. The Catholic Estates rejected it on July 5th and the Protestants did the same on the 12th. The Emperor's failure at Augsburg of eleven years before, with all its bitter disappointment and mortification, was now repeated at Regensburg. Charles was anxious to leave Germany to take up an offensive against the Turk by an attack on Algiers, and he rushed through a series of agreements with the Diet to cover for the time being the *de facto* German situation. In return for some concessions he received a promise of 10,000 infantry and 2,000 cavalry for three months. The grant was made on July 29th, the very day that Suleiman the Magnificent took the city of Budapest, and Charles left Regensburg to seek success in other parts of his Empire.

During this last fateful period of the Diet, Peter sealed the bond of his union with the Society of Jesus by pronouncing his vows as a Jesuit, as Ignatius and the other Fathers at Rome had done the previous April. On July 9th at the high altar of the church known as Alte Kapelle, located not far from the Dom of Saint Peter's, Favre pronounced the following formula:

I, Peter Favre, promise to You, Almighty God, in the presence of Your Virgin Mother and the entire celestial court, and to reverend Father Ignatius of Loyola, who holds the place of God in the Society of the Name of Jesus, perpetual chastity, poverty and obedience according to the manner of life found in the Bull of the Society of Our Lord Jesus and its Constitutions already

110

promulgated and to be promulgated in the future. Besides, I promise special obedience to the Supreme Pontiff in regard to the missions as contained in the Bull; and again, I promise obedience in regard to the instruction of children in the elements of the faith according to the same Bull and Constitutions.[44]

On July 26th, Peter and Doctor Ortiz started on the road for their original destination, Spain.

A history of the Colloquy at Worms and the Diet at Regensburg within the restricted framework of diplomatic give-and-take, political maneuvers and theological debate would give but meagre mention, if any at all, to the name of Peter Favre, contributing as he did nothing to the progress and development of the religious conferences. When imperial might could accomplish nothing better than a theological impasse and left the trend to Lutheranism, observed by Morone, unchecked, Peter's positive and constructive activity toward the creation of a spiritual renovation was the first wave of what in years to come would be the great floodtide of Jesuit effort in the Catholic Reform in Germany. In assessing Peter's work the attempt must be made to estimate things that in many ways elude examination. He gave what he learned from Ignatius and brought to Germany a promise of renewal of that country's spiritual forces. His labor was not without its recompense, because he could find consolation in the persevering fidelity of those who had placed themselves under his direction. "Of all those about whom I have written to you," he told Ignatius, "be they the ones who have made the *Exercises* or those who at any time have been my spiritual sons, not one, as far as I know, has turned back or lost his fervor." [45] Peter gave his heart to Germany and confessed that very frequently he felt penetrated by what he called "great rays of love and charity" for that nation.[46]

VI. *Weighing the Needs of Spain and Germany*

THE ROAD from Regensburg to Madrid was a long one, and three months were to go by before the three travelers, Peter, Doctor Ortiz and a lay companion whose identity is unknown, would reach their destination. Before they entered France they went into the rugged mountain country of upper Savoy and there they remained for about nine days. Peter was once more back in familiar country-side. It was summer and the shepherd boys had their flocks out in the fresh green fields. At Alex, on the route between Annecy and Thônes and beautifully located on the northern side of Mount Cenis and opposite La Tête à Turpin, they received a gracious welcome from the lord of the region, Mark d'Arenthon. D'Arenthon, of one of the best-known families in Savoy and a close friend of Duke Charles, insisted that the travellers interrupt their journey and remain at least a short while as his guests. They stayed for three days at lovely Alex from where they were able to look through the peaceful passes of Morette and Sainte-Claire and into the exquisitely graceful valleys of Thônes and Dingy.[1]

Peter explained to his host the aims of the Society of Jesus and brought him up-to-date on the religious problems of Germany. Mark served Peter's Mass in the chapel of the château. Whether he realized it or not, Peter was under close scrutiny during those three days. By his gracious manner he made a lasting impression on d'Arenthon's daughter Wilhelmine. When he was in his room, she and other young ladies of the château used to sneak up to a hole in the door and peek through. There they saw Peter completely absorbed in prayer and for long periods lifted above the floor in ecstasy.

One of Mark's servants, Jacques du Merat, had been ill for a year and a half with quartan fever. Peter visited Jacques, heard his confession, gave him Holy Communion and recited some prayers over him. Within a few days he was cured and this, he was convinced, was a grace received through the holiness of Father Favre. At Peter's departure from Alex, Mark, his wife and family knelt to receive his blessing; then the gracious host accompanied Peter and his two companions for a league along the road to Villaret.

It had been eight years since Peter had last seen his home, and now he spent six days in the villages of Villaret and Grand Bornand, visiting his friends and relatives. To the families in the valley of the River Borne, Peter's return was a memorable event and fifty-five years later some of them were able to recall the highlights of those six days. There was a sense of pride in which they spoke of him, one of their own, as a founder of the Society of Jesus. The things they remembered were the things that would impress a simple, devout people of a region far remote from the world that lay at the foot of their mountain homes. They remembered how Peter offered Mass each day after Doctor Ortiz had first offered his, how he created a burst of devotion to the rosary of the Blessed Virgin, how he personally showed them the way the rosary ought to be said. They recalled his sermons, his hearing confessions, his visits to the sick.

High up on Chinallion, Jeanne Favre, an aunt of Peter and mother of several children, had been ill for eight months. Peter climbed the mountainside to her home, prayed over her and said Mass for her intention. Within three days

Jeanne was cured, and the rumor spread through Bornand that Peter had performed a miracle. When the time came for Peter to leave Villaret, the people of the village gathered around, knelt and asked his blessing. There in the majestic peace where neighbors remembered him as the shepherd boy of years ago, Peter in the power of the priesthood raised his hands in benediction over these good people. At Grand Bornand the same scene was repeated. Then the villagers went with Peter and his companions as far as Thônes on the River Fier where he had first gone to school. Peter preached at Thônes and had to decline an invitation to delay there because of the necessity of moving along on his journey.[2]

The three travellers left the mountains of Savoy behind them, crossed the Rhône, only to fall into the arms of the soldiers of His Christian Majesty, once again at war with the Emperor. For seven days they were kept in detention at the little town of Nantua on the River Semine, a short distance west of the Rhône. Prospects for an early release were not promising, and Peter became anxious about Doctor Ortiz. Then an opportunity came Peter's way to speak to the commanding officer. The military might of France broke before the charm and graciousness of the Savoyard prisoner. The officer made his confession to Peter, and the gates of the prison were thrown open. "I hope," wrote Peter, "that I shall never be unmindful of the great goodness of Our Lord, Who by His favor freed us from our captors and gave us the grace of an occasion to speak with them and to help them spiritually."[3] With Nantua behind them the travellers turned westward toward Lyons. More than likely they followed the course of the Rhône southward. Toward the end of September they were at Narbonne, and for the first time Peter caught sight of the Pyrenees disappearing far into the western horizon and into the lands of Cerdagne and Foix.

* * *

Peter must have learned a great deal about Spain during the years he lived so close to the Basque Ignatius, the Navarrese Xavier, the Castilians Laínez, Salmerón and Bobadilla. This was the time when a united Spain was still in the making. The Kingdom of Aragon, facing eastward ever since the capture of the Balearics in the thirteenth century, and the Kingdom of Castile, having launched from its mountain bastion in the Asturias the *Reconquista* that swept past the Tagus, the Guadiana, the Guadalquivir to the gates of Granada, were now slowly being formed into the unity presaged by the marriage of Ferdinand and Isabelle. The two kingdoms, like separate pieces of gold being hammered together into one beautiful *chef-d'oeuvre*, were gradually being moulded and fashioned into a single unit by the government of Charles V. Peter's recollection of his entry into Spain, as recorded in his *Memorial*, reads like a page from the Roman Martyrology:

That same year while I was entering Spain, I experienced remarkable devotion and inspiration in calling upon the Principalities, the Archangels, the Guardian Angels and the saints of that country. I felt attracted in a special way to Saint Narcissus of Gerona, Saint Eulalia of Barcelona, Our Lady of Monserrat, Our Lady of the Pillar, Saint James, Saint Isidore, Saint Alfonsus, the holy Martyrs Justus and Pastor, Our Lady of Guadaloupe, Saint Engrazia of Saragossa. I asked all of them to deign to look with favor on my journey into Spain and to help me by their prayer to bring forth good fruit. . . . I resolved to adopt the practice, in whatever kingdom or jurisdiction I should happen to be, of commending myself to the principal angels, archangels and saints who are honored in a special way in that particular province or kingdom.[4]

115

Favre was not the first Jesuit to enter Spain since the approval of the Society by Paul III. That distinction belongs to Antonio Araoz, native of Vergara and nephew of Ignatius. Araoz had come from Rome to Guipuzcoa to carry out some business and had left Spain on his return to Rome only two months before Peter and Ortiz had quit Regensburg.

Peter and Doctor Ortiz made the initial stages of their trip through Spain in rapid fashion. Through incredible Monserrat to Saragossa and its El Pilar they passed; through ancient Medinaceli, sentry at the border of Aragon and Castile on perpetual watch over the deep valley of the Jalon far below, to remote Sigüenza with the imprint of Burgundy on its Romanesque Cathedral; then through Guadalajara, proud of its strangely beautiful gold-studded Palacio del Infantado, to venerable Alcalá de Henares, throbbing with the intellectual ambitions of Jiménez de Cisneros. But not an adjective fell from Peter's pen to tell his reaction to some of the world's most wonderful scenery, the starkness of the parched tablelands, the twisting gorges, or to the antiquity of the towns, each a multicolored gem reflecting light from the manifold cultures of Spain's past. He mentions places where he stopped with the casualness with which he might tell that he passed from one side of the street to the other. Delays were few. He had a very special reason, however, to tarry a bit at Medinaceli, since the son of the Duke, Don Hernando dela Cerda, had been one of his spiritual sons at Regensburg. Of the Duke, Peter wrote to Ignatius: "The Duke took me aside and opened his soul with the utter sincerity of a man at the point of death." [5] One thing Peter desired especially to do was to visit the family of James Laínez at Almazán, only twenty miles north of Medinaceli. But Ortiz vetoed the idea, and Peter had to content himself with writing a letter to James' father.

The day after their arrival at Alcalá, Peter had an opportunity to speak with the Vicar General and future Cardinal of Toledo, Gaspar de Quiroga, when he sought permission to say Mass at the Church of San Guisto. The Vicar General's few initial questions expanded into a prolonged conversation, primarily about the work of Ignatius and the Jesuits. "It was remarkable," Peter informed Ignatius,

how delighted and edified he was by all that I had to say. After an hour or two he personally guided me to the church, gave instructions that I be afforded every courtesy and invited me to return at eleven o'clock to dine with him. This I did, and after the meal we were closeted together for another hour or two. Meanwhile more than forty people who wanted to see the Vicar General were kept waiting in the hall.[6]

Doctor Ortiz and Peter had hardly started on the road from Alcalá to Madrid when they met one of the key men in the government of Spain, the Cardinal Archbishop of Toledo, Juan Pardo de Tavera, on his way to Alcalá for a few days' rest. When this capable and most trusted of the Emperor's Spanish ministers greeted Doctor Ortiz, the latter then and there lost no time in telling His Eminence about the Jesuits —*suo more*, Peter observed. The Cardinal requested the two to return to Alcalá with him because he desired to consult with Doctor Ortiz. At least one result came of the conferences between the two men: the Cardinal, more fully schooled in the ideas and work of the Jesuits, extended his expression of good will to them in any work they might take up in his Archdiocese. At long last, toward the close of October 1541, after three months on the road, the two arrived at Madrid.

Peter's first impressions of the city were favorable, and he saw it as a place that gave promise of special opportunities

117

for the success of the Jesuit apostolate. There were a number of factors that would ease his introduction to the people of the city, such as the good will evident in the circle around the Primate and the influence of two gentlemen whom he had directed at Regensburg, Pedro de Castilla and Don Francisco Manrique. Peter reviewed his journey from the time he passed over the Franco-Spanish border and could not help but reflect on how the courtesy and charity he everywhere received contrasted with the contempt and distrust that Ignatius met years before. While writing his report to Rome he had in mind the time Ignatius had been burned in effigy.

I have jotted down all these details, confused as they are, so that you might see that the Spaniards have not burned me in effigy and that our work here is respected in a way that defies description. I am convinced that the peace we enjoy was merited by the persecution suffered by Ignatius. In fact, the depth of the suffering he endured years ago is the measure of the depth of our tranquillity here. May it please the Divine Clemency of Christ Our Lord to grant us the grace never to grow weary of labor in His Vineyard for which He gave Himself up even unto death.[7]

Despite Ortiz' plans to set up a Jesuit residence in Spain, the prospects of Peter being able to settle down in one place were remote. The good Doctor was indefatigable. Ignatius and Polanco may have thought him too obese to take on the labors of a Jesuit, but the pace he set for Peter would have wearied any well-bodied man. Within a few days after his arrival at Madrid, he took Peter to Galapagar, a small town committed to his priestly and spiritual care and located on the Guadarrama River to the North. After Galapagar the Doctor was thinking in terms of an itinerary that included a return trip to Madrid, visits to Torre de La Laguna, Toledo

118

and Salamanca. Over and above the question of these journeys there was the further problem of just where he would ultimately make his fixed residence. About this particular point the Doctor was not sure, one possibility being Galapagar, another being Salamanca, where a professorship might be awaiting him. One consequence at least, if no other, Peter assured Ignatius, would come out of meeting so many people in so many different places. "No one will have ground for the claim that our plans are not publicized in the chief centers of Spain or that the leading people of this country are in ignorance of what we intend to do. . . ." [8]

As things turned out, Peter did not have to leave Galapagar with Ortiz. As soon as he had arrived there, he started to teach catechism to the children and to give the *Spiritual Exercises* to some priests. So pleased was Ortiz with the success that Peter was enjoying in this work that he modified his original plans, told him to finish the task he had started, while he himself went to Ocaña to visit the daughters of Charles V, Doña Maria and Doña Joanna.[9] Teaching catechism to the young was specifically written into the Jesuit Constitutions as a work proper to the Society, and in his teaching experience at Galapagar Peter found a deepened conviction of its value and importance. "Nine days have gone by," he reported to Ignatius,

since I started to teach the commandments here at Galapagar. This I do at the second hour after dinner after I have first rung the church bell to announce the class. Ordinarily each day the little ones number about a hundred, both boys and girls. The fact that they also come from a nearby community, about a league from here, accounts for the large number. On feast days the number is doubled. During the period when I am teaching the youngsters, I usually develop more at length certain aspects of the subject matter for those who are older. For this reason it is

ordinary to find men and women, even priests, in attendance.
. . . So gratifying is the fruit of all this that I feel that up to
now I have not appreciated with deep interior conviction how
very worthwhile is this profession of ours of teaching the commandments.[10]

One day an ecclesiastic from a nearby town happened to
hear Peter preach the eulogy of a highly respected citizen of
Galapagar who had died. Pleased with the sermon, he
invited Peter to speak at his own town the next Sunday.
Peter never thought much of his preaching powers and
probably smiled as he wrote to Ignatius. "I promised him
that I would go, the thought all the while running through
my head that he will certainly suffer no loss of prestige
because of any sermon that I shall deliver there." [11] Peter
rounded out his duties at Galapagar by the work at which he
was most adept. At least two priests, one of whom was
Doctor Ortiz' representative in the town, made the *Exercises,*
probably the first to do so within the borders of Spain since
the foundation of the Society.[12]

The year 1541 was hardly a time when people would
have been inclined to think kindly of the great ones of
Europe. Henry VIII had been married for the fifth time and
had set himself up as *caput Ecclesiae Angliae,* Suleiman the
Magnificent was firmly established in Hungary and was
looking toward Vienna, the contest between Charles V and
Francis I was somewhat paralleled by the distrust that had
grown up between the Emperor and Paul III. On November
19th, Peter wrote in his *Memorial:*

On the feast of Saint Elizabeth, Queen of Hungary, I experienced great devotion. Eight personages came to mind and I
felt the desire to remember them in prayer and to overlook their
faults. They were the Supreme Pontiff, the Emperor, the King of
France, the King of England, Luther, the Turk, Bucer, Philip

120

Melanchthon. I felt that they were being made targets of criticism by a great number of people, and at the prompting of the good spirit there rose up within me a certain feeling of compassion for them.[13]

Through November, December and part of January Peter stayed at Galapagar. A year and a half had passed since he had been with James Laínez at Parma, and since that time he had not seen any of his Jesuit companions. Letters from Ignatius were not reaching him. The recurring note in his correspondence from Galapagar was his desire to hear about the men of the Society. "May God grant," he wrote to Ignatius,

that you receive at least some of the letters I send and that you may realize the desire we have to learn all about you and through you about all the rest of our men and houses. So far we have received not an iota of news, nor have we laid our eyes on a single letter since we left Regensburg. . . .[14] Each week, indeed each day, I feel new pain because I am not receiving your letters.[15]

In his watch for the courier with mail from Rome, Peter never anticipated the kind of message that was handed him in January 1542. In accordance with the instructions of Doctor Ortiz, Peter was leaving Galapagar to visit the court of the Infantas at Ocaña when word reached him that the Pope had ordered him to return to Germany.[16]

In October, 1541, Cardinal Contarini and Cardinal Aleander were assigned a twofold task: to draw up proposals regarding the time and place for a General Council of the Church and to outline a program of reform of the Church in Germany. Under the latter heading they were to make specific designation of the men they thought fit for the task. Because of Aleander's illness, Contarini had to carry the

121

burden alone, but he worked fast and by the middle of the month he made his recommendations. It was proposed that Giovanni Morone should be designated Nuncio and that Robert Wauchope and two Jesuits should be named his assistants. Contarini's suggestions were adopted, except that three Jesuits instead of two were assigned. The three were Nicholas Bobadilla, Claude Jay and Peter Favre. On January 4, 1542, Morone left Modena for Germany. Favre's orders were signed by Cardinal Farnese under date of December 22, 1541.

At the time the Supreme Pontiff ordered our Lord, the Bishop of Modena, to go to Germany to attend to the affairs of the Christian religion, it seemed proper to His Holiness to give him as associates, men who by their wisdom and good example could be of assistance to him in the spiritual succor of souls. Since His Holiness is cognizant of your fitness for the achieving of this purpose and since you have lived for an appreciable length of time in that country, as well as for other considerations, it is his wish that you create no difficulty about returning to Germany. He has therefore commanded me to write you and enjoin you in virtue of holy obedience that on receipt of this communication you immediately take the road to Speyer, or any other route that in your judgment will enable you to reach the said Bishop more rapidly. . . .

A. CARDINAL FARNESE [17]

Brief as Peter's visit to Ocaña had to be—it was for three days only—he did have the opportunity to speak with some of the more influential people in Spain, Ferdinand de Silva, Count of Cifuentas and Majordomo for the Infantas, and his sister Doña Isabel de Silva. The Count was very emphatic about his wish that Ignatius station a Jesuit in Spain, and preferably Favre.[18] The capable and devout Doña Leonor Mascarenhas, who had shared the responsibility of training

Prince Philip, gave Peter a gracious reception and impressed him particularly by her devout earnestness and heartfelt loyalty to Ignatius. How she regretted, she told Peter, that she was not a man so that she could become a member of the Company of Jesus! Doña Leonor had been an important part of the Portuguese influence at the Spanish court ever since she had come to Spain as lady-in-waiting to Doña Isabel at the time of her marriage to Charles V. Born at Almada on October 23, 1503, she and her sister were received into the court of King Manuel after the death of their father. She met Ignatius in 1527 when he was passing through Valladolid on his way to Salamanca, and after that time till her death in 1584, ever remained a generous and devoted benefactress of the Society. Ignatius called her "the mother of the Society," and Francis Borgia wrote to her as "*mi señora charissima hermana en Xto.*" [19] Before Peter took his leave of Ocaña, he gave a talk in the presence of the younger Infanta, Doña Joanna, and the staff of the court. The elder sister, Doña Maria, who was ill at the time, asked Doña Leonor to communicate her respects to Father Favre and her request that he say three Masses for her mother and commend her to the entire Society.[20]

Peter could not very well leave Spain without paying his respects to the man who had brought him there. Doctor Ortiz was at Toledo at this time, so Peter took the road westward for the thirty miles or so from Ocaña. Ortiz was distressed by the news of Peter's recall to Germany and he promptly sent off a message of protest to Cardinal Farnese. Peter's departure from Spain meant the frustration of his fondest hopes, and twice in his letter to Farnese he used the expression "*yo esparava,*" something of an echo of the *sperabamus* of the crestfallen disciples on the road to Emmaus.

123

In regard to Master Father Favre's leaving here I cannot but give humble obedience to the orders of His Holiness. . . . However, I cannot just simply ignore my deep feelings on this matter because, even though I know that Father Favre will achieve great things in the service of Our Lord anywhere he may happen to be, nevertheless what he has accomplished here is outstanding, and I was hoping, *yo esparava,* that it would become even greater. So true is this that, if His Holiness had been accurately informed, I believe he would rescind his order. Another reason for cancelling this command is that it means a great deal to the service of Our Lord and the Apostolic See that His Holiness have a residence founded in Spain with many learned men of the virtuous life and calling of Master Favre. . . . This very residence I was hoping, *yo esparava,* with the help of Our Lord, would soon be established through the spiritual labor and diligence of Master Favre. . . .[21]

It is small wonder then that Favre wrote to Ignatius that his leave-taking of Doctor Ortiz, after three days in Toledo, was "not without intense sorrow of heart." [22] It was a moving picture that Ortiz drew for Cardinal Farnese, of Jesuits, ever at the disposal of the Holy Father, fanning out through the length and breadth of Spain. But when all arguments for both sides were placed in the balance, it was clear that Germany's need of learned and holy priests outweighed that of Spain. In a debate on the subject, Cardinal Contarini certainly would have carried the day against Doctor Ortiz.

An integral part of the story of Peter's departure from Spain is what might be called the episode of the two chaplains. The Infantas, in a charming gesture of courtesy, sent one of their court chaplains to accompany Peter as far as Toledo. After Peter had already left Ocaña, Doña Leonor sent still another priest to catch up with him and to go with him even beyond Toledo. Little did the good women realize

124

what their thoughtfulness would cost them. Contact with Peter of the briefest kind was enough to send the two chaplains along the road back to Ocaña to ask permission to go with him all the way to Germany. These two priests were Father John of Aragon, a Spaniard, and Father Alvaro Alfonso, a Portuguese. Peter himself was not too hopeful about a favorable reaction at Ocaña because he realized how highly esteemed both priests were at the court. So, alone and on the mule provided through the generosity of the Papal Nuncio, he continued on his way. This time he made sure to include Almazán on his route, and there he paid a visit to the parents and two sisters of Diego Laínez. It was about a day's journey from Almazán to Almunia, a small town about nine leagues from Saragossa. Here Peter made a brief stopover. After he had offered Mass in the church of the town, he detected, much to his surprise, Father Juan and Father Alfonso coming through the church toward him. The court at Ocaña had actually given its blessing to their project. "*Y gratissimamente y con muchas lagrimas,*" Peter wrote Ignatius, "they gave me a large batch of letters. They are men gifted for the achievement of every sort of good." [23]

A Jesuit arriving at Barcelona at this time was sure to receive a most gracious welcome from no less a person than the charming Viceroy of Catalonia, Francis Borgia. Francis, a great-grandson on his father's side of Pope Alexander VI and on his mother's side of Ferdinand the Catholic, personal friend of Emperor Charles V, devoted father of eight children, polished grandee of exquisite courtesy, was four years younger than Favre. Whether the Viceroy's first contact with the Society of Jesus was through Father Araoz or Father Favre is uncertain. When Araoz made his first trip to Spain from Rome he arrived at Barcelona on October 19, 1539, about six weeks after Francis had arrived there to take up his duties as Viceroy. But whether the two men met at that time, or in the summer of 1541 when Araoz returned to Rome is not known. Nor is it clear whether Favre met Borgia when he came from Germany to Spain in the early fall of 1541. No doubt remains, however, after March of 1542, for it was then that Francis made his debut in Peter's correspondence. In his report to Rome, Peter advised Ignatius,

> We arrived at Barcelona on Saturday night and were put up through the personal courtesy of the Marquis of Lombay. Both he and his wife, the Marquise, are deeply attached to all of our Company. For this reason all of you in Rome should keep them very much in mind. And meanwhile do not forget us since you can see that our needs are mounting. . . .[24]

Some time after Peter and the two chaplains left Barcelona, Antonio Araoz arrived there on his second mission from Rome to Spain. This time there was no doubt about his having met Borgia. Antonio went about Barcelona in a blaze of glory, heralded for his eloquence in the Cathedral, in the churches of Nuestra Señora de la Mar and Nuestra Señora del Pino, and in constant demand as director of the *Spiritual Exercises*. So many wanted to make the *Exercises*, Antonio told Ignatius, that "ten Fathers would not be enough to take care of all the requests." When Ignatius ordered Araoz to return to Rome, the Viceroy was one of those who took the lead in voicing protest, even to the extent of writing to Ignatius.[25] From these almost casual associations Francis' respect and admiration for the Jesuits grew into the deep love which was eventually sealed by his own entrance into the Society of Jesus.

After Peter left Barcelona in early March, he turned north toward France by way of Perpignan, where he happened to meet Lawrence García, a Spaniard, who had joined Ignatius'

126

group of companions in Rome in 1538. Inconstant, sickly, somewhat light-headed, he did not last very long with Ignatius and returned to Spain. Peter, hearing that he was then at Perpignan, desired to see his former companion. But from his description of what followed it seems that he had his regrets that the meeting ever took place. "He came to the house," Peter told Ignatius,

and immediately on his entrance, highly excited and with tears pouring from his eyes, he threw himself on his knees before me. He begged my pardon and would rise only when I insisted on it. I was not able to get away from him until he had tagged after me for four leagues, all the while telling me of the sufferings he had endured since he quit Rome and of his inmost desire to again be a member of our Company. He insistently asked me to write for him and in his name to beg your pardon and present his plea that you receive him even as one of your hirelings. I believe that without question he will soon be on his way to Rome.[26]

The unpleasantness of this experience was offset by the gracious courtesy of the Spanish military commander of the area, Don Juan de Acuña, who personally escorted Peter and the two chaplains to the French border.

Only five months had passed since Peter had crossed that same border on his way into Spain. The nature of his achievement during those short months in Spain, marked as they were by nothing spectacular, can probably best be portrayed by certain words that appear in his letters to Rome, such as *communiqué, hablé, familiar conversación, por communicar,* words that tell of intimate and personal conversation with persons like the Duke of Medinaceli, the Cardinal of Toledo, the Vicar General of Alcalá, the Majordomo of the Infantas. The Society of Jesus was introduced to the Spaniards by two men who cut their paths by different methods, Araoz, whose fiery eloquence brought him before the public eye, and

127

Favre, whose quiet priestliness gained for the Society the benison of some of the key persons in Aragon and Castile. Each supplemented the other. And the reception Spain accorded her visitors was symbolized by the courteous and thoughtful gesture of the commander of Perpignan who attended Peter personally on the road to the border.

❀   ❀   ❀

Peter and his two companions took about six weeks to make the journey between Barcelona and Speyer, reaching Lyons, the halfway mark, by way of the Rhône Valley by March 20th. Once more he ran afoul of the French military. At Valence a French knight and his retinue on their way to the King's court stopped them, emptied their pouches and took their letters for inspection with the promise that they could be reclaimed from the postal authorities at Lyons. The only apostolic work that Peter mentioned after his departure from Perpignan was some preaching that he did at the village of Serrieres, near Turnon on the Rhône. From Lyons they traveled into Savoy, but they did not stop at Villaret even though they passed within but six leagues of that village. Holy Thursday and the morning of Good Friday were spent at the city of Solothurn on the Aar River in the Swiss Confederation. The Ambassador of the French to the Swiss resided there and Peter had the opportunity of meeting him.[27] On Easter Sunday they brought the consolation of the Holy Sacrifice of the Mass to the people of a place which Peter did not identify and which had no priest. When the three travellers reached Speyer on April 14th, one of the first things that Peter did was to write to Ignatius to ask him to join them in thanksgiving to God

for bringing us here and for carrying us along on such a prolonged journey through places teeming with all sorts of intense dangers. I am speaking of dangers from thieves, from the clash of warring princes, from heretics, soldiers and the great pestilence which had gripped cities through which we passed. This was especially true in Germany. From all of these we were saved by Our Saviour and Our Hope, Jesus Christ.[28]

By the time Peter had arrived at Speyer the plan for the reform of Catholic life in Germany, conceived in its broad outline by Cardinal Contarini and under the immediate authority of Cardinal Morone, was already set in motion through the missions assigned to Claude Jay and Nicholas Bobadilla, the two other Jesuits picked with Favre for this work. Jay had been sent into Bavaria and the area of the upper Danube, where with the Primate of Armagh he was to be active in the cities of Regensburg, Ingolstadt, Dilingen and Salzburg. Bobadilla had left Speyer just a few days before Peter arrived and was headed for Regensburg and a tour that would eventually take him to Vienna. Awaiting Peter at Speyer was a letter from Bobadilla with a brief of the instructions received from Cardinal Morone. These instructions, as it turned out, were not at all definite and left a great deal of freedom to Peter. Morone suggested that Peter might go to the court of Ferdinand, King of the Romans, and work with Jerome Verallo, the Papal Nuncio accredited to Ferdinand, or he might assist the Cardinal of Mainz, Albert of Brandenburg, if he should judge that to be more feasible. It was up to Peter to undertake whatever he felt inspired to do until the time he received more definite word from either the Pope, Verallo or Morone himself.[29]

Peter was keenly disappointed to learn that he had arrived too late to see Morone personally. He wrote to Ignatius that the report of Morone's absence from Speyer came as "news more in keeping with the spirit of the Passion than that of the Resurrection." If only he had been given a specific date on which he was to arrive at Speyer, he would have been sure to be there on time. In this somewhat anomalous situation Peter asked Ignatius that he send him instructions.

> The reason is that I want to know what I ought to do. You well know that there is a difference between being moved by the dictates of self-will and being prompted by the way of holy obedience. This way of holy obedience is, to put it succinctly, perfect prudence and wisdom, total devotion, fortitude and charity for those who receive the guidance of that virtue in a spirit of perfect humility, patience and joy.[30]

These words show how strongly Ignatius had imprinted on Peter's heart the ideal of obedience years before he delineated it so masterfully in his famous letter on that subject in 1553. For Peter, obedience was the *sine qua non* for progress in other virtues. Ignatius held the same when he wrote: "As long as this virtue shall flourish, all others doubtless will flourish, and bring forth such fruits as I desire in your hearts." It was the basic and radical Jesuit need to put aside self-will and to know the will of his superior that motivated Peter to write from Speyer to Ignatius for instructions.

On the advice of the local Bishop, whom he knew from his brief visit of the previous year, Peter decided to remain at Speyer for the time being. There was no end of priestly work to be done there; it was one of the more important centers in the upper Rhine area and a likely starting point for any effort toward reform.

As Peter settled down, he could have had no illusions about the nature of the task ahead of him, knowing Germany as he did from his sojourn of the years before and having observed much to discourage him on his return trip from

130

Spain. In his first letter to Ignatius from Speyer there is an insistent note of sorrow that always came to the fore when he spoke of Germany.

It is a terrifying thing to see the numerous places that there are in Germany, and I include those that are free of corruption, where there are no priests to say Mass. Other places there are with but one priest. This situation has been brought about either because of the pestilence or because of the corroding effects of heresy toward which many are inclined. May it please Our Lord Jesus Christ to send us workers to care for these souls . . . workers who will in person visit these places and behold with their own eyes, touch with their own hands and hear with their own ears the condition of those objects that are consecrated for the divine service and the carrying out of the divine worship. . . . They would see corporals, altar cloths and coverings of the chalice in such condition that they might very well be moved to a greater solicitude about the state of the coverings of the spiritual altars, the souls of men where the Lord God should dwell. In fine, they would see such a picture that they would never again be surprised at anything they might run into, except the puzzling fact that there are not more Lutherans. . . .[31]

The man who seems to have done most to make Peter feel at home in Speyer was a canon of the cathedral, Otto Truchsess von Waldburg. Otto, to whom Peter was no stranger, the two having met at Regensburg in 1541, opened his home to the recent arrivals from Spain and introduced them to his friends and relatives. His esteem for the men of the Society of Jesus which began at Regensburg deepened as the years went on and as he came to rely on them more and more once he had assumed the responsibilities of the see of Augsburg. The welcome by Truchsess was, in its expansiveness and cordiality, in sharp contrast to the widespread suspicion and distrust that the priests and people in general

131

had about Peter's purpose in settling among them. The news had been circulated that Peter was a cog in a machine of reformation that had been set up by Cardinal Morone during the latter's stay in Speyer. The people with an instinctive reaction against the professional reformer, aggravated no doubt by the widespread nationalism stirred up by the humanists with their jaundiced view of things Roman, turned on Peter and his two companions with vigorous displeasure. The fact that Jay, Bobadilla and Favre were working in three different areas of the Empire was a perfect setting for the gossip that pictured the Jesuits fanning out through Germany as Papal spies. One of Peter's objectives, so the people were led to believe, was to search out the secret evils of Speyer and its clergy in order to inform the Pope. Despite the atmosphere of suspicion and hostility, Peter recognized a fundamentally good people and a group of priests that did not compare at all badly with the priests in other parts of Germany. "I, for my part," he wrote to Ignatius,

discredit these murmurings and I attribute the blame for them to the evil spirit and not to these people who by nature are not bad or evil-minded. I have in mind especially the priests of Speyer who carry out their obligations satisfactorily. Among the people there is a natural spirit of devotion which is not evident in other areas and which is seemingly on the increase. . . .[32]

Otto Truchsess and others, in their anxiety to dispel the cloud that hung over the three newcomers, took up the accusations that were being noised abroad and assured their fellow townsmen that these foreigners were not what they thought them to be. Rather were they men dedicated to the attainment of personal holiness and to the task of personal reformation, carried on, as Truchsess expressed it, "day by day according to the sevenfold gift of the Holy Spirit." [33] So convincing was Truchsess and so quickly did Peter steal into the hearts of the priests of Speyer that in a month's time their murmurings had ceased.[34]

Again it was the *Spiritual Exercises* that took up a great measure of Peter's time. The Vicar General, who had made the First Week a little more than a year before, again took up the same meditations in order to prepare for a General Confession. Truchsess himself had started to make the *Exercises* under Peter the previous year at Regensburg but was forced to interrupt them. He now placed himself once more under Peter's direction and started anew from the very first exercise. The Bishop of the city, pressed by the duties of his office, put aside an hour a day when Peter went over to his castle. Then there were the chaplains from Spain. To break in as understudies to Peter and to learn his approach to the spiritual life, there was no better way than to make the *Exercises* under him in their entirety. No time was wasted in starting the retreat. They began within a few days after their arrival at Speyer, having found in the Carmelite convent the place of seclusion they desired. The two men were wholehearted in their generosity and Peter could report to Ignatius that they

have been on retreat eight days now, and I have been so gratified with them that I could not possibly exaggerate in giving you an appreciation of even a small measure of the good I find in them. Although they have not yet made their general confession, they are excellently disposed and they show that alacrity of spirit that one looks for in a person who would make a good election.[35]

In the same letter Peter intimated to Ignatius that the two chaplains were thinking of entering the Society. His intuition was correct, for by the time the *Exercises* had been

133

finished the two chaplains had become Jesuit novices and Peter found himself with the responsibility as their Novice Master.

One of the "experiments" exacted of a Jesuit novice was a pilgrimage. With insistence on traveling without money, on begging food and lodging, the pilgrimage was designed as a test of the sincerity of the novice's spirit of detachment from comfort, ease, self-seeking. The first of his two charges that Peter put on the road was Father Juan, with Cologne as his objective. Interesting and many were the experiences that Father Juan had.

One of them was particularly unpleasant, especially for a gentleman accustomed to the courtesy and etiquette of the Spanish court. It happened on the journey down the Rhine to Cologne. He went aboard a river boat at some unidentified place. A good number of people were making the trip, including a Lutheran who closed in on the poor foreigner and turned into a dismal experience what could have been a delightful ride along one of the most historic waterways of Europe. Past the famous Mäuseturm, where wicked Bishop Hatto of Mainz was supposed to have been eaten alive by mice, past the Schloss Rheinstein looking across the water on beautiful Assmannshausen, past Saint Goar, named in honor of the sixth-century missionary to the sailors of the Rhine, past age-old towns, large and small, they sailed. But all this could have meant very little to Father Juan, constantly badgered as he was by the Lutheran who kept up a barrage of nagging criticism of the idea of pilgrimages and other Catholic practices. Juan did not remain silent and did his best to counter the false notions of his tormentor. At the end of the journey, Juan, who did not have a single coin with him, found himself in the embarrassing situation of not being able to pay for his passage. The woman—for it was a woman

134

who was in charge of the boat—demanded either the fare or his cloak, much to the glee of the other passengers. The Aragonese, unable to express himself in German, startled his Lutheran heckler, who was conversant with Latin, by asking him if he would kindly act as interpreter for him and say to the others that he in his poverty was asking for an alms for the love of Christ Our Lord. The Lutheran was taken aback by the request, but, to his credit, his better self came to the fore and he did as Juan had requested. The requisite money was raised. But the unexpected did not stop there. When Juan tendered the money to the woman she, suddenly distressed by her own importunateness, would not take the alms, but, begging Juan's pardon, asked him to pray for her.[36]

Such an "experiment" as an experience in poverty, humiliation and even positive ridicule was a unique opportunity to carry out the Jesuit pledge of honor made to Christ the King. Peter knew that it was an exacting trial that he was asking Juan to undertake. Some friends had even warned him that his novice might not get back to Speyer alive. When he sent Alvaro Alfonso on his pilgrimage to Trier on August 25th he described it to Ignatius as a journey "most difficult and arduous." But Peter, who had been very close to Ignatius during similar experiences, knew that the Ignatian way was to prefer poverty with Christ poor and insult with Christ contemned, and all out of personal love of Him and the desire to be more like to Him.

Pilgrimages, such as these made by Juan and Alvaro, were hardly in keeping with the temper of the times in many parts of Germany, where the value of good works was a point of ridicule by the Protestants. As a reaction to such doctrine Peter's viewpoint was the larger one, which saw in pilgrimages not only an instrument for the formation of his novices

135

but also a means of reparation for the widespread disrespect among the Germans for such pious practices. He wrote in his *Memorial*:

On the feast of Saint Alexius a certain reflection came to mind while I was going over the mysteries of Christ's life and considering the story of the Three Kings. I was moved by a great desire that Master Juan's pilgrimage be a recalling of the pilgrimage made by the Three Kings when they came to adore Christ. And I reflected on how proper it was that they who had given so much honor to God be visited in their relics. My hope was that pilgrimages of this kind would be acceptable to Our Lord and all His saints, especially in these times and in this country when so few undertake them as a consequence of the heresies which reject the value and worth of such works. . . .[37]

A day or so later Peter again wrote in his *Memorial*:

One day when Master Juan was getting ready to start on his pilgrimage to Cologne I had the very intense desire that his pilgrimage would be acceptable to God Our Lord, to His Mother, all the angels and saints, and especially to the Three Kings, Saint Ursula and her companions. Also, that all would work out well for Master Juan and that the fruits of the pilgrimage would be a sort of return payment for the blessings that the Germans received in Spain when they used to make their numerous pilgrimages to the shrines of Saint James, Our Lady of Monserrat and Our Lady of Guadeloupe. . . .[38]

✿ ✿ ✿

While the two novices were absent Peter paid a brief visit to Albert of Brandenburg, the Cardinal Archbishop of the great see of Mainz. Albert was none other than the prelate who in 1517 had delegated John Tetzel to preach the special indulgence that provoked Martin Luther to placard his famous theses on the door of the university church at Wit-

136

tenberg. After some initial vacillation, he aligned himself with the work of Cardinal Morone in clearing away the dry rot in the German Church and so called down upon himself one of Luther's choicest maledictions. The Bishop of Mainz, said Luther, was

a plague to all Germany: the ghastly, yellow, earthen hue of his countenance—a mixture of mud and blood—exactly fits his character . . . if thieves are hanged, then surely the Bishop of Mayenne deserves to be hanged as one of the first, on a gallows seven times as high as the Giebenstein.[39]

When Peter went to Mainz, he and the Cardinal were not meeting for the first time. They had become acquainted at the Diet at Regensburg in 1541, and there the seasoned prelate of many a stormy battle became one of Peter's warmest admirers.[40] One of the tasks he assigned Peter was the review of certain writings that he feared might be harmful to the faithful of his diocese. What this particular literature was is not known, but it is clear that the Cardinal was quite uneasy about it. He called in several reviewers. Difference of opinion developed among them on a number of points, but in his final decision the Cardinal sided with Peter. To express his gratitude to Father Favre he offered him a valuable silver vase. Expensive as it may have been, a vase was hardly the most suitable gift to give a man who was without a fixed abode and who was so frequently on the road. Peter politely declined the gift and tried to explain that he was not quite accustomed to carrying silverware around with him. The Cardinal, however, would not be denied making some present. When the two were together a short time later, he took hold of Peter and stuffed into a small pouch that hung from his cincture a hundred gold florins. Peter could not very well object in the face of such insistence and he wrote Ignatius, "I, thus confounded and overwhelmed by such magnanimity, asked his blessing and took my leave of him." [41] He sent sixty of the gold pieces to the Jesuit students at Paris and used the remaining forty for alms and other pious purposes.

On his return to Speyer, Peter found the two novices back from Cologne and Trier with many a story to relate of dangers they encountered from thieves and beasts of the forest, of the risk of contracting the plague, of the discomfort of hunger and thirst, of sleeping in bug-ridden beds or under the open sky. Peter told Ignatius that he felt the "experiment" had been a success.[42]

Peter could not have been back at Speyer but a few days when Cardinal Albert sent him an insistent summons to return to Mainz. This order, as it turned out, brought to an end his work at Speyer. When he and his novices left the capital of the Bavarian Palatinate on October 10th, they could look back with gratitude to God on the great change that had been effected in the attitude of the priests and people. A feeling of resentment had given way to one of widespread friendliness. After his arrival at Mainz, Peter wrote to a friend,

> May God be blessed for granting us the favor that our final days at Speyer and our leave-taking were in circumstances more pleasant than at the time of our arrival. For there was no one at Speyer, layman or priest, who had not become kindly disposed toward us. Even those who apparently were farthest removed from us on questions of faith, once they saw our manner of speaking and our attitude, showed themselves to be very gracious. Thus it was with sorrow that we left Speyer and, as for the future, in spirit we shall ever belong to her.[43]

It was not only the change of attitude of the people that made Peter happy but also the many signs of a rebirth of

138

fervor in the old Rhineland city. "God knows," he had written to Ignatius, "what I went through at Speyer in fighting against despair for the well-being of Germany." [44] But as the months passed, the return of the people to the practice of the faith was manifest. With growing frequency they approached the Sacraments of Penance and Holy Eucharist; they participated in processions; they did not hesitate to preach the Church's doctrine. The crowning joy was a report that the parish priests issued the next year, stating that more people had received Holy Communion during the Easter time than the entire twenty years previous. What Peter's share was in writing this page of Speyer's history it is impossible to measure. But the tenor of his correspondence shows that, as he came to know its people through his own priestly work, he could feel the pulsation of a new life throughout the city.[45]

Sorry as Peter was to leave Speyer, his summons to Mainz at least meant that he would remain with the German people, for whom he felt a growing affection. He confessed to Cardinal Contarini that he was grateful to God for being allowed to know intimately two nations so different in their *"essere christana"* as Germany and Spain, and that despite the warmth of the Spaniards' response to his work among them, so much in contrast to the dispirited mood he met among so many of the Germans, he nevertheless felt greater inspiration and a deeper devotion in Germany than when he had been in Spain.[46]

*   *   *

Cardinal Albert's first intention was to send Peter along with his suffragan, Michael Helding, to the General Council which the Pope was trying to assemble at Trent. While waiting for the time to leave for the Council, Peter made arrangements to give the *Exercises* at Mainz. One of his retreatants was a priest of the cathedral who felt that God had brought Peter into the Empire precisely for the salvation of the Germans. On November 7th, Helding and Julius Pflug, Bishop of Naumburg, started the *Exercises* under Peter's guidance. To Peter the two Bishops were stars of hope in the darkened German skies: "The good I look for from these two Bishops is more than I would deserve to see *en esta pobre Alemaña.*"

In early December the Cardinal gave Peter another assignment, the delivery of a series of public lectures on the Psalms, to be held at the school of the theological faculty. How Peter treated his subject matter is not known, a particularly tantalizing circumstance because he attracted audiences three times as large as those who listened to most doctors of the university. This fact, he told Ignatius, was "a miracle in the eyes of those who know the indifference of this city." [47]

Juan of Aragon was at Peter's side giving the *Spiritual Exercises* and through them he induced a priest to give up a life of concubinage. Peter sent Alvaro Alfonso to Louvain sometime in November. Alfonso remained there but a short time before he left for Cologne, where he arrived in early January of 1543. It was Peter's idea that both priests do further studies, and he was most anxious, under pressure as he was for caring for their support, that he would not be constrained to send them to Rome. He hoped to be able to see his way to hold them in Germany since "their mere presence and their good desires" meant so much to the Catholic cause there.[48]

At Christmastime Peter learned that the Cardinal had altered his plan to send him to the Council of Trent. He was to remain in Mainz and to start preaching in Latin on Sundays as well as to continue his Scriptural discourses and personal direction of those who sought his counsel. During the Christmas holidays the lectures on the Psalms were suspended and Peter took this opportunity to visit His Eminence at Aschaffenburg, about forty miles east of Mainz on the River Main. For many years Albert had made his residence at Halle in the diocese of Magdeburg, but in 1541 he was forced to move to Mainz and Aschaffenburg when the Protestants closed in on Halle under the leadership of Luther's friend, Justus Jonas. Albert was glad to receive Peter as his guest at Aschaffenburg and went out of his way to show him the fabulous collection of relics which earned him the reputation of being, along with Frederick of Saxony, one of the greatest relic gatherers in Germany. This collection was a particular target for Luther's attack on Albert. Luther claimed that, when the relics were being transferred from Halle to Mainz, they were augmented by others such as "a fine piece of the left horn of Moses and three flames from the bush of Moses on Mount Sinai," each indulgenced by the Pope.[49] What Peter saw at Aschaffenburg was not, however, the entire collection, since in the transfer from Halle the relics had been distributed throughout a number of cities. But he saw enough to fill him with great awe, and this apparently without the least suggestion to his mind to question their authenticity. He wrote to the Jesuits at Rome,

I do not want to be too wordy in describing the way His Reverence received me and the kindness he continues to show me every day. He was anxious that I see his relics taken from the bodies of the saints as well as his other spiritual treasures. . . . He has a chapel so adorned that I really believe that there is not another in the world like it. I said Mass in this chapel and His Reverence saw to it that all the relics were arranged as though we were celebrating a great feast like Our Lord's Nativity. He

141

attended my Mass and has given other manifestations of his boundless kindness. . . .[50]

In this letter to Rome Peter contented himself with painting a picture of Cardinal's courtesy and reserved for his *Memorial* his innermost thoughts amid the splendor of the lavish chapel.

On the octave of the feast of Saint Stephen, I celebrated Mass in the chapel of his Reverence, the Bishop of Mainz, which on my account was extensively adorned with all his relics and other treasures. On the following day, the octave of the feast of Saint John the Evangelist, I offered Mass in another chapel belonging to His Reverence. This one is in the cathedral and it too was elaborately adorned. In both these chapels, even though they were embellished in this exceptional way, I experienced very little devotion as I entered the sanctuary. Even greater was my utter aridity as I ascended the altar, during my entire time there, and as I left. It thus came about that through the grace of Christ Crucified I lost completely all desire of seeking after external helps as manifold and ornate as these in order to foster my interior devotion and to find more surely Christ Crucified. For it frequently happens, as I have found out on these occasions, that when one receives the unusual favor of men, still more does he lose in his interior life familiarity with Christ and the Holy Spirit. I consequently felt in my soul a certain aversion to receiving the favor and esteem of men of influence, realizing how much more efficacious for obtaining God's grace is a life of closeness to the Crucified and of abandonment by men. All human favor, if it is to be sought for or accepted when tendered us, should be referred and directed to the help of our neighbor and not to our personal gratification. . . . There is, therefore, an unending need of turning one's spirit toward the road that leads to the Cross, since Christ Crucified is the true way to the glory of both soul and body; indeed, not only the Way but also the Truth and the Life.[51]

VII. Along the Prince Bishops' Highway

IN THE spring of the same year, on a day that must ever loom large in Jesuit history, May 8, 1543, and which certainly must have been one of the happiest in Favre's life, one of his retreatants, a young Dutchman named Peter Canisius, made a vow to enter the Society of Jesus. The meeting of Canisius and Favre was one of those meetings, like that of Paula with Jerome, or of Augustine with Ambrose, or even of Favre himself with Ignatius, that meant for a richly gifted soul the finding of a destiny.

Peter Canisius, the son of Jakop Canis and Aegidia van Houwenigen, was born at Nymegen on the very day that Martin Luther was placed under the ban of the Empire through the Edict of Worms, May 8, 1521. Peter's father had been Bürgermeister of Nymegen, and was elected to that position nine successive times. His mother died when he was young and his father married a second time. Peter learned to love his stepmother, Wendilina van der Berg, and spoke of her with affection. On one occasion, when Peter was a boy, he happened to be visiting some relatives at Arnheim when a certain lady, known for her holiness of life, met the young visitor from Nymegen and made the extraordinary prediction that a new order of priests would soon take its place in the Church and that Peter would become one of its members. A beautiful insight into the spiritual experiences of the young Canisius with his surrender to the appeal of sin, hours of repentant prayer and the graces of God gratefully recognized, is revealed in his *Confessions.* Peter wrote these *Confessions* when he was about fifty years old and when he was able to look back on the failures of his youth through the eyes of a saint. It is with this caveat in mind that the *Confessions* should be read. A few passages will give some appreciation of the soul won to Ignatian ideals through the influence of Peter Favre.

What shall I say of those early years of mine when, in my foolishness, I spent my boyhood profitlessly and stupidly in things that were utterly mean and inane? . . . I am not able to take to myself the words that Tobias merited to be said of him, that when he was young never did he do a puerile thing. Nor can I compare myself to Augustine who, even while he acknowledged and lamented the sins of his childhood and youth, attained to extraordinary holiness in his manhood. Indeed many were the things of which a Christian lad is ashamed that I in my boyhood thought of and desired. And many too were the things that I carried out and planned for which I deserved not only a reprehension but frequent and severe chastisement. The age of boyhood has its own particular beauty in its modesty, its guilelessness, its innocence, but in none of these can I take pride. This age also has its faults and I, O Lord, at that time began to soil the nuptial robe You entrusted to me.

Alas for me, how many were the hours, the days and the nights, the weeks, months and years that I wasted. How vain, mean and obtuse I was, leading my life without any thought of the fear and love of You, as though I were in complete ignorance of You, the Source, the Guide and Conserver of my life. . . . Now I plead for Your grace, Lord Jesus, Who, when You were a Boy, advanced more than other boys in age, wisdom and grace before God and men. . . . Lord, Who finds joy in little ones when they come to You even though they be sinners, remember not my wickedness and my transgressions. . . . What other offering can I make for those early years . . . except that by

144

which You are gladly appeased, the sacrifice of a contrite heart and a humble spirit?

It happened that one day while I was still a boy I was praying in the Church of Saint Stephen, the Protomartyr. I lay prostrate and I adored Your Sacred Body, O Lord, reserved in the tabernacle near the main altar. It is impossible to forget the grace You gave me. With an insight, I know not how, of the vanities and the deceitful excesses of the world and of the many dangers to my life and salvation, I poured out my heart's desires to You and I called on You in all earnestness and, I think, not without tears. I prayed that You would be near at hand when I was at the brink of danger and my prayer seemed to have been formed in these words: *Show, O Lord, Thy ways to me, and teach me Thy paths. Direct me in Thy truth, and teach me; for Thou art God my Saviour.* Later on, when I was living next to the Church of the Golden Martyrs in Cologne, I felt this same prayer rise up anew within me. . . . I truly believe that You, O Lord, brought forth in my soul this spirit of fear and holy watchfulness, and that You kept it alive so that my inconstant and wanton youth might stray less frequently into evil paths with such fear as a teacher and guide. During this same period of my youth it came about, and this I am sure not without the help of the Angel Guardian You gave me, that I next began to find pleasure in pictures of sacred things and in the ceremonies carried out in the churches. I therefore gladly served the Sacrifice of the Mass. Indeed, boy that I was, I pretended that I was a priest and I used to imitate the priest's duties by chanting, offering the Mass and praying. In the presence of my comrades I used to carry out the sacerdotal functions as far as I knew how. These actions of a boy indeed seem foolish but they do sometimes reveal the future trend of a man's thinking. . . .[1]

It was in a school near this same Saint Stephen's Church where he prayed with such heartfelt earnestness that Peter received his earliest formal schooling. At fourteen, directed by the choice of his father, Peter entered the University of

Cologne. The new student from Nymegen was particularly fortunate in being placed under the care of a holy priest named Andrew Herll, who counted among his friends another priest of rare spiritual endowments, Nicholas van Esche. Van Esche, schooled in the spirituality of the Brothers of the Common Life and its ardent devotion to the Person of Christ, became a light for Peter in the years of study at the University. Another friend of Father Herll with whom Peter developed a tender and lasting friendship was a young man from Lübeck, Laurence Surius. One love that Peter and Laurence had very much in common was the Charterhouse of Saint Barbara, where both found spiritual refreshment and strength. Surius soon discovered that his vocation was to be a son of Saint Bruno in that very monastery. The Prior of Saint Barbara's, dedicated though he was to the hidden life of the Carthusians, became nevertheless one of the most stalwart pillars of the Cologne church in one of the stormiest periods of its long history. He was Gerard Kalckbrenner from the Belgian village of Hamont.[2] In Prior Gerard's monastery Peter imbibed a spirit that was essentially the same as that of Nicholas van Esche, a refulgence of the spirituality of the Brothers of the Common Life.

These were the precious friends that Peter made as he pursued his studies at the University. He took his Licentiate in 1539; then followed a short stay at Louvain for studies in canon law; at nineteen he was made a Master of Arts at Cologne. This was in May of 1540. The vow of chastity that Peter made a few months before becoming a Master and the decision to study theology indicated the direction of his thoughts. He felt a strong attraction for the Carthusians, but he held back from joining Surius at Saint Barbara's because of the memory he had of the holy woman of Arnheim and her prediction. Sometime about January, 1543, Alvaro Al-

146

fonso had arrived at Cologne to take up further studies.
He and Peter soon crossed paths. He explained to Peter what
he, a Portuguese, was doing at a German University and he
unfolded the story of the recent beginnings of the Society of
Jesus. The new Society of Jesus! What Peter heard was like
a shaft of light to his perplexed mind. He began to see the
cloud of mystery about the Arnheim prophecy dissipate. The
news that one of Ignatius' first companions was at that very
time at Mainz was all that was necessary to start him on the
journey up the Rhine.

Cor ad cor loquitur. The two Peters met and each recognized in the other an image of his own aspirations and ideals:
the soul of the Savoyard, touched in his impressionable years
by the Charterhouse of Reposoir, and the soul of the Dutchman, ennobled by the spirit of the Charterhouse of Cologne.
The touching reverence and devotion of each for the other,
so evident in their correspondence from the time of this their
first meeting, was that of saint for saint. Canisius made the
Exercises in their entirety under Favre's direction. In the
conviction that his search for a new order of priests was over,
he made a vow to become a member of the Society of Jesus.
It was his twenty-second birthday, May 8, 1543. How
completely Canisius was captivated by the person of his retreat master he revealed in a letter to a friend, written most
likely immediately after he finished making the *Exercises*.

My trip to Mainz was not at all unpleasant, and to my great
profit I found the man whom I was seeking, if indeed he is a man
and not rather an angel of the Lord. Never have I seen or heard
a more learned and more profound theologian or a man of such
striking and remarkable holiness. His paramount desire is to
labor with Christ for the salvation of souls. No word of his, be
it in private conversation or in friendly greeting, or even while at
table, is not filled with God, and never does he become weari-

147

some or irksome to his listeners, so eloquent is he. The respect that he enjoys is so great that many religious, Bishops and Doctors have placed themselves in his hands for guidance in their spiritual lives. In that number is Cochlaeus, who affirms that he shall never be capable of making a return for the direction he has received. Many priests and ecclesiastics of different ranks have either stopped living in concubinage, or have retired from a worldly life, or have broken away from their shameful habits to live a life of virtue, and all is due to his influence and zeal. As far as I personally am concerned, I can hardly find words to tell how fully I realize that my soul and my way of thinking have been changed by those very *Spiritual Exercises*, that my mind has been enlightened by new rays of grace from heaven and that I have been imbued with a certain strength, so much so that in the overflow of the divine blessings into even my body I am completely invigorated and seem to be changed into an entirely new man.[3]

What Favre in turn thought of his retreatant is shown in a letter he sent to Gerard Kalckbrenner while Canisius was still going through the *Exercises:*

Meanwhile I am enjoying the company of Master Peter and I find it beyond me to tell you how charming it is. May He be blessed who planted a tree so beautifully developed, and may they be blessed who in any way nurtured it. I do not doubt but that Your Paternity is among those for whom I make this prayer since you aided this young man in so many ways to be what he is and unlike the other youths of his generation. I have grown in my love for our Cologne which found within itself to rear such a pure soul. . . .[4]

Years later when there was a Jesuit Novitiate at Mainz, two stone statues were placed in the vestibule of the house, one of Peter Canisius and the other of Peter Favre. They were reminders to the German Novices of what the Society of Jesus in their country owed to these two men. The young

148

German Jesuits were not to be allowed to forget the two Peters, the two rocks from which they were hewn. *Attendite ad Petram, unde excisi estis.*[5]

*　*　*

During his thirty days of retreat one of the graces that young Canisius asked of Almighty God was that of being able to imitate Christ in bearing insults and wrongs so that his likeness to his Divine Master and Model might be the more perfect. On his return to Cologne, completely on fire with a Novice's dedication to the principles he learned in the *Spiritual Exercises,* he was to find more than one occasion which would be an answer to this prayer. The driving force behind many an anxious and harassing day for Peter was none other than the Elector and Archbishop of Cologne, the vigorous Hermann von Wied, who was doing his utmost at this time to bring his great diocese into the Lutheran camp. The city of Cologne with its 60,000 souls had an importance appreciated by both Catholics and Protestants, and this made both sides all the more determined to control the metropolis that had grown out of the old Colonia Agrippina of Roman times.[6] Like large expanses of land suddenly sinking into the ocean, areas of Germany, quite near to Cologne, were becoming inundated with Lutheranism. To the northeast there were the bishoprics of Münster, Minden and Osnabrück whose Bishop had applied for admission into the Schmaldkald League in January of 1543. To the northwest Duke William of Jülich-Cleves indicated that he was anxious to be associated with the program of protestantizing Cologne.[7] In those days when, frequently enough, the army commander and the theologian walked together arm in arm, Cologne received a high priority rating in the list of places that Protestant leaders felt must be drawn into their orbit. Philip

149

of Hesse voiced the mind of the Schmaldkaldian League when he said that Cologne had to be taken over by any means whatsoever because "if it really comes to war much will depend on this town." [8]

What Cologne needed was an Athanasius, heroic in his devotion to the apostolic faith and undismayed by the power of the opposition. Instead, the great see, known in history as a "true daughter of Rome," had a pastor who opened his arms wide in welcome to Melanchthon and Bucer. Hermann von Wied, one of the six children of Fredrick von Wied and Agnes von Virneburg, was born on January 14, 1477. In 1493 he matriculated at the University of Cologne, but next to nothing is known of his formative years except that he was a great lover of the hunt. The dignity of Archbishop and Elector of Cologne came to him early in life, in his thirty-eighth year, when he received the temporal regalia from the Emperor Maximilian and the pallium from Pope Leo X.

The Emperor Charles could very well have been out of sorts when he made his oft-quoted observation on the Archbishop. "How would the good man go about doing any reforming? His knowledge of Latin is nil and during his long life he has not celebrated Mass more than three times. He does not even know the *Confiteor*." [9] Aside from the question of his theological aberrations, Hermann was perhaps not as ignorant as the Emperor might have believed. He at least kept up with the fashions of men who would be well thought of in those days of the Renaissance, and he lined his rooms with works by such authors as Saint Augustine, Savonarola, Thucydides, Petrarch, Fortunatus, Erasmus, Marsiglio of Padua, Sebastian Franck. He was on good terms with a number of the humanists.[10] Sturm dedicated a volume of his edition of Cicero's speeches to him as "the friend of learning and scholars." [11] The prince of the sixteenth-century human-

150

ists, Desiderius Erasmus, planned to dedicate his edition of Origen to the Archbishop, an intention realized after his death through the efforts of Beatus Rhenanus.[12] Von Wied had given his resounding *approbo* to the Dutchman's criticisms of the current failings within the Church. "Carry on," he urged Erasmus, "to the best of your ability to cleanse with the winnowing fork of the gospel-teaching the threshing floor, for a long time now filled with chaff. . . . As far as in us lies we shall direct our energies to this enterprise. . . ." [13] In the early days of the Lutheran movement the Archbishop championed the cause of Catholicism with vigor, but as the years passed he began to waver in his convictions. It was well to cleanse the threshing floor of the chaff. But it was another thing to scatter the wheat also. Erasmus understood the distinction and saw the compelling need of preserving the unity of the Church even while the movement of reform was pushed forward. Von Wied did not, and under the influence of two Lutherans, Bruckner and Medmann, whom he had brought to his court, he came to believe that the two men most fit for anything like executing a program of reform were Melanchthon and Bucer. The author of the *Augsburg Confession* was not able to get to Bonn, where von Wied held court, until May of 1543, but the way was prepared for him by Martin Bucer, who started to preach there in December of 1542.

Powerful as he was, the Archbishop was not able to overawe three men of more than ordinary courage who became the soul of the Catholic resistance in Cologne, Johann Gropper, the head of the Cathedral Chapter, Eberhard Billick, the Provincial of the Rhineland Carmelites, and Gerard Kalckbrenner, Prior of the Charterhouse of Saint Barbara.[14] Once the direction the Archbishop was taking became clear, the Chapter, spearheaded by the vigilant Gropper, demon-

151

strated that there was among the Catholics of Cologne a consciousness of the seriousness of the situation and a determination to withstand betrayal from within.

Eberhard Billick, whose family name was Steinberger, was born at Bilk near Dusseldorf. Soon after his entry into the Carmelite Order, he became one of the key defenders of Catholicism in the lower Rhine area. In 1540 he attended the Colloquy at Worms, where it is possible he met Favre and where Cardinal Morone asked him to draw up a refutation of the *Augsburg Confession*. Two years later at Aachen he was named Provincial of his Order for all Germany.[15]

With the unobtrusive effectiveness of a contemplative, perhaps the most influential of all three was Gerard Kalckbrenner, the Carthusian Prior. Gerard had a genius for making friends, and with Saint Barbara's as the center he formed a constellation of men and women of rare personal holiness whose spiritual intensity enlightened the city and who by the sheer radiance of their purity and charity checkmated the spread of heresy. Kalckbrenner was born in Hamont, a town of Limberg west of Roermond. As a boy he attended the school run by the Brothers of the Common Life at Herzogenbusch and in this way he came in contact with the spirit of the *Devotio Moderna*. After working as a notary in the Marienstift in Aachen, he eventually went to Cologne and joined the community at Saint Barbara's. In 1523 he was made Procurator, in which office he had charge of the temporal affairs of the community and the administration of its property. In 1530 Gerard had occasion to go to Herzogenbusch on some business, and during this trip he learned of a group of people interested in the ideals of a deeper spirituality and interior life who used to meet in the little nearby town of Oisterwijk.[16]

Oisterwijk, a town rarely, if indeed at all, recognized in

152

the considerations of the great religious movements of the sixteenth century, in its quiet and noiseless way contributed in a measure far beyond its size to the beginnings of the Catholic reform in the realm of the Empire. From Oisterwijk came a number of the dedicated souls who rallied about Gerard Kalckbrenner and became a great beacon shining in the darkness of the region of the lower Rhine. The founder of the group was the priest who, as we have seen, became the spiritual director of Peter Canisius at Cologne, Nicholas van Esche.

Nicholas, born at Oisterwijk in 1507, the son of a cloth merchant, attended the school of the Brothers of the Common Life at nearby Herzogenbusch and eventually joined the Brothers. Ordained in Liége in 1530, he began his priestly work as the spiritual director of the Beguines at Oisterwijk. The superioress of the Beguines was a remarkable woman, Maria van Hout, whose interior life was focused in a special way on the Passion of Christ and who contributed to the spiritual literature of the day by her *Der rechte Weg zu evangelischen Vollkommenheit*. Kalckbrenner would not rest content until he brought Saint Barbara's and van Esche's group into contact with each other, and soon there was a lively correspondence between the two places. In September of 1530 the Carthusian made arrangements for the support of Maria van Hout and two other Beguines at Cologne if they would but come to that city from Oisterwijk. The General Chapter of the Carthusians and the Father Visitor gave their approval of the plan, and Maria with two others named Ida and Eva settled at Cologne. Nicholas van Esche soon followed and, but for reasons of health, would have entered Saint Barbara's. He made his residence with another noble-minded Brabantese, Andrew Herll, canon of the famed collegiate church of Saint Gereon. Herll was born in 1476 at

153

Beardwijk, not far from Oisterwijk, and before going to Cologne had been associated with the spiritual activity of the Oisterwijk group. His home near Saint Gereon's became a sort of spiritual dependency of Saint Barbara's, and it was here that young Peter Canisius received such a warm reception when he first came from Nymegen for his university studies.[17]

The Charterhouse had become a veritable fountainhead of spiritual literature characterized by a simplicity, tenderness and warmth of feeling that placed it in the tradition of the *Devotio Moderna*. Johann Justus of Landsberg in Bavaria, popularly known as Lanspergius, had been Sub-Prior at Saint Barbara's from 1536 to 1539 and published such works as *The Epistle of Jesus Christ to the Faithful Soul* and the first Latin edition of the *Revelations* of Saint Gertrude. Another of the authors at Saint Barbara's was Lawrence Surius. Surius, a year younger than Peter Canisius and his intimate friend at Cologne, came from the city of Lübeck. At twenty years of age he became a monk at Saint Barbara's and filled his thirty-six years of Carthusian life with the tireless work of writing popular lives of the saints and of translating into Latin the works of the German and Flemish mystics of the fourteenth century. The works of Surius were the salt that gave savor to the traditionally Catholic practice of devotion to the saints, just when the Protestants would cast it aside as spiritually insipid. His literary output merited for him a salute from that other great student of the saints, John Bollandus, whose name is immortalized by the awesome enterprise of the Bollandists. A great contemporary of Bollandus, Robert Bellarmine, once made the observation that his was an age of saints. Bollandus concurred with Bellarmine and then went even further. Not only did their age produce saints, but no other period in the Church's history,

154

he thought, was comparable to it in its interest in the editing and publicizing the lives of the saints of centuries gone by. "And no one so far," he continued, "has matched the assiduity and application of Lawrence Surius, the Carthusian." [18] By his Latin translations of the works of Ruysbroeck, Tauler and Suso, Surius made countless persons, laymen and religious, debtors to Saint Barbara's for putting into their hands classics that would otherwise have remained closed books. Small wonder that Kalckbrenner's community became a rallying place for those who would save Cologne from the loss of her heritage.

It was a versatile triumvirate, Gropper, Billick and Kalckbrenner, which was at the head of the Catholic forces in Cologne. Their determination was matched, however, by the relentless drive of Archbishop Hermann, of whom one sympathetic observer wrote to Duke Albrecht of Prussia,

The Elector of Cologne, a right worthy bishop, is throwing himself energetically into the work of having God's word preached in all purity and simplicity, and yet among all his councillors, as I know for a fact, he has not more than two who help and support him in his endeavors. But the good old lord does not let himself be deterred or frightened by anything or any one, neither by the Pope, the chapter, nor the Emperor.[19]

The lines between the Catholics and the Lutherans were becoming more sharply defined, and it was becoming increasingly clear that the impact of a head-on collision was inevitable.

* * *

Peter Favre at Mainz knew of the tense and anxious situation at Cologne, at least in its salient features. Peter Canisius undoubtedly must have given an eyewitness account of the ominous signs that were appearing in the city when he came to Mainz in the spring of 1543, and Alvaro Alfonso, continuing both his novitiate and his studies at the University, almost certainly stayed in touch with Favre. By the time of Canisius' retreat, Peter had been corresponding with Gerard Kalckbrenner. Good apostolic fisherman that he was, Kalckbrenner cast his net in Peter's direction and tried to catch him for Cologne as he had before caught so many others.[20] The first of Peter's extant letters to the Prior is a lengthy one that ranges over a number of subjects of mutual interest to the two men, such as the reasons for the wide-spread tepidity in so many parts of Germany, the effectiveness of good example, the need for courage in the struggle against heresy, the inspiring nobility of soul of young Canisius.

HONORED FATHER IN JESUS CHRIST AND DEAREST BROTHER:

Your letter has been delivered and, brief though it is, I treasure it for many reasons. What I especially prize is the realization that I am remembered by Your Paternity in your spirit of charity and love. I feel this way not because I believe or have the desire that your remembrance of me will give me any standing among men, but because I hope that Your Paternity's prayers to God, His Mother and the saints will be a source of many graces for me. . . .

The second reason why I received your letter with a grateful heart is that in it I could sense that there is aglow within you and your disciples a fire of zeal that has been extinguished in others. I could sense too that you are reaching to heights of perfection even while others are falling away. Would, my Father and Brother, would that the great number of those who now slumber amid the frighteningly great dangers would awake to an understanding and realization of this situation! Oh, that all of Cologne would have ears to hear and harken to the words now

156

spoken to her: "Do the former works; or else I come to thee and will move the candlestick out of its place." Would that every single person, be he in the city itself or in the suburbs, were penetrated with the conviction that these further words of the Apocalypse are being shouted at him personally: "I would that thou wert cold or hot. But because thou art lukewarm, I will begin to vomit thee out of my mouth." Few there are who have an appreciation of the Church, which is the candlestick, in the belief that it is possible to retain the candle and to disregard the candlestick; but then the candle would have no place in which to be firmly fixed once the golden candlestick is missing; for outside the Church there is no salvation. . . .

May Your Paternity, therefore, in your holy fervor, so vital these days, continue to be a source of help to the ignorant and the wayward. . . . Let Your Paternity exhort, strengthen and influence as many as possible so that they, themselves being made strong, might encourage still others. Be courageous in the service of God because violence is being done to His Honor . . . Be of strong heart in the service of Christ, His Only Begotten Son, because all sorts of questions are being raised about the devotion to His Humanity. And finally, be fearless in the service of our holy Mother and the other saints because the veneration of them is being called into doubt with an eye to its eventual destruction. . . .

I am really grieved to hear that there is anyone at Cologne who believes that I can be of assistance to him, or even more, that my presence there is a necessity. Not that I am unwilling to be of assistance to each and every one of Cologne's citizens. It is rather my dread of the evil that should come about if Cologne were deprived of something that would be of help to her sons. . . . Look, Reverend Father, look into the corners of the city and you will find hidden treasures of sound doctrine and piety. . . . I have grown in my love for our Cologne, which found it within herself to rear such a pure soul as Peter Canisius. . . . Nor can we doubt that there are at this very time other unknown plants

157

which are being nurtured for the inspiration of the masses of the people. . . . For in this is Christ made manifest, that out of the mass of such widespread confusion He puts aside some individual souls as vessels of election to be formed and enriched by the Holy Spirit. . . . Carry on with courage, therefore, Reverend Father, and be of good heart. Ask God to deign to bring about the cure of the spiritually infirm through the labor of the spiritually sound. But do not think that the beginning in this kind of work should be made by, first, converting the greatest sinners and then moving on to the less sinful. It is far more advisable that, first, those who are not so bad be turned into men of virtue; but even more important is it that the man of virtue . . . even though he has reached a high degree of holiness, be made still more holy and be more richly endowed with the grace of the Lord. For how can the sinner be induced to adopt a virtuous life except that he see, in the example of good men, that the advance from one degree of holiness to another that is higher is possible of achievement, and that indeed with a certain amount of ease. . . .

May Christ be your daily Food and Drink for the hunger and thirst of your soul. In His Name I would love to visit Your Paternity. But if we cannot have the consolation of sharing our bread together, we can at least find joy in writing each other of our desire to do so, *et si quidem non poterimus consolari in communicatione panum nostrorum, gaudebimus saltem in communicatione nostrae famis.* Let us conclude at this point in Christ Jesus Our Lord in Whom I again wish you Adieu. In haste, Mainz, April 12, 1543. Your Reverend Paternity's servant and brother in Christ Jesus.

PETER FAVRE [21]

Peter's letters only whetted the Carthusian's desire to pry him loose from the hold of Cardinal Albert and to have him come to Cologne. And Canisius' stories on his return from Mainz did not help any to dispose Prior Gerard to feel resigned to what seemed to be the inevitable impossibility of his seeing Favre. A letter of Kalckbrenner to the Prior of the Charterhouse at Treves shows how this was preoccupying his mind during that spring of 1543.

VENERABLE AND VERY DEAR FATHER AND FRIEND IN CHRIST:

Amid the storms by which all of Christendom is shaken in these sorrowful times, God has not deserted His Church, but has raised up some apostolic men, filled with His Spirit and endowed with heavenly virtue. This I have learned from a number of learned men. By their fervor they call back those who are lost and lead sinners to the path of salvation. Their labor is blessed with great fruit, and through the workings of the Invisible Master in the souls of men, their words, like sparks cast off a piece of glowing metal, touch men's hearts and inflame them. . . . One of them, a man of great holiness, is at Mainz in the service of the Cardinal. His name is Master Peter Favre and he is a theologian of Paris. He guides men of good will, who place themselves in his hands, through certain amazing exercises by means of which, within a few days, they attain to a true knowledge of themselves and their sins, the grace of tears, a courageous and real turning from creatures to God, progress in virtue, intimate familiarity with, love of and friendship with God. Would that the occasion would arise for my making a journey to Mainz! A man might very well go as far as the Indies in search of such a treasure. I hope that before I die God will grant me the blessing of seeing this man, His Divine Majesty's wonderful friend, so that I might receive his direction for my interior renovation and life of union with God.[22]

What Gerard could not have in person he would have in writing, and from Saint Barbara's he penned frequent requests to Peter that he charter for him the course to the port of higher religious perfection. The saintliness of the Carthusian was evident to Peter and he was understandably diffident about suggesting any spiritual direction to a man of Gerard's breadth of experience. "I clearly see from all your letters," he wrote the Prior in July, 1543,

indeed, from nearly every sentence in them, that I am unable to give you any satisfaction through the answers that I have been sending you. I wish that there were some hope of my actually being able to do so. But then, who is able to satisfy the hunger that Your Paternity experiences except the Divine Word? . . . And who can gratify your thirst except the waters of the Divine Spirit? . . . You say that you have disposed yourself to receive guidance from me. I suggest that you first put your mind to figuring out what arrangement we might make for the mutual exchange of information about our respective spiritual resources and needs. Immediately you would find yourself forced to wonder whether you ought not to undertake the guidance of my soul. . . .

It is hard for me to see what I possibly could do for your spiritual consolation. For I am sure that the rudiments of the spiritual life are already known to you, and I would be doing hardly anything else except trying to turn a rhetorician into a grammarian or a logician into a dialectitian.[23] And would this not be contrary to Saint Paul's teaching: "Forgetting what is behind I strain forward to what is before"? We also have the experience of knowing what an oppressive thing it is for one who has tasted the higher things to return to the lower.[24]

During his months at Mainz, when the days were filled with lectures, retreat work, correspondence and spiritual direction, Peter was most faithful in jotting down his "lights" in prayer and the inspirations he received from the Holy Ghost. It was a period when his entries in his *Memorial* are most uninterrupted and complete. A few random selections follow:

On the vigil of the Apostles Simon and Jude, when I rose in

the silence of the night to pray, I felt deeply inspired to throw myself wholeheartedly into the work of gathering the destitute sick who are wandering about Mainz and of taking them to a hospital where they might be cared for and be made well again. At the same time I had a consciousness of my frequent negligence, forgetfulness and carelessness in regard to certain poverty-stricken infirm whom I had come across in the past and had at times visited, but with remissness and little concern for what I was doing. Although at these times I personally was without resources, I could have been a help to them by going from door to door begging alms. . . . I could have intervened with the prelates, doctors, surgeons, the authorities and the magistrates of the localities where these infirm and destitute people were living. At this time I was intensely moved to ask the Blessed in heaven who had experienced bad health during their life on earth that they deign to be the advocates of the poverty-stricken sick of Mainz, and indeed of every place else. I was also moved to ask them to obtain for me anew the grace to be of help to these poor people.[25]

On the feast of All Saints, from the time I began to prepare for Mass until I had finished, I felt deep devotion, such as I never before had on this day, in reflecting on the faithful departed. . . . It was given to me to have an abundance of tears as my thoughts turned to my parents and relatives, my deceased brothers of the Society, my benefactors and the parents of all my brothers. . . .[26]

On the solemnity of the Conception of the Most Blessed Virgin Mary, I felt a certain renewal of interior strength and sureness of judgment. As a consequence, I seemed less vulnerable to the force of the waves of temptation. It was not that I experienced much devotion in the sensible part of my soul. . . . And yet I was freed from the all too usual piercing thoughts suggested by the unclean spirit of evil. And this was because I was strengthened and made firm by some new grace sent by God. . . . It is as though someone would announce that his house had been redone by the strengthening of the foundations,

161

the walls and the columns. . . . May Jesus, Most Perfect Saint of saints, grant through the intercession of His Mother and all the angels and saints of heaven that I may be renewed each day, grow in grace and advance in the work of cutting down the number of my imperfections. . . .[27]

On the feast of Our Lady's Purification, I received a deeper insight into the meaning of the Gospel and much devotion from the ceremony of the blessing of the candles. I felt a strong desire not to die until I had come to an intimate knowledge of Jesus Christ and to the realization of His presence in my soul, reducing all to peace in the face of the attacks of the enemy, freeing it from all peril, enlightening it in everything that touches on His service. . . . On that same day I had in manifold ways a sense of my imperfections and failings, especially in the fulfillment of my obligations. My sole comfort against such thoughts of sadness was in the assurance that God looks upon me with favor. If I but cling to Him and be not remiss in my recollection of His presence within me, He will see to it that I attain to the ideal for which I should strive. This day also brought to me a certain joy even as I reflected on my spiritual poverty and indigence, for thus an occasion was given the Blessed Virgin Mary to have pity on me as she looked upon me with my shortcomings.[28]

On the transferred feast of Saint Hyginus, Pope and Martyr, while I was preparing to say Mass for the intention of the Sovereign Pontiff, Paul III, my mind was filled with wonder at the goodness of Jesus Christ, Who showed His liberality to the point of giving Himself entirely and in so many different ways, not only to the just and the holy but also to sinners, as at the Last Supper He gave His whole Self in Holy Communion to the traitor. Here I was reminded that just as Christ gives Himself to me each day as I celebrate Holy Mass and is ready to do the same during my prayer and other pious works, I too should surrender myself to Him in every way. I should give myself not only to Him directly but also to all my neighbors, good and bad,

out of love for Him, preaching, teaching, doing good and opening to all the joys of consolation. . . .[29]

On the transferred feast of Saint Gilbert, confessor, I felt the
deepest devotion during Mass in thoughts of compassion for the
departed souls in Purgatory. The flow of my tears was unceasing.
Before I began Mass, I felt very strongly the desire to be united
to Christ, and during the Mass I saw that an admirable way of so
staying in union with Him was to experience what He experienced in His Passion, both in body and spirit. . . .[30]

✿ ✿ ✿

During the months when Peter and Prior Gerard were
corresponding with each other, the momentum of the Protestant program in the electorate of Cologne was accelerated
and its forces were appreciably augmented. Sometime after
the turn of the year, Bucer, who had started to preach at
Bonn in December, 1542, sent out a call for assistance.
Lesser lights like Hedio, Steuper and Pistorius responded
from Strasbourg, Geissen and Hesse.[31] Melanchthon arrived
on the scene in May, and Bucer, elated by the new power
brought to the Protestant cause by the presence of the
"*Praeceptor Germaniae*," wrote to Justus Jonas in breathless
enthusiasm,

We are suffering at the hands of the Cologne clergy, university and senate the very same things that the Apostles suffered
in Jerusalem at the hands of the Priests, Scribes and Elders. . . .
But God has shown His mercy to us, and that in a magnificent
way indeed, by bringing here His Proto-doctor and uniquely apt
instrument, Master Philip. . . .[32]

Philip looked over the situation and in his first letter from
Bonn wrote to the secretary of the Prince of Nassau, "I see
that something of a conflict is shaping up." [33] It was in reality
more than just "something of a conflict." It was a large-scale

battle, with the Catholics shoring up their defenses in Cologne proper and the Protestants building up their forces at Bonn. Actually, ever since Bucer's arrival at Bonn there had been some skirmishing, started by the indictment of the Strasbourgian's teaching by the Cathedral Chapter of Cologne. In this work the hand of Gropper was evident. On January 27th Gropper presented in the name of the Chapter a plan for reform that would be accomplished within the framework of Catholic teaching. But von Wied would not be deterred, and Bucer continued to preach at Bonn while the pulpits at Andernach, Linz and Kempen were taken over by other Protestant preachers.[34] On March 10th Bucer defended himself against Gropper in a work entitled: *What is Being Taught and Preached at Bonn in the Name of the Holy Gospel.* From then on the attacks and counterattacks became more frequent, and the printing trade, hardly out of its infancy, was kept busy turning out the polemical literature in both Bonn and Cologne. Like two armies behind their redoubts, they bombarded each other over the twenty miles or so between the two cities.

The Archbishop did his part to heighten the drama of the contest. Like Goliath taunting the Israelites, Hermann von Wied on Easter Sunday gave a demonstration of his derision of the things Gropper and Billick stood for when he celebrated Mass in German and distributed Holy Communion under both species.

During the heat of the battle Peter Canisius joined his voice to that of Prior Gerard and urged Peter Favre to join them at Cologne. Some people in the city—it is not known who precisely—sent a messenger to Mainz to argue personally the importance of Peter's presence among them. In spite of pressure put on him, Peter was not able to act immediately because Cardinal Albert, whose permission to leave Mainz was necessary, was absent at the time. No better way could be found for the messenger to spend his time while awaiting the Cardinal's return than to make the *Spiritual Exercises* under Peter's direction. This he did and finished with the resolution to become a Jesuit. When the request from Cologne was finally presented to the Cardinal, he gave his permission for Peter to leave, and by the middle of August Favre had arrived among the people who had closed ranks in the uncertain contest for their city.[35]

Peter found a city tense with expectation. About the same time, with an almost *Deus ex machina* effect, on the horizon of the field of battle appeared a new and different force. All eyes were turned down the Rhine because the report was abroad that the Emperor had returned to Germany and was now not far distant in his march at the head of a powerful army in the direction of the duchy of Cleves. Charles had indeed re-entered the Empire, the first time since his disappointed departure from Regensburg in the summer of 1541, and was now leading a force of 35,000 men against the Duke of Cleves. Duke William, counting on French military assistance, contested the imperial claim to the principality of Guelders. Charles repudiated the Duke's pretensions and, after the failure of diplomatic negotiations, decided to force the issue by armed might. The Emperor's approach was, therefore, the news of the hour, and Peter was very probably reflecting the mood of the city of Cologne when he wrote to Cardinal Morone, "On the Emperor's current arrival it seems to depend alone, *pro dolor,* whether nearly all the German people will have deliverance or annihilation, peace or destruction, and this even in things spiritual." [36]

As soon as he had arrived at Cologne, Peter entered the lists. He wrote, at the request of some of the citizens, to John

165

Poggio, the Papal Nuncio accredited to the court of the Emperor, as well as to the Emperor's confessor. In his letters he pleaded for protection for the Catholics of Cologne and the breaking of the impasse that had developed between the Archbishop and the men around Gropper. These letters, along with one from the University to Granvelle, were delivered at the imperial headquarters which by that time had reached Mainz. Their effectiveness was immediate. Charles sent word to the University and the Senate, exhorting them to fortitude in the faith and promising definite help against their opponents. Poggio too sent a message of hope to the University. At the same time he advised Peter that he wanted to see him personally.[37] Just when these heartening words were tracing a silver lining around the cloud that had hung over Cologne for so many months, further encouragement came in the form of messages from Pope Paul III to both the canons of the Cathedral Chapter and the members of the Senate. Paul had heard, among other things, the story of the way von Wied had celebrated Mass in the vernacular on Easter Sunday, and was deeply troubled. From Bologna on June 1st he wrote to assure the canons and senators of Cologne of his fatherly solicitude for them in their trial and of the comfort he found in their fortitude. The responsibility of seeing that these letters were delivered was given to Peter.[38]

Both the Senate and the University rose up like fresh troops for whom there is not the slightest shadow of doubt about victory. The Senate promulgated an edict making it a serious offense to receive or even to listen to a Lutheran preacher. This was directed chiefly against those people who used to cross the Rhine to the village of Deutz to hear a Lutheran who had set himself up there with the benediction of Archbishop Hermann. The University determined to set aside all vacillation in their opposition to von Wied. Impressed by the wisdom of close rapport with the Papal Nuncio, it also decided to keep a personal delegate at Poggio's side to care for their interests. This office they asked Peter to assume for them. Peter argued against their choice of himself and pointed out what he felt would be an impropriety, that he, practically a stranger in Cologne, should represent that august body. The men of the University were convinced by Peter's argument and contented themselves with the simple request that he carry a memorandum for them when he would leave to see Poggio.[39]

The Emperor Charles and his retinue arrived at Bonn on August 17th. Peter made the short journey there from Cologne on the same day. He made a personal report to the Nuncio and to the Emperor's confessor, and this information was in turn passed on to Granvelle. Peter just missed seeing Melanchthon, who had withdrawn from Bonn on the 28th or 29th of July, but he did have the opportunity that was denied him at Worms and Regensburg in 1541 and 1542 of a face to face debate with Bucer and other Protestant leaders.[40]

Sober thoughts indeed must have been running through the archiepiscopal head of Hermann von Wied during these days, for on the next Sunday the people of Bonn were treated to a sight wonderful to behold. Hermann offered the Holy Sacrifice of the Mass, and under the watchful Hapsburg gaze of the Emperor he carried out the ceremony with the utmost fidelity to Catholic practice. The joy among the faithful was widespread. When the Mass was over von Wied was told by both Granvelle and Poggio that the Emperor wanted to speak with him. During this interview Charles was adamant. Three things he wanted from the Archbishop: first, a promise to remove all Lutheran preachers from the diocese; second, the suppression of Bucer's plan of reformation; third, a

167

promise not to make any innovations in matters of faith in anticipation of imperial decree, and then to follow the Emperor's decisions. It looked as though Charles had definitely brought Hermann's program to a halt, and Peter hastened back to Cologne to pass on the good news to his friends. "I related everything to the doctors and the others who were eagerly awaiting my return," he wrote Morone.

Their delight is intense and they are new men, filled with a fresh and profound hope. I do not doubt that all this brings out clearly how much confidence, strength and energy the solicitude and letters of the Nuncio, Pope and Emperor have brought to the people of Cologne.[41]

Meanwhile the Emperor moved on into the duchy of Jülich, where on August 24th the stronghold of Düren fell to his troops. Left to shift for himself by the French, Duke William saw his territory completely taken over within a few days and himself forced into the position of begging the Emperor for mercy.

Now that this quasi-diplomatic experience was over, Peter gave his entire time among *"esta pobre gente"* to the same work in which he had been engaged in the upper Rhineland, hearing confessions, giving the *Spiritual Exercises* and outlining points of spiritual direction. He also did some preaching in Latin. One of his penitents was Anthony Schauenburg, a canon of Cologne, brother of the Coadjutor Bishop of the city and himself destined to become Archbishop of the see in 1556. There was, however, a big question mark which hung over Peter's work and threatened its continuity at Cologne. What of his obligation to return to Cardinal Albert of Mainz, whose permission to leave for Cologne was not without its restrictions and its limits? The Nuncio, John Poggio, took it upon himself to instruct Peter not to

168

hurry back, and he assured him that he would see to it that an explanation was made to the Cardinal, "so that," as Peter explained to Morone, "I shall not merit a rebuke because of my prolonged absence from Mainz, although I personally do not believe that I shall be wandering far from the Will of Christ as long as I shall be at work in the Rhineland." [42] When word got about that Peter might find it necessary to leave Cologne, some of the people, more than likely Kalck-brenner and his circle, let the Nuncio know that they had some very strong ideas of their own on this matter. They addressed him in a formal petition.

MOST HONORABLE LEGATE:

Since your most gracious sense of duty in advancing the faith and in the winning of souls is sufficiently clear and proven in so many instances, it seemed to us to be a well-advised move to present a petition to Your Reverence. . . . We ask, indeed with all respect we implore through Jesus Christ, that it be given us to continue to enjoy the singularly delightful presence of the very distinguished theologian, Master Peter Favre of the Society of the Name of Jesus. This we ask that this holy city of Cologne may be kept safe and sound. . . . Although he never before lived among us in Cologne, he immediately won the admiration and the more than ordinary love of the faithful. Employing a method that is divine, he is leading not a few to higher virtue. He continues to gain, as the days go by, more and more souls for Christ. Indeed, as we have heard him say himself, his work here is more fruitful than anywhere else he has been in Germany so far.

Therefore, in view of this rich harvest . . . and also for the preservation of the purity of the city of Cologne, surrounded as it is on all sides and enticed by a thousand wiles to become heretical and schismatical, it is of the utmost importance that this man remain here to help by his wisdom the hard-pressed people of this city who themselves are the mainstay of weaker regions.

169

. . . We hope that through God's favor we shall obtain this request from Your Reverence, judging as we do that you, from the power granted you, can satisfy these holy desires of ours. And if it be necessary to do so, we ask Your Reverence to intercede for us with the Servant of Our Lord and His Vicar, Paul.[43]

Such a poignant and touching confidence in Peter was a beautiful return for the completely unselfish and sympathetic way in which he took Cologne to his heart. "I now rejoice in the Lord," he wrote Cardinal Morone,

that during these crises it was given me to be with the people of Cologne for whom I have made a dedication of my energies and life itself. . . . My work here has been blessed with far more success than anywhere else I have been in Germany, and I see a vastly greater number of fish ready for the catch here than elsewhere.[44]

*　*　*

One day in late September or early October, Andrew Oviedo, one of the Jesuit scholastics at Louvain, stumbled into Cologne, severely beaten and wounded by robbers whom he had encountered on the road. He carried a message for Peter that had come from Rome and which terminated his stay at Cologne with the suddenness of a clap of thunder on a clear summer day. Peter was to go to Spain by way of Portugal.[45]

The chain of events which eventually led to this abrupt interruption of Peter's work in the lower Rhine was set in motion by the generous impulse of Father Simon Rodriguez, at that time laying the foundations of the Society in Portugal. One of the social highlights of 1543 in the life of the European nobility was the coming marriage of Prince Philip of Spain and Princess Doña Maria of Portugal. Simon conceived the idea of having some Jesuits accompany Doña

Maria into Spain, where, with her kind favor, they could establish the Society. Simon took his plan to King John, who gave his hearty approval. He then wrote to Ignatius in January, 1543, recommending that Peter Favre be chosen for this mission. The King alerted his ambassador at Rome, Baltasar de Faria, about what was afoot.[46] The Society owed a great deal to King John, who had taken so spontaneously to the Jesuits as soon as he had met Francis Xavier and Simon Rodriguez. It would not be easy to turn down the request of a prince who had already sponsored two houses of the Society, one at Lisbon and the other at Coimbra, and so Ignatius went along with the plan. Orders were sent to Favre, while de Faria wrote to the Portuguese agent in Flanders to see to it that the expenses of the journey were cared for. Communications were slow, however, and by the time Peter received his orders it was impossible for him to get to Portugal in time to accompany the Princess. This did not rule out, however, the possibility of following her to the court at Valladolid and working out from there in the establishment of the Society in Spain. This he decided to do.

Within a few days Peter took leave of Cologne and the many friends he had made there. His part in the defense of the faith in the city was not extensive—he had been there less than two months—and he had not experienced the ordeal of the long and uncertain siege. But what he did do was important.[47] His arrival had coincided with the dramatic turn of events in the wake of the Emperor's march into Bonn, and he pressed home, by letter and by personal interview with the imperial advisors, the critical state of affairs. He had hardly begun his usual and normal kind of apostolic work when he received the orders to go to Spain. It must have been with some misgivings that he observed that already the Archbishop was beginning to vacillate in his

171

action against the heretics. Although Bucer, Pistorius and Hegio had withdrawn, he did not move against some other Lutheran preachers who were still within the diocese. Time was to show that the Hermann who was brought up directly before the famous Hapsburg chin and the Hermann who was well beyond the clutch of the imperial hand were two different men. Peter had noticed the few birds of ill omen that augured unquiet times ahead for Cologne, and his mind could not have been completely content as he turned westward for Louvain, Antwerp and the sea lanes to Portugal.[48]

✿ ✿ ✿

The written work that is always associated with Peter's name is his *Memorial*. In the middle of June 1542, while he was at Speyer, Peter decided to keep a journal in which he would record the varied experiences of his interior life. "On the octave of the feast of Corpus Christi in 1542," wrote Peter,

I was prompted by a strong desire to do from now on what I have in the past failed to do through sloth and carelessness. This was to jot down, lest I forgot them, at least some of the graces given me by God for the betterment of my prayer, my contemplation, my understanding, my work. . . .[49]

He first looked back in retrospect over his past life and briefly summarized the most memorable of God's blessings during that period. This part fills fifteen pages of the *Monumenta Fabri*. Then, in the years that followed, he marked down, sometimes uninterruptedly day after day, sometimes less regularly, the interior movements of his soul, his temptations, his desires and hopes. This part fills one hundred and eighty-nine pages of the *Monumenta Fabri*.[50] The *Memorial* might be described the same way as Ignatius' diary: more

172

the record of God's love for Peter than Peter's love for God. Because of the nature of the *Memorial* the same caution should be given that Ludolf the Carthusian gave in the introduction of his *Life of Christ:* "Take heed that you do not hurriedly read such a life as this, but taste some part of it each day." [51]

The *Memorial* reveals a personality that was candid, affectionate, introspective, contemplatively inclined. It is a work of moving simplicity. Yet, striking as are some of its passages, they are no match for the sublimely intense and often rhythmical sentences of Saint Augustine; nor can they compare with the skillfully chiseled and ringing phrases of Saint Bernard. The *Memorial* is not, in short, a literary masterpiece.

More important, however, than the question of its literary graces is the grave interior struggle waged in Peter's soul that the *Memorial* reveals. Peter did not meet the German religious crisis with the forcefulness and intrepidity of a naturally dynamic spirit. He recoiled from it. His nature was a retiring one and destined by its very sensitivity to keen suffering because of the brutal, coarse and immoral conditions by which he was surrounded. Saint Peter Canisius, thirty-seven years after Favre's death, in a memorial to the General of the Society, Father Claude Aquaviva, on the subject of the Jesuit apostolate among the Protestants, recalled that a very severe trial for Favre had been the thought of the futility of his efforts.

Let this be a basic principle behind the entire ministry of our men among the heretics, be it in Germany or elsewhere, that they be assiduously on guard against the spirit of timidity and diffidence which severely distressed Father Favre and other pious men, a spirit that would make out their work among heretics to be fruitless and as futile as trying to change an Ethiopian into a white man.[52]

During June of 1543 when he was at Mainz Peter confessed that he had the temptation to flee from the whole cataclysm that was developing before his eyes.

> I reflected on the suffering that has been unceasingly mine ever since I came to Germany because of the rebellion of these people. May God forbid that what has suggested itself to me so often ever come to pass! For I have had the thought, originating certainly not with the good spirit but rather with the spirit of diffidence that has distressed me in so many ways, to give up hope of achieving any good here and to flee from the Rhineland which has been assigned me as my field of labor.[53]

That Peter carried on in Germany was a victory of grace. The anchor that held him secure and gave him confidence was his vow of obedience. By virtue not of his own will but of that of his superiors, Germany was his province of apostolic labor. Peter's love of obedience is one of the keys to his character. Conquering timidity and fear, obedience created an apostle distinguished for zeal, perseverance and courage.

In the *Memorial*, Peter does not stand forth as a many-sided man in the sense that he shone as a theological or philosophical star, or as a promoter of humanistic studies, or as a lover of the arts. Not that his spiritual principles relegated these interests to the gehenna of Puritanism, for in Peter's makeup there was not a gram of the rigidity and formalism of the Puritan. But such interests, if ever they made a bid to be heard, were bound to be silenced by the very nature of his external life and by the pressing sense of immediacy in Germany's crisis which demanded that he throw all his energies into the direct apostolic work of administering the Sacraments, giving spiritual counsel, conducting the *Spiritual Exercises*. Peter's absorption in the ideal of his Jesuit vocation was absolute, but his single-mindedness of purpose did not turn him into the grim, witch-hunting type of religious zealot. Ever the affable, friendly, gentle priest, he would have shuddered if anyone, to reward him for his work against Protestantism, had called him a hammer of heretics. Père Dudon in his *Saint Ignace de Loyola* likened Peter to a meteor flashing through the skies of Europe. This is not the happiest of similes, because the light of the meteor suggests a resplendence and an awesome magnificence. And the light cast by Peter was the soft, tranquil, comforting light of the candle.

VIII. Jesuit Roots in Belgian and German Soil

O NE OF the places on his route where Peter planned a short stopover was Louvain, where there had been a Jesuit community since August of 1542, the sixth to be organized in Europe, following upon those at Rome, Paris, Padua, Lisbon and Coimbra. The formation of the Louvain community had been forced on the Jesuits because of the hostilities that had broken out between Charles V and Francis I that same summer.[1] Only four years had passed since Charles and Francis had met on the deck of the imperial galley in the harbor of Aigues Mortes and assured a wonder-struck Europe that they had at last buried their royal hatchets. But the Hapsburg-Valois rivalry was soon resumed and the two princes were again at war in July, 1542.

Francis gave orders that all the Emperor's subjects should be out of France within a month under penalty of death. This decree touched home for eight Jesuits who were part of the Paris community which had been set up in September, 1540, by a group of scholastics under the rectorship of Father James d'Eguia. In November of that same year Father Jerome Doménech, Peter's friend from the days at Parma, brought another group of young Jesuits from Rome, and in March of the following year he succeeded d'Eguia as Superior. Father Doménech hoped that he would be able to hold his little group together despite the wrath of the Valois by an appeal to the university privileges by virtue of which all students, regardless of place of origin, were classified as citizens of Paris. The President of the Parlement, however, as well as the two Cardinals, Charles of Bourbon and Antoine de Médon, thought that it would be too risky for the foreign members of the community to remain at Paris. Doménech could do nothing else but pack up and take along with him the subjects of the Emperor, Andrew Oviedo, Aemilian de Loyola, Pedro Ribadeneira, James Spech, Anthony and Francis Strada and Lawrence Dels. Their objective was Louvain. There they sought asylum in the land whose fortunes were now tied to those of Spain and whose brilliant Burgundian inheritance, received from Charles the Rash, was now eclipsed by the grandeur of the Hapsburg eagle.

Arriving at Brussels on the 28th of July, Doménech discovered that it was necessary to delay making the final lap of the journey to Louvain, because in the escape from France he had actually walked into one of the theatres of the farflung war between Charles and Francis. The French King had dropped the usual offensive in Italy, had launched attacks at Perpignan in the south and in the Netherlands in the north, where one of his most vigorous allies was the hardhitting Martin van Rossem, leader of the troops from Guelders. Van Rossem spread devastation about Antwerp and Malines and was threatening Louvain when Doménech and the other Jesuits arrived at Brussels. The students of the University dropped their texts of Aristotle and Saint Thomas, armed themselves, and in a gallant sortie routed the Gueldeans and opened the Brussels road. On August 13th the Jesuits entered Louvain and found the students and even the religious of the town drawn up in squads, prepared for any new designs that van Rossem might have on their city.

Doménech obtained a house on the Rue des Recollets and had his charges enrolled in the *"pédagogie du Faucon."*

Severance from the Queen of Universities on the Seine was not at all a serious setback to the intellectual formation of the young Jesuits. The University of Louvain, situated at the crossroads of French and German civilizations, had been in the fifteenth century the chief center of the literary reawakening in Western Europe and had realized much more smoothly and easily than her sister universities the transition from the Middle Ages to the Renaissance. Parisians might look down on Louvain as a *parvenu* in the university world, founded as it was only in 1425 by Duke John of Brabant, but it would be hard to match the glory of those three decades between 1490 and 1520 when Erasmus, Adrian of Utrecht, Van den Dorp, Luis Vives, Costers and Palude lived there and initiated reforms in the studies in the faculties of Arts and Law. And how proud were the citizens of Louvain of their University! They placed at the disposal of the students the beautiful Halle aux Drapes, the town's glory until the sad days of 1914.[2]

Despite the many attractive features of the University, Ignatius had decided, nevertheless, that the Jesuits there should withdraw, some to go to Rome and the others to Coimbra. These were the standing orders when Peter arrived at Louvain with the intention of taking with him the scholastics destined for Portugal. That Peter would be at Louvain for a full three months, and that the Jesuits would not be completely uprooted from Belgian soil were developments that were a direct reversal of all that Ignatius must have anticipated when his instructions had gone out from Rome. The gremlin who was waiting in Louvain to do his mischief among the Jesuits was a lovable and childlike priest named Cornelius Wischaven.

178

Cornelius, one of seven children, six boys and a girl, born to Sebastian Wischaven and Anna Wens, came into the world at Mechlin in 1509, probably in the month of October. His early schooling was in his home city. In addition to the Latin course, the school included in its curriculum a training in choral singing that gave young Cornelius an excellent opportunity for developing the beautiful voice with which he was gifted. As a youngster he felt attracted to the priesthood and directed his studies to that end. Ordained on May 17, 1533, at Brussels, when he was twenty-four years old, he then began a period of fourteen years of priestly work in Louvain. Here he displayed an unusual aptitude as confessor and spiritual director. He stressed the frequent reception of Holy Communion and made quite a name for himself by his success in filling the religious houses about Louvain with vocations. At the same time he made the Cathedral Chapter his debtor by the superior way in which he carried out the office of deacon. This office involved the singing of the Gospel at all the High Masses, a practice that consumed practically the entire morning. Cornelius' early training in sharps and flats stood him in good stead, for his singing of the sacred text was a delight to hear. In 1541 he was invited to take over the pastorate of a hamlet called Oerschoth that was due to be vacant in three years. He accepted, but one day, just about the same time, he had a strange and unusual experience that convinced him that his future was not to be that of a parish priest. A flash of light crossed his mind, an intuition of some sort, in which he saw a society of missionary men, not tied down to one region but ever on the move from country to country. He felt sure that he was to become a member of this society. Where this group of men might be he did not have the slightest idea, but he was now unshakably convinced that his life was to be spent neither at

179

Oerschoth nor at Louvain. One day late in June, 1543, this Society came to his doorstep in the person of the ubiquitous Francis Strada.[3]

Strada arrived at Wischaven's home by the most circuitous of routes. Nicholas van Esche, Peter Canisius' saintly director in his early days at Cologne, had by this time gone to Diest in the duchy of Brabant, where he assumed the guidance of the Beguines in that town. How Canisius would like to have seen van Esche become a Jesuit! He hoped that he might be induced to make the *Spiritual Exercises* and in this way find his way into the Society of Jesus. Young Strada, who was among the scholastics who had come from Paris to Louvain with Jerome Doménech, found out about Canisius' designs and in June, 1543, went to Diest to invite the experienced spiritual director to make the *Exercises*. Van Esche gave Strada a warm reception, but it was with the warmth of indignation and not of friendliness. He bristled when he heard what Strada wanted. What could his dear friend Peter Canisius be thinking of to have such confidence in a retreat master as young as Strada! Gradually, however, he calmed down and invited his caller to spend the night at his home. Strada, realizing that he had run against a stone wall as far as van Esche was concerned, did venture, however, to ask his host whether he could suggest some young man or some other priest who might be willing to make the *Exercises*. Van Esche recommended Cornelius Wischaven of Louvain and wrote a note of introduction which contained a sentence or two that would surely catch the attention of Father Cornelius: "His [Strada's] outlook on things is just like yours. Never has it happened that I have met anyone who is more like you."

This introduction was all that was needed to open the door to intimate conversation between the two men. In the

180

garden of Wischaven's home, they exchanged their ideas on such subjects as the ideal of holiness and the spirit of apostolic zeal. In Strada's portrayal of the aim of the Society of Jesus Cornelius saw the realization of his own personal aspirations. He was convinced that his future lay with Strada and his companions. He had found the group of apostolic men which it was given him to see in the memorable illumination he received in 1541. Later in the month, on the 26th, Wischaven started the *Spiritual Exercises* under the direction of Strada. In a secret place, unknown even to his sister Katherina, who was his housekeeper, Father Cornelius passed through some severe tests of his generosity from feelings of loneliness, from thoughts against his decision to enter the Society, and from anxiety about the people who were dependent on him for spiritual guidance. During the retreat Martin van Rossem had again brought his forces entirely too close for comfort; about the same time the order from Ignatius for Strada to ready himself for the trip to Portugal had reached Louvain. Wischaven was, therefore, not able to go through the *Exercises* in their entirety and finished his retreat on August 10th, but not until the battle had been won and he had determined to sign a promise to enter the Society of Jesus.[4] He then invited some of the Jesuits to reside at his home, among them Andrew Oviedo, who shortly afterward went to Cologne with Ignatius' instructions for Peter Favre to make the trip to Portugal.[5]

It is more than likely that Oviedo accompanied Peter along the road from Cologne to Louvain and told him about the Belgian priest whom Francis Strada had won for the Society. Peter certainly was familiar with Wischaven's story because, when he reached Louvain and was introduced to him, he greeted Cornelius in somewhat the same way Our Lord had greeted Nathaniel: "Master Cornelius, I have known you even before laying eyes on you." Cornelius was delighted to have Peter as his guest and was anxious to keep him at Louvain for some little time. Peter, however, would not be delayed and left for Antwerp to make arrangements with the shipping authorities for passage to Portugal. Cornelius, not to be discouraged, had warned Peter that he intended to pray that God would keep him at Louvain even if it meant reducing him to sickness. At the bustling seaport, Peter discovered that no ships were sailing in the immediate future. He turned back to Louvain and he arrived there on the feast of Saint Luke, October 18th. At dinner he felt a fever coming on, but tried to hide this from the others at table. Francis Strada, however, was quick to observe that something was wrong and after the meal put Peter to bed. When Cornelius came to his room to see him, Peter had to admit that his host had won the day. "Master Cornelius," Peter remarked with a smile, "God has heard your petition. I came here to take the others with me to Portugal, but God has decreed otherwise. His Will be done." [6]

The doctors started their treatment by draining three small dishes of blood. The sickness proved to be a lingering one and they were at a loss to hit upon a remedy. It dragged on through November. Not until early December did Peter recover, but only after he had charged his host, "Master Cornelius, you prayed that I be delayed here and your prayer was heard. Now pray that I get better." Much to the amazement of the doctors, once Wischaven had prayed as he was told, Peter began to recover and was able to walk about the house. As Father Polanco penned his chronicle of the Society he added this little observation on these happenings in Louvain: *ipsius aegritudo multis sanitatis causa fuit,* Peter's bodily sickness was the occasion which brought to many a person in Louvain his health of soul.[7] And Father

182

Polanco was correct, because Francis Strada, who was repeating in the pulpits of Louvain his successes at Montepulciano and Brescia, directed any number of his listeners to Peter's sickroom to make their confession.

Even before Peter arrived at Louvain, Francis had made a deep impression at the University by his eloquence. No one less than the Vice-Chancellor of the University, Ruard Tapper, wanted to be the first to place himself under his direction. Sometime after Peter arrived, the President of the Collège du Pape requested the Inquisitor, Theodore van Heeze, that Strada be allowed to give a public exhortation. This request was submitted to Peter, who gave his approval. On the 9th of November Francis spoke for an hour and a half in Latin with such satisfaction that he was asked to give an exhortation every Sunday. There was a danger, however, that his studies would suffer because of the time that he would necessarily devote to the preparation of the sermons. This difficulty was met by a division of labor. Peter assumed the burden of *scriptor* and Francis that of *praedicator*. While Strada was busy learning his Aristotle, Peter, as ghost writer, prepared and arranged the material of the sermon. Strada then carried on from there with his personal warmth of feeling, radiant imagination and sonorous voice. As the audiences grew, three times the need was felt for a larger church, until finally he was delivering his sermons in the Church of Saint-Michel.[8]

Not the pulpit alone, but the more private and hidden work of giving the *Spiritual Exercises* gave play to Strada's talents. Perhaps the most widely known of those who made the *Exercises* under him was the Inquisitor, Theodore van Heeze, onetime secretary and confessor of the last non-Italian Pope, Adrian VI. Van Heeze's generosity, sublimated by the power of the meditations proposed by Strada, carried him to the point where he placed himself entirely in Peter's hands for the chartering of his future life. Peter decided that the Inquisitor, in view of his age and experience, should remain in his office and there employ his talents for God's greater glory.[9]

Father Cornelius, who had so graciously received Peter to his home, found himself, as a novice, in the somewhat anomalous position of being host to his Novice Master, for on Peter, from the very nature of the circumstances, fell the responsibility of the formation of the new aspirant to the Society. Novices are of course supposed to be tested. Besides, Father Cornelius had been a priest ten years, had enjoyed considerable freedom of action, and it therefore remained to be seen how sincere was his grasp of such principles as obedience, mortification and humility, so essential in Jesuit life. Peter was able to concentrate a somewhat awesome amount of testing into a short time. While Strada held forth with all his eloquence in the Church of Saint-Michel, Cornelius had to sit on the steps of the pulpit, in full sight of the congregation, with an hourglass in his hand. Peter had him do some writing and then took him to task for lack of neatness or failure to follow exactly the correct external form. Not once did Cornelius express regret that he had ever prayed that God would delay Peter at Louvain, and he came through these and other testings with flying colors. But not so his good sister Katherina, driven to distraction at the sight of her brother so treated. If she but knew how tame Peter's testings were, compared to the more robust methods of Ignatius that could drive such a stalwart as Father Nadal to tears and make Father Laínez exclaim in prayer, "Lord, what have I done against the Company that the saint treats me the way he does?" She condensed all her feelings against Peter and the others into the phrase "those Spaniards," a

184

little spark of the ire of the Netherlands toward the men from Aragon and Castile that was to turn into a general conflagration in the days of Alba and Farnese. At Peter's bidding Cornelius consulted Katherina on the procedure to be followed in the surrender of his worldly possessions and benefices. Katherina, at the prospect of her brother and herself reduced to poverty, broke into tears and exclaimed that she wondered at her patience with "those Spaniards" who were bent on the destruction of her Cornelius. If she could have only persuaded Cornelius to give his assent, she would have turned the guests, one and all, out of the house. But, as it turned out, these incidents were just passing squalls and Katherina later showed that she entertained no grudge against Peter.[10]

Peter's delay in Louvain also proved to be an unexpected blessing for the Papal Nuncio in Germany, John Poggio. Poggio knew the diplomatic world intimately and had resolved to use his influence to bring Peter back to Germany. On November 12th Peter received a letter from him which threw the whole project of his mission to Portugal into doubt.[11]

❊   ❊   ❊

Poggio was adamant in his conviction that Peter should not be lost to Germany, and he had a strong point when he argued that the Empire should receive prior consideration to Spain. Peter's sickness gave him the time needed to send his grievance to Rome and to receive through Cardinal Cervini the assurance that he would soon be given definite jurisdiction from the Pope to recall Peter to Germany and to keep him there. This was the news Peter received on the 21st of November while he was still ill. By the 28th of the same month, the authority that Poggio sought from Rome reached him, and he dispatched a secretary to tell Peter. At this point the liaison between Ignatius and the Holy See failed. Cardinal Cervini, Poggio's intermediary in Rome, knew nothing of the orders Ignatius had sent to Peter. Ignatius in turn knew nothing of the negotiations between Poggio and the Holy See. With Poggio and Ignatius working at cross-purposes, Peter was caught in the middle. In early December he sent a plea for help to Ignatius.

So far I have not seen the letter to Poggio from the Holy See and just how the extent of his authority has been formulated. I continue to be perplexed, faced on the one hand with the command of Your Reverence and on the other by the opposite wish of His Holiness. I am decidedly surprised that this message was received from His Holiness without Your Reverence's knowing about it, especially since Cardinal Cervini acted as intermediary. In a letter to me it was clear that he knew nothing of my instructions to go to Portugal. I am telling you all this, not because I am inclined more one way than another, but that Your Reverence may know what is going on at Rome unknown to you. If I clearly discern in the letter to Monsignor Poggio the voice of His Holiness, I shall not be able to do anything except to stay in this area until I receive a reply from Your Reverence. I ask you very earnestly for the love of Christ to be prompt in sending me an answer with your decision. . . .[12]

As things turned out the Nuncio's order prevailed and Peter began to make arrangements for his return to Cologne and the dispatch of the students to Portugal.

The story of the Jesuits' approaching departure was bruited about and the fire of the Holy Spirit sped on the word as it spread through the town. Louvain experienced a little Pentecost of its own as a group of nine of the university students, their horizons broadened to the measure of the Jesuit ideal, presented themselves to Peter and sought admission into the Society of Jesus.[13] It was a moving exhibition of generosity and idealism. Opposition developed when the fathers of two of them became violently indignant, one of whom even threatened to have his son thrown into jail. But both were soon won over, although one lamented that he did not know just how he would be able to comfort the boy's mother. Some men of influence in the University tried to dissuade one of the group, but their arguments came to nothing. A great spirit of detachment and selflessness was demanded of these young men that they leave their families, suffer the discomforts of a long sea voyage, and face the uncertainty of life in a foreign country. They had their courage with them—but *horum omnium fortissimi sunt Belgae.*

Another young man, not of the group, who came to see Peter at the news of his departure was Maximilian La Chapelle, nineteen years old, from the city of Lille. He had no intention of asking admission into the Society and his whole idea was merely to make a visit of courtesy before Peter should leave. A student of law, he had become one of Strada's most eager listeners and had chosen Peter as his confessor. Through the months he had felt somewhat attracted to the Society, but at least twice he had definitely decided that it was not his vocation. He was strengthened in his decision by the public attack of a celebrated preacher against "the curiosity seekers and featherbrains" who flocked to hear Francis Strada. Yet, a sense of courtesy prompted Maximilian to come to say goodbye to the man who had so often heard his confessions. He went to the home of Cornelius Wischaven and there found Peter, who greeted him with the question, "And you, Maximilian, do you want to go along with us . . . ?" The words that came through the young man's lips ran far ahead of his firmly reached decision.

187

"Why, it is just what I desire, Father," he blurted. He went upstairs where he found the others. Maximilian would not even return to his dwelling, but gave his key to a friend who was to gather up his belongings and send them to his parents at Lille.[14]

A short time before these happenings a student named Oliver Manare asked Peter to receive him into the Society. Peter refused. Little did he realize that in this refusal he was turning away a future Rector, Provincial and Assistant of the Society. Manare was twenty years old and from the area about Douai. He had heard Francis Strada preach and asked him to hear his confession. Strada explained that he was not yet ordained and took him to Peter. He has left a record of his own personal recollection of his meeting with Father Favre.

He [Favre], although afflicted with a fever, was endowed with such affability and zeal for souls that he most kindly heard my confession. When I finished my confession, since I was completely on fire and hardly knew what to say, I humbly begged through Christ that I be received into their group. The Father, in his prudence, judged my fervor to be still immature, and, since I was in the middle of my philosophy course, he told me that I should wait.

Peter then advised Oliver to place himself under Cornelius Wischaven's direction. As it turned out, after Peter had left Louvain, unusual difficulties of one kind or another made it impossible for Oliver to see Father Cornelius, and he lost contact with the Jesuits, but he never forgot the *"infixa species et imago cujusdam divinae modestiae"* of Favre and Strada. Years later he went to Paris, where he again met the Jesuits and was received into the Society in 1551. He lived to the age of ninety-one, having served as Rector of the Roman College, Commissary for France and Germany, Assistant and Admonitor for Father General Mercurian, Vicar General between the death of Mercurian and the election of Claude Aquaviva, Visitor in Austria, Germany, Belgium and Provincial of the Provinces of Belgium and the Rhineland.[15]

The Jesuits at Louvain planned a three-way division of their community. Eleven, including the quasi-veterans Andrew Oviedo, Francis Strada and John of Aragon, as well as eight new Novices, were to go to Portugal. Peter was to return to Cologne with Aemilian de Loyola and Lambert de Castro, a young student of the University whose home was in Liége. And at Louvain itself, where the previous summer it seemed that not a single Jesuit would be left, Cornelius Wischaven was to remain.[16]

On the feast of the Epiphany, 1544, just before the larger group left for Antwerp, Peter gathered them together in his room after supper and gave them a beautiful exhortation on the imitiation of Christ and the practice of perfection. It was the close of a day of special spiritual preparation for the enterprise that lay ahead. Peter was clearly happy when he wrote to Francis Xavier.

> There is cause to praise Jesus Christ because of the deep consolation that each of these young men has found in the Holy Spirit by reason of his vocation. On the feast of the Epiphany all of them went to confession and received Holy Communion. Each gave me a detailed account of his conscience and they all listened to my discourse with careful attention.[17]

On the 8th these gifts of Northwestern Europe to the Society of Jesus started on their way, Peter de Smet from Hal, Leonard Kessel from Louvain, Hermes Poen from Renaix, James Favre from Douai, John Couvillon and Maximilian La Chapelle from Lille, Daniel Paeybroeck from Termonde and Thomas Poghius from Tournai.[18] At the very

189

last moment their number was augmented in an unexpected way. An insistent young lad wanted to go along, was denied by Father Favre, but refused to take no for an answer. He was a nephew of Cornelius Wischaven, of the same name as his uncle, only fifteen or sixteen years of age and from the town of Mechlin. The night before the departure, young Cornelius, on his knees, begged Peter to let him accompany the others. Peter refused because he felt that the boy was not sufficiently prepared for such an undertaking. This did not stop the young Mechlinese, for the next day he hitched onto the wagon and rode along with the others through the flat countryside to the port of Antwerp. Peter did not learn immediately what came of the tenacity of this spiritual soldier of fortune, but he discovered later that in the face of such constancy the others gave in and took him along for the entire journey. The rich promise of this generous soul was cut short with tragic suddenness in the spring of 1546 when young Cornelius was drowned in a river in Spain.[19]

With the group Peter sent to Father Simon Rodrigues a letter of explanation. It is a revealing letter, for it shows that Peter was not one to measure priestly timber by initial enthusiasm. His sure norm was the acceptance of the principles of the *Spiritual Exercises*, detachment, aversion for sin, personal love of Christ to the point of preferring humiliation with Him humiliated. He prepared Rodrigues for the want of formation that he probably would soon detect in the new recruits. "This group will give you some trouble," wrote Peter,

and you may possibly come to the conclusion that all do not measure up to standard. Circumstances forced us to accept them without a close examination since we did not have time to remain here any longer. Before all else they should make the *Spiritual Exercises*. Then the dispositions of each one will be

190

made evident. . . . I beg you for the love of Christ Our Lord to embrace in love each one of them. . . . Their spirits are not yet formed to the point that they are intent on the persevering search of that Holy Spirit by Whom their souls have been visited. . . . There is, therefore, the need of working the harder with them so that they will be fully disposed to persevere in their vocation. Similarly, you will have to watch some more, some less. Some, you may judge, will have no further need of study. If I had any certainty about my residence, just where I would be and for how long, I would take some with me so that you would not have such a large number on your hands to take through the *Exercises.*

Peter could not refrain from putting in a word for Germany and the need of priests there.

I beg you to make it your concern that Germany will soon receive trained couriers of the word of God. If you should find that you are unable to receive others at Coimbra because of the number I am sending you, send us in exchange some men of holiness who by their example will inflame the spiritually cold of these regions.[20]

On the next day, the 9th, Peter left Louvain for Saint-Trond on the road to Cologne.

❊   ❊   ❊

At Saint-Trond the abbot, temporal lord as well as spiritual head of the area, joined his monks as they assembled to hear Peter preach in Latin three times during his stay there. From Saint-Trond Peter turned southeast on the road to Liége, where his arrival was awaited by Theodore van Heeze and where the parents of Lambert de Castro had their home. Van Heeze gathered together the canons of the cathedral to hear his guest preach. The stopover at Liége gave Lambert an opportunity to visit his parents, which, as it turned out,

191

was the last time he saw them since he died at Cologne the following September. Travel in that part of Europe was somewhat like stepping from ice floe to ice floe in a frozen stream, so broken up into little jurisdictional segments was the area washed by the Scheldt, the Meuse, the Rhine and the Ems. From Liége the travelers moved down the Meuse to Maastricht, across the duchy of Luxembourg to Aachen, then across the duchy of Jülich to Cologne, where they arrived on January 22, 1544.[21]

Peter Canisius was not at Cologne to greet them because he had returned to Nymegen toward the end of December to be with his critically ill father in his last hours. After his father's death, Canisius hurried back to Cologne as soon as he was able to do so, arriving at the early part of February. Before his departure from Nymegen, he gave part of his inheritance to the poor and the rest he brought with him for the sustenance of himself and his companions at Cologne. With this money the Jesuits rented a house that had recently been the residence of the auxiliary bishop, situated near the old walls of the city and popularly known as *"auf der Burgmaur."* [22] The comfort and security that the little community derived from Canisius' inheritance, however, brought little contentment to Peter's stepmother back in Nymegen, and she let him know of her hearty disapproval of his open-handed use of his money. Besides, she was sure that he was caught in the snares of a foreigner whose whole idea was to take away the inheritance. Favre did what he could to rescue his novice from the asperity of Wendelina van der Berg and wrote to the unhappy woman.

RESPECTED AND DEAREST LADY IN CHRIST OUR LORD:

You loudly complain that Master Peter Canisius, up till now ever the dearest of sons, has of late become a decidedly unworthy

192

one, and you judge that this is my doing. On the other hand, seeing as I do this most virtuous young man joined to me in the closest bond of spirit and affection that makes us one in mind and will, I cannot help but wish him every good from the bottom of my heart. This feeling carries me to the point of making me look upon myself as a debtor to all his relatives. . . . Thus it is that I pray much and frequently for the soul of his recently deceased father, for you that God may comfort you, and for your children and those near to you.

"But why is it," you will ask, "why is it that you have taken Master Peter from us when you could not but be aware what his presence, his advice, his help, his comfort mean to us?" I in turn ask you a question, O Christian Lady. What would you do, if, on the one side, you beheld Christ Jesus desirous of taking His pleasure in the intellectual and spiritual progress of this young man, and, on the other side, you beheld his friends and relatives taken up with the desire of basking in the glory of his presence, his transitory possessions and every other sort of passing thing? As I interpret the situation, it is completely a matter of worldly interests. Few there are who care for Peter's soul. But many there are who take it ill that he gives away what is justly his by title of inheritance.

Favre continued his defense of Canisius by the assurance that his own pockets were not being lined with her son's gold. What distribution of money had been made had been for purposes of charity. Peter then closed his letter on a personal note that was an effort to broaden somewhat Wendelina's narrow spiritual horizon.

As far as the stories that are spread abroad about me are concerned, I think that they are too empty to merit your credence. . . . I do not disavow the charge that I am an unknown stranger. That is indeed true, as it is true of all our Fathers. I am a stranger in this land, and a stranger I shall continue to be to the end of my days in any land where the Divine

Goodness will place me. My confidence is—and to this I am wholeheartedly dedicated—that I shall one day be made a servant in the household of God and a citizen in the realm of the saints.[23]

Peter made his chief concern at Cologne the student body of the University and the clergy of the city. His objectives and methods remained unchanged: the formation of a vigorous Catholic life through the endless labor of giving the *Exercises* and of hearing confessions. At this time he gave more than his usual emphasis to preaching. The program of sermons that he delivered in Latin opened on Septuagesima Sunday in one of the schools of the University. Holy Week and Easter Week were especially busy periods for preaching. Students, priests, canons, doctors of law, licentiates in theology, city consuls, the exiled Bishop of Lund, on occasion the Vicar General, came to hear this voice tell of the truth and the beauty of the things that von Wied, Bucer and Melanchthon had been trying to steal from them. To his great missionary brother, Francis Xavier, at this time working in the area of Tuticorin, Peter wrote of his own mission in Germany.

As a result of my sermons I have had many students come to confession. There are about a dozen who receive Holy Communion every week, or at least every two weeks, and this has given considerable edification. There are also some citizens and distinguished ladies of the city who used to have this practice of frequent Holy Communion, but who, in the face of the general apathy all around, began to grow remiss. I should mention especially some students whose faith was completely corrupted, but who have now experienced a true resurrection and have come to an acknowledgment of their errors.[24]

Through the *Spiritual Exercises* a young man named

194

Peter Kannegesser, son of one of the leading women of Cologne, was inspired to join the Society.[25] The novice from Louvain, Lambert de Castro, also made the *Exercises* as part of his formation and finished with the wholehearted determination to carry out his dedication to the Society.[26] A veteran pastor of the city made the *Exercises* and of him Peter wrote to Xavier:

> I am at a loss how to express the broad and deep knowledge that this man has gained of Christ Our Saviour. He praises God for the mercy His Divine Majesty has shown him in not letting him die before his soul felt what he has experienced in the *Exercises.*

Another priest, a man of importance in ecclesiastical circles of the city but with the reputation for a scandalous and vain life, became ill and was visited by Prior Gerard of Saint Barbara's. The Prior evidently drew an attractive portrait of Peter because one of the results of his visit was the wish that the sick man expressed that he be visited by Favre. Peter did so a number of times and also sent Canisius. The two Peters brought the sick priest to the point that he resolved to cut himself off from all business so that he could make at least the First Week of the *Exercises,* with the intention, as he conceived it, "of making an example of himself to the world." [27]

Meanwhile, the other members of the little group carried on their studies. Aemilian de Loyola did exceptionally well in the disputations in the colleges, and Lambert de Castro, after he finished the *Exercises,* joined Canisius in the study of theology. By March there were seven mouths to be fed at the Jesuit residence, and several loyal friends, especially two women and the Carthusians, saw to it that there was always food on the table.[28] In May Peter Canisius noted on his expense sheet that he had paid just under eight marks for the brewing of some beer and that the balance of the bill was taken care of by Gerard Kalckbrenner.[29]

* * *

Kalckbrenner's charity received its reward, in part at least, through the presence of Peter Favre in Cologne. The Prior had written rather wistfully in 1543 to the Carthusian Prior of Treves of his desire to make the *Spiritual Exercises,* and now, at last, he had his opportunity. Peter conducted a retreat at Saint Barbara's for the monks and, as a pledge of his affection for them, gave them a copy of the *Exercises* written out in his own hand. As late as 1764, the Jesuit historian of the Society in the Rhineland, Frederick Reiffenberg, recorded that he had seen the little book that was guarded carefully by the Carthusians.[30] Kalckbrenner contributed his own bit of authorship to keep the memory of Peter alive at Saint Barbara's. He observed Peter closely, listened carefully to his words, and then put to paper some of his impressions. Written in no particular order and covering a wide range of details, these recollections, with sentences that are frequently tortuously long, are without any pretense at literary grace or excellence.[31]

The Peter that Kalckbrenner recalled was a man who had walked through vast areas of the blighted German Church and who had seen many heretics in action, but who, nevertheless, far from being goaded to a spirit of vindictiveness and strident argumentativeness, preserved an attitude of radiant charity and gentleness. "Master Peter says," wrote Kalckbrenner,

that the door should be closed to thoughts that dwell on the evil of others. We should rather find excuse for that evil, give it a good interpretation and in our prayer seek to extenuate it by

196

speaking to God of whatever good can be found in those men. . . . By this practice he often received the great grace to pray for Luther, Melanchthon and Bucer that they might be converted and saved even though they were perverse heretics. . . .

Favre remained in the Carthusian's memory as a priest of sensitive feeling for men in their failings and weaknesses and of uncommon capacity for entering into the distress of others and suffering with them.

Master Peter says that his desire is to be zealous in the cause of mercy rather than in the execution of God's Justice, even though it should happen that God would give him power to punish the wicked. . . . He wishes to be ever moved by a heart of mercy and compassion for all and to win them over by words of sweetness. If at times in a spirit of charity severity of word is necessary, never should we keep feelings of anger in our hearts. . . . The very time we experience an interior feeling of indignation is just when we should hold back from making a correction until a later occasion. Besides, we should imagine the wretchedness and afflictions of the poor and the unfortunate as being our very own so that we might suffer with and be moved to the desire of bringing succor to all of them. . . .

Then there was Peter the apostle. The unending toil of helping others was of a piece with his interior spirit of universal charity. It was a labor of patience with individual souls, knowing each, studying each, seeking what would most help each. In what Père Guitton calls *ce morcellement de soi*, Peter was giving a wheat that had been ground into the pure bread of Christ, not indeed by beasts as had been the aspiration of Saint Ignatius of Antioch, but by the millstones of self-forgetfulness and travail. "Take as your model," wrote the Prior,

this man who was so inflamed with charity for his neighbor's
197

salvation that he was ready to expend himself for each and every one, forgetful of his own needs and even without thought about the time for meals and sleep as long as the salvation of his brother demanded it. . . . Varied are the means and the ways that Master Peter employs in correcting and bringing back sinners and the wayward, perseveringly, by degrees, and in the measure of each one's capacity, until at length they are won for Christ. He never leaves off in his efforts. His doctrine is that there is never room for despair of the amendment of anyone, be he ever so perverse. The wayward soul should be taught step by step, both by word and deed, and should be generously assisted in a spirit of charity until a complete reformation is achieved. A beginning should be made in little things, because it was in little things that the soul first fell, and then gradually into more serious offences. Insistence should be placed on prayer, almsgiving, fasting and works of piety. Let these works and similar ones be adopted with a view to creating a disposition to receive greater graces. He who perseveres in this way will ultimately gain victory.

Then there was the memory of Peter echoing what he had taught in season and out of season in Parma and upper Germany, the essential place that Confession and Holy Communion have in a vigorous Catholic life. It was a memory of a Peter who was constructive and positive in his thinking, free from anything like the grimness and mercilessness that can easily mark a purely negative program of assault on sin.

Master Peter says: Let us encourage men of the world to take up the practice of recollecting themselves at least once a day, in the evening, of examining their conscience and of noting the offences of that day and then asking forgiveness and pardon. Let us also encourage them to weekly or bi-monthly Holy Communion. The result will be that in this practice of frequent Holy Communion, both before and after receiving the Blessed Sacrament, they will be more careful about avoiding sin and checking

198

their evil inclinations, because they will be learning how to recognize and confess what otherwise they possibly would never correct. Let us encourage these men to educate their families, and others also, in these same practices and draw them to a love of God. . . . Let us urge them to visit the hospitals, minister to the sick, help the poor and give themselves to other works of mercy. . . . Instruct the men of the world in the love of God above all things, in fear of Him and in the love of their neighbor as themselves. Make clear to them the meaning of the commandments and how to observe them. Urge them to attend Mass devoutly, daily if possible, to recite a fixed number of prayers, say the rosary of the Blessed Virgin, to honor their Guardian Angel and their other patrons, and to be ready for death at any hour. . . . Urge them to reflect often on the Passion of Christ and His Love and to abstain on Wednesdays and fast on Fridays in His honor.

It would indeed be strange if Prior Gerard had written naught about the Peter who could see God in all things and who could find nutriment for a life of prayer in the very objects that might be for others a source of dissipation. It is, therefore, not surprising to find the Carthusian writing the following.

Master Peter says: From everything you see or hear always draw some fruit, and turn it into an occasion of either a feeling of compunction, or the recitation of a prayer, or an expression of God's praise, or an incentive to reproduce in one's own life what is worthy of imitation. Should someone show his respect to you, you, in return, arouse a holy desire for his well-being or say a prayer for him. If you should happen upon any sinful men or women, say a number of *Paters* or offer some mental prayer for them. As you tread the earth, fear hell hidden within its depths; as you look up to heaven, sigh for its happiness. You can find God hidden in all creatures, in the very food and drink you consume. . . . For ourselves and the citizens of any particular

199

city we should call upon the angel of that city, the guardian angels of its inhabitants, the saints who have ever lived there and taught there by word and example. We should give thanks to God for all corporal benefits as well as for the gift of those holy and saintly persons. We should ask the Divine pardon and forgiveness for men and offer ourselves to bear injuries for their salvation. Thus it is, that, at any time, we can walk among creatures—*spatiari per creaturas*—and turn all to the glory of God and the salvation of souls.

If he had had the blessing of Peter's companionship for a longer time, Prior Gerard might very well have become what the good Lord Jean de Joinville had been for King Saint Louis. But this pleasure was denied him, since Peter remained at Cologne but a very short while. Brief as they are, and silent as they are about such things as Peter's stature, voice, gesture, Prior Gerard's memoirs do give, nevertheless, a fairly full picture of a prayerful, selfless, hardworking priest, ever busy in the streets, the homes, the pulpits of Cologne. They highlight qualities that show why Peter won the affection of men and commanded more than just their respect. They were not the qualities of the dashing, colorful crusader going forth to battle. It was rather his modesty, gentleness, radiant charity, a certain distinct impression that he was in contact with the supernatural world, which made men love him and share with him their most secret thoughts.

✿   ✿   ✿

One of the first things on Peter's list of *agenda* after his return to Cologne was a letter to be written to one of the canons of Saint Peter's Church in Louvain. Cornelius Wischaven was in trouble and needed help. And it was all due, ultimately, to his beautiful voice. Cornelius had tendered his resignation as Deacon at Saint Peter's with the accompanying responsibility of singing the Gospel each day at the High Masses. His object was to be free to devote his time to the pulpit and the confessional. The Chapter did not take kindly to Cornelius' action and they began to think about how they might retain him. They were determined not to lose one whose voice meant so much to the beauty of the liturgy at Saint Peter's. The President of the Collège du Pape, the assistant Pastor of Saint Peter's, and a number of others devised a little plot to trap Cornelius. A dinner party was arranged and Cornelius was invited. He said that he would prefer not to be present at the dinner but that he would join the company at the end of the meal. This he did, and the conversation took a curious turn. Father Cornelius heard his friends sing his praises and make much of what an excellent fellow he was. Complimentary and flattering remarks of all sorts fell on his ears. Something was decidedly rotten in the state of Brabant, and eventually Cornelius sensed the way the wind was blowing. His hosts were using honey, and perhaps a little appeal to human vanity, to lure him back to the cantor's lectern in Saint Peter's. When the diners realized that they were getting nowhere by this approach, they pulled off the mask and argued openly against his decision. Cornelius remained unmoved. Then in one last supreme effort, they appealed to the name of Father Favre. "We know," said they, "that if Father Favre were here he would not deny us what we want. As a matter of fact, he would make you take on this responsibility." Cornelius was not dismayed and shot back his riposte. "Why did you not put this request to him when he was still here in Louvain? Here is my suggestion. Write to him at Cologne. I am under his direction and, if he orders me to do this in virtue of obedience, I shall be willing and happy to do so." [32] Before Peter had reached Cologne, while he was still at Maastricht, the canons had a letter in his hands pressing their side of the case.

Peter came to the defense of his besieged novice. His reply was so angry, even belligerent, that it demands much mental effort to believe that he would have written it. He had seen laziness in high places in the Church and an external formalism empty of the interior spirit of zeal and charity. He was exasperated and his habitual mildness could not conceal the indignation he felt. He addressed the letter to a certain Canon Walter, spokesman for the others at Saint Peter's.

REVEREND MASTER AND DEAREST BROTHER IN CHRIST:

May the grace of our Lord Jesus Christ and His peace be always in our hearts. I have not replied sooner to your letter which I received when I was leaving Maastricht because I was then in a hurry to move on. Besides, I did not know at the time just what I ought to say about the problem you brought to my attention concerning Master Cornelius. If I should deny what Your Lordship requests in the name of the Chapter of Saint Peter's in Louvain, I fear that I shall be subject to some rather serious criticism. And yet, if I should accede to what you piously ask, I am afraid that I would be acting contrary to the admonition of Saint Paul: "Strive for the higher gifts."

There is no question that the office which our Cornelius has up till now fulfilled by singing the gospel is a holy one. But it strikes me that the more holy occupation would be to give that time to the hearing of confessions and helping those who go to him for assistance. The canons, it is true, claim that no one can be found to chant the gospel with as pleasing a voice as his. . . . My reaction to that is this: if the canons but looked around for someone who would give himself without reserve to apostolic labor they might very well find themselves in an even more difficult situation. It is my impression that no matter where you

202

turn it is always much easier to find priests singing beautifully in the church than to find priests who as workers are giving freely of what they have received. Besides, the perquisite, I am given to understand, is not large, just a stiver a day. Yet each day he had to sing the gospel several times, a work that fell on him alone, with the result that no time was left him in the morning to bring consolation to the numerous souls that sought his counsel. Let Your Lordship recognize, therefore, wherein lies the greater service to Christ, especially in this affair of Master Cornelius, whether it be in the singing of the Gospel or in the living of the Gospel.

I do not know what more I should add about these things that touch immediately the question of helping souls. . . . I am not grieved because the very best singers are sought so that the divine worship, embellished in every way, will attract tepid souls to the practice of piety. But what does cause me sorrow is this, that the very things of greatest worth and consequence are not appreciated and fostered by men who count. . . . I am grieved at the sight of the leading men of our age busying themselves with trifles, the men of greatest talent fussing about what is paltry, and men of distinction all wrapped up in what is inconsequential. To feed the sheep of Christ is the supreme duty of the ministers in the Church. Yet, there is no one who has any desire to assume this obligation except for the advantages that are connected with it. Positions in the Church are evaluated by the scale, not of the good works that can be accomplished therein, but of the wealth and honor that can be picked up in them.

Peter realized that his position laid him open to criticism, especially on the grounds that he had little regard for the beauty of the liturgical life of the church. This he met with straightforward frankness.

Your Lordship will counter: In effect, then, you do not want to see the most minute care taken to maintain and enhance the external worship of the Church. You are averse to making any effort to find the best singers, the most competent organists and the neatest sacristans for the sanctuaries. My answer to all this is: Quite the contrary. I decidedly want to see all the things you have enumerated. I wish to see everything of this nature carried out with external decorum and order. But over and above all these externals I would like to see an interior awareness of what it is all about, in the application of all our faculties of a clear mind, a vivid memory and an ardent will to the words and actions of the liturgy. I insist that it is my wish to see all these services carried out in the most perfect manner possible. But what I desire far more is that we apply ourselves to those things that are essentially interior with a fresh measure of whole-hearted attention. . . .

But mind you, I am not asserting, as do the enemies of the Church, that the external liturgy should be turned into a sort of internal divine worship. But I do say that, along with the preservation and even the amplification of the external liturgy, there should be a decidedly reawakened concern for the things of higher moment. . . .

There is one result that I would like to see achieved by all I have said here. Inasmuch as the gentlemen at Louvain whom I have in mind are not troubling themselves to discover a Cornelius who will be an apostle as well as to find a Cornelius who will be a singer, it would please me if Your Lordship would spell out this answer for their benefit. Certain it is that they would find someone with a voice better than that of our Cornelius if they but looked hard enough and raised the salary. . . . We behold the spectacle of the very ones who receive the highest pay for the office of caring for souls manifesting the least interest in their work. Therefore, let one who is working gratis be free to busy himself with the higher things. Such is my judgment and answer to your letter about Master Cornelius.[33]

The canons at Saint Peter's must have gasped when Canon Walter delivered this message to them. It was terribly blunt, perhaps too blunt. Not many days passed before Peter had to write to Louvain again. Once more Cornelius was in trouble.

This time Cornelius ran afoul of a regent at the Collège de Lille at the University. The regent, a venerable-looking gentleman named Armentarianus, was seething inside with all the potential fury of a Vesuvius because four or five of his students were in the group that had joined the Jesuits and left Louvain in early January. One of them, Hermes Poen, had given the key to his room to Father Cornelius so that he could gather up his personal belongings and take care of them after his departure for Coimbra. One day Cornelius made his way to the Collège de Lille to carry out his commission. He was not there very long before he met Armentarianus. The regent, in no uncertain terms, told him to get off the premises and promised that he would be tossed down the stairs if he was ever again found in the building. The incident was soon reported to Peter, who took his attention off the affairs of Cologne long enough to write a few words of advice and encouragement to Cornelius. Peter was clearly nettled by the regent's want of sympathy for the idealism of his former students. The tone of his letter to Wischaven equalled in sharpness his censorious reply to Canon Walter of the previous week. And his judgment of Armentarianus, harsh and severe, was strangely alien to the general temper of his thinking. He wrote in part:

I am sorry to hear that there are some people who fail to recognize, as we do, the special workings of God's grace, by the power of which Christ has drawn to Himself some of their former charges. It is these former students who can now in the name of their regent make up for the numerous ways in which he was possibly negligent in his past life. If this man, who really should have expressed his thanks to you, takes you to task because of a work of virtue, you in turn admonish him because, unable as he may be to follow in the actual footsteps of his students, he fails to be one with them in their aspirations. These very aspirations should have been deepening in his own soul as he advanced in years. If such is not the case, it behooves him to see to it that, in union with his former students, they now come to life in his soul and grow. Otherwise, how does he think he will escape the divine judgment, if at death in his old age he had never, either actually or in spirit, carried the cross of poverty and detachment from the goods of this world? . . .[34]

However, it was impossible for Peter to continue for long in this critical vein and he tempered the sharp tone of his words by an admonition to Cornelius to try to pour oil on the troubled waters in a spirit of charity.

Visit the old man, greet him for me and pay him my respects. Do this not only to him but to everyone who feels that we were responsible for taking away some of their friends at the time the group left for Portugal. If they love us the less for this, it is now incumbent on us to love and reverence them all the more, because they are now more intimately joined to us by reason of our common friends. Take care, my Cornelius, take care that you do not close your heart in the slightest way to anyone.[35]

There was no end of letter writing. The post between Liége and Cologne was kept busy with Theodore van Heeze's frequent letters on his problems in the spiritual life and with Peter's replies.[36] Then there was the correspondence with the court of the Emperor. Those about Charles could not be allowed to relax in their concern for Cologne, because Hermann von Wied, despite his turnabout of the previous August, was keeping alive the embers of Lutheranism against the day when he might fan them into a great blaze. Much had developed in the relationship between the Emperor and the Protestant princes during Peter's absence

206

from the Rhineland. Another one of those imperial Diets that occurred with almost the same monotonous regularity as the turn of the tides was summoned to meet at Speyer at the end of 1543. Each side learned to assess the weaknesses of the other as the time again came around to approach the bargaining table. Charles' victory in Jülich had made quite an impression on the Princes of the Schmalkald League and it also revealed the lack of cohesion in their ranks. Philip, the Landgrave of Hesse, told Bucer that he was not at all sanguine about prospects for even a small number of them voting together at the Diet. But Charles too had his Achilles' heel. He was determined to press the war against France to the finish and this he could not do without the aid of the Princes of the Empire. Carl van der Plassen observed,

The Princes of Saxony and Hesse knew through Granvelle and other bribed imperial councillors that the less they gave in the more they would obtain in matters of religion, for the Emperor has set his mind determinately on the war against France, and in order to get help for this purpose he would be ready to concede all that was possible.[37]

This appraisal of the Emperor's position was borne out by the agreement reached at Speyer that, "a general Christian free council of the German nation" was the proper medium for healing the religious conflict.

Pope Paul III, who was trying to open a General Council of the Church at Trent, sent to Charles a scathing criticism of the way the Catholics had jettisoned the principle that religious questions were outside the competence of the layman. The Diet, which was protracted through the spring of 1544, had its repercussions in Cologne. Some members of the University, as well as other loyal Catholics of the city, were afraid that the stage was again being set for the

Archbishop to show off what he had in his bag of innovating tricks. The story was abroad in the city that a plan of the Archbishop for the reformation of his see had been shown to the Emperor. A few well-placed propagandists could make this story the starting point for a rumor that Charles, having seen the plan, found no cause to condemn it. Peter was anxious to strike at the root of any such vague and damaging talk about imperial suffrance of von Wied's planned innovations. He wrote to his friend, John Poggio, and asked for written assurance of the Emperor's unequivocal opposition to the introduction of Lutheran practices into Cologne. "You must pardon our dissatisfaction," he told Poggio,

unless we see it written in black and white that the heretics are lying or are mistaken if they should say that the Emperor remained mum or that he is not opposed to them. What the leaders of Cologne want is this: a clear statement from His Imperial Majesty that he in no way wants the reformation admitted into the states of this diocese, nor indeed anything else that would not receive the confirmation of the authority of the Roman Church.[38]

Peter judged that this kind of work was one of the most important things he could be doing for Cologne and he told Francis Xavier that it was not without its dangers.

I know from experience that there is no little trouble involved in writing to the court of His Majesty. But if we did not do so, this city would be lost. It also means that I am exposed to danger to life and limb more than anyone else here. May the Creator of the universe, its Redeemer and Glory, be praised and acknowledged in all and by all. May His grace and His strength never be without their fruit in us.[39]

✿ ✿ ✿

There were two big uncertainties that faced Peter during

these months in Cologne. The first was his inability to say how long he would be able to stay there. The possibility of new orders to go to Portugal was a real one and could not be simply brushed aside and forgotten. After all, Poggio might not have the last word, and sixteenth-century monarchs, be they good or bad, were accustomed to having their own way. The second perplexity rose out of the first. What should he do with the younger Jesuits in the eventuality that he was ordered to Portugal? His love for Cologne inclined him to leave Canisius, de Castro, Kannegesser and the others there so that they could become pillars of the faith in that sorely tried city. On the other hand, his concern for their spiritual and intellectual formation disposed him to send them to Portugal, where they would receive a training superior to that at Cologne. In his indecision he wrote to Ignatius about the hope he had of seeing settled in Cologne some of the Society "who would daily cry out, pray, weep and die for this people." [40]

I cannot but yield to the feeling that I sometimes experience in Our Lord, that their presence here would be the more advantageous thing and that under Our Lord's guidance some way will be worked out by which the Society might take root in Germany.[41]

In the spring of 1544 both doubts were resolved for Peter. And it was out of Portugal in each instance that the solution came. The representations of King John III at the Vatican prevailed, and in May Peter received word from Ignatius to move on to Portugal.[42] Then, of a sudden, nine scholastics appeared on the scene to take up studies at the University. By their sheer number they settled then and there the question of the formation of a community at Cologne. Five of the new arrivals were of the group that had left Louvain the previous January and the other four were Spaniards and Portuguese. The twelve who had sailed from Antwerp the past winter had disembarked at Corunna on February 2nd and then walked to Santiago de Compostela. While still on the road between Santiago and Coimbra, Simon Rodrigues heard of their coming and sent some of his community to meet them and guide them to their new home. For some reason or other that is not clear, possibly the inability to accustom themselves to the Portuguese climate, or possibly the difficulty of taking care of so many newcomers in a community already numbering forty-five, Rodrigues, a few months later, sent nine to Cologne to carry on their studies. They matriculated at the University on June 25th.[43]

The appearance of the group of strangers, Belgians, Spaniards and Portuguese, caused a stir in the official circles of the city. If there was anything that would irritate any latent belligerence of Cologne's officialdom, it was the settlement of a new religious order in their midst. Cologne had a satiety of religious communities, and in the opinion of the civic leaders any new group would be a burden to the citizens, *onus quam ornamentum*. Apparently the house *auf der Burgmaur* created no misgivings until the arrival of the men from Coimbra. Two days after their matriculation at the University the city senate conducted an inquiry into the nature and character of their community. On July 4th, a report was drawn up which itemized the statements made by Father Favre and the others, that they were not a new sect but adhered to the Catholic faith, and that they followed a form of life approved specifically by the Holy See and so requested that they be not hindered in their work.[44]

Eight days later, on the 12th, Peter and Aemilian de Loyola left Cologne for the port of Antwerp. Friends wanted to make sure that Peter would never forget them and their

210

city and gave him some relics that included seven heads of the companions of Saint Ursula.[45]

Peter was never to see again in this world the devoted Prior of Saint Barbara's, nor Johann Gropper, nor his novices, Peter Canisius, Lambert de Castro and Peter Kannegesser. When in the lands of Southern Europe his mind would turn back to the North, he could think of this group of friends in their luminous holiness as an aurora borealis, and he could then know that it was not wholly night in Germany.

IX. Clear Iberian Skies

THE ocean-going ships of the King of Portugal rode at anchor off the town of Veere on the western end of the island of Walcheren, one of those innumerable and irregular bits of land that make Zeeland appear on the map as a disordered collection of pieces from a jigsaw puzzle. Antwerp, which had taken the sceptre of commercial supremacy in Flanders from the once thriving medieval towns of Bruges and Ghent, was about sixty miles away on the Scheldt River. There passengers boarded the smaller river craft that carried them out to Veere. From Diest, where he more than likely visited Nicholas van Esche, Peter wrote to Cornelius Wischaven and instructed him to go to Antwerp. Cornelius' sister, Katherina, now more tolerant toward the idea of her brother's vocation and in a spirit of letting bygones be bygones, wanted to say farewell to Peter and went along to Antwerp with Cornelius. When they arrived there, they found Peter and Aemilian de Loyola already in the riverboat, ready to sail. Peter told Cornelius to get aboard. Teasingly he said to Katherina, "I was not wrong in surmising that you would come along with your brother to say good-by to me." Poor Katherina! Left by Cornelius, she went back to Louvain, not knowing whether he was heading for Portugal or whether he would shortly return to her. Actually, Peter's plan was to have Cornelius accompany him only as far as the transfer place to the main fleet. Very little time was left them to be together and they made the most of it. They passed the night in conversation and in the disclosure to each other of the secrets of their interior life. A brief stop was made around noon of the next day at Ter Neuse, a town on the south bank of the Scheldt, halfway between Antwerp and Veere. After they left Ter Neuse a deep calm fell over the waters. Rowing the large, round river craft called *een hue* was difficult, and the exhausted crewmen chided the two priests for chatting together rather than praying for a breeze. Peter did not understand the Flemish tongue, but Cornelius translated for him the jibes of the men at the oars. Their feelings were understandable enough and Peter said, "Let us pray." They knelt and had scarcely finished the Our Father when a delightful breeze came up. At Veere Peter wrote some letters for Cornelius to deliver, and made some last minute purchases for the trip. Cornelius asked Peter for a memento and received from him two little knives. They gave each other the kiss of peace. Then Peter entered the boat that was to take him out to the Portuguese fleet. Cornelius stood on the shore, head uncovered, as long as he could see the figure of Peter, who raised his hand in frequent benediction toward the good Belgian. It was the last time that Cornelius saw Peter. So tender was his memory of the man who had brought so many blessings to Louvain and himself that after Peter's death his frequent prayer was: "Holy Father Peter, pray to God for me, a sinner." [1]

More than likely Peter was on the high seas the 15th of August, the tenth anniversary of the vows at Montmartre. As his ship ploughed through the waves, he had some respite from the monotonous journey from country to country, from city to city. There was time to reflect on the many memories associated with all those other August 15ths since the first one in 1534. On the first and second anniversaries there was the return to Montmartre, the renewal of vows at the Chapel of Saint-Denis, the new companions, Jay, Codure and Broet. The third was spent in the solitude, the poverty, the recollection of the old broken-down Hieronymite monastery at Vicenza with Ignatius and Laínez. The fourth was passed in the Eternal City while the storm of calumny raised by Fra Agostino was breaking about the heads of his friends. On the fifth and sixth he was in Parma, the city that gave to the Society Paolo D'Achille, Elpidio Ugoleti, Giovanni Battista Viola, the brothers Palmio, and which became a center of Eucharistic devotion. The seventh saw him on the long road from Regensburg to Spain with Doctor Ortiz. Speyer was his home on the eighth, Speyer, that ancient town where he felt such keen discouragement at the plight of Germany and where he gave the Long Retreat to the two chaplains from the Spanish court. On the ninth he was at Cologne—or almost there on his journey from Mainz—the city where he lived with Peter Canisius, learned to know and revere Gerard Kalckbrenner, worked side by side with John Gropper, the city with its famous chapel of Saint Ursula, with its relics of Saint Gereon and the Magi. And now he was on the high seas headed for Portugal. The whole story had a unity. A single thread ran through all he had seen, heard, and experienced: the thread of selfless service to the Greatest and Most Lovable of Kings.

On the feast of Saint Bartholomew, August 24, 1544, Peter came in sight of the giantlike tower of Belem, the fortress-shaped convent of the Hieronymites. For the Portuguese, Belem stands as a monument to the daring of their explorers of the fifteenth and sixteenth centuries; for the Jesuits it is a reminder of the zeal that took Francis Xavier to the Far East. From the spot where Belem was later erected, Vasco da Gama started on his great expedition of July 8, 1497. King Emmanuel vowed to erect a memorial in honor of Our Lady there if the expedition was carried through with success. Construction began soon after da Gama's return in

1499, and the Tower of Belem became a symbol of the prowess and fearlessness of the sons of Portugal. From this same place Francis Xavier started on his long sea journey to the Indies a little more than three years before Peter arrived.

The men of the sea from Leiria and Braga and Oporto siphoned off the wonders of Cochin, Sumatra, Java and the Celebes, filled their galleons and then emptied them into the enchanting city of Lisbon. A certain Damiao de Gois, a writer of the sixteenth century, noted that there were then two cities that could justly be hailed as queens of the ocean seas, Lisbon on the Tagus and Seville on the Guadalquivir.[2] Lisbon was indeed a queen who looked down from her throne of precipitous heights onto the waters below, the rendezvous of the ships that flew the banner of Saint Vincent and came up over the horizon from the South Atlantic, the Indian Ocean, the China Sea to pay their homage to this fair city. As Peter's ship eased its way into the great roadstead, he looked upon one of the most beautiful metropolises of Europe. It has been said. *"quem não tem visto Lisboa, não tem visto cousa boa*—He who has not seen Lisbon has no idea what beauty is."

Peter was not faced with the same task in Portugal that he found in Germany—breaking ground for the establishment of the Society. The generous and noble-minded monarch who had been on the throne of Portugal since 1521 was John III, whose knowledge of Ignatius and his group dated from 1538. It was in February of that year, as we have already seen, that Doctor Diogo de Gouveia, the President of Collège Sainte-Barbe, made his recommendations of the men around Ignatius as the ideal missionaries for Portugal's overseas possessions. The insistence of de Gouveia played a major part in the eventual dispatch of Rodrigues and Xavier to Portugal in 1540. For nearly a year before the fleet of

1541 sailed for the Indies, both Simon and Francis showed by their zeal and their love of poverty the beauty and strength of Jesuit life as they had blueprinted it for the King in their first audience with him. Delighted with his two Jesuits, the King entirely on his own—Francis Xavier was most emphatic about that—decided to establish a college for the Society in Coimbra and a residence in Evora. The monarch began, in fact, to think that he might keep both Fathers in Portugal, where there was so much to be done by zealous priests. Less than a month before he sailed Francis wrote to Ignatius,

> The King in his affection for our Company and in his desire for its increase, as though he were one of us, as well as by the fact that he is doing all this solely for God's love and honor, has placed on us the obligation of being his servants forever. . . . In our prayers and unworthy sacrifices, therefore, let us recognize this debt of such great magnitude with the realization that we would be guilty of the sin of ingratitude if we fail to pray for His Highness as long as we live.[3]

Eventually, however, the King decided on an equal sharing of his two Jesuits by the homeland and the overseas possessions. Simon was assigned to the former, and Francis to the latter. The actual organization of the community at Coimbra was not carried out until June of 1542, more than a year after Francis had sailed, when Simon Rodrigues arrived there with twelve aspirants to the Society. The community grew with a rapidity not experienced up to that time anywhere else in the Society, and by February, 1544, when the scholastics sent from Louvain by Favre arrived, it numbered forty-five.

Peter did not arrive in Portugal a complete stranger. He had been mentioned prominently in de Gouveia's correspondence with the court, and Simon Rodrigues, who had inaugurated the whole business of Peter's assignment to Spain, had prepared the way. Ignatius decided to augment the Jesuit mission to Spain and sent Antonio Araoz to be companion to Peter. Antonio wrote to Ignatius from Almeirín in May, 1544, that Peter's coming was anticipated at the court "*con mucho deseo.*" [4] The news that Peter was in Portugal was soon at Coimbra, and Hermes Poen, one of the Louvain scholastics, rushed off the greetings of the men from Flanders and an earnest invitation to Peter to come to Coimbra and visit his friends there. "I can scarcely tell you," wrote Hermes,

how much joy the news of your arrival has brought me. In the way of sons who have a burning desire of seeing their father, I have awaited you with deep affection these many months. . . . Please give us the pleasure of your presence among us. The soul of Hermes languishes with love of you; the son is seized with a desire of his father. For you are my father in Christ, you have begotten me, you have removed me from the allurements of the world by His aid Who draws all things to Himself. You have snatched me from the jaws of the devil. It was you who first fed me with the Word of Life, and I therefore beg that you continue to nurture your son whom you did not disdain to beget in the spiritual life. [5]

Peter's first obligation, however, was to go to Evora, about sixty miles east of Lisbon, to present himself to the King. There he found both Father Rodrigues and Father Araoz. In his audience with John III, Peter thanked the monarch in the name of Ignatius for the many unusual favors he had granted to the Jesuits both at home and abroad. King John, for his part, began to think about Peter the way he had thought of Xavier and Rodrigues when they first arrived

in Portugal. It might be better, he reflected, to keep him in
Portugal rather than to allow him to carry out his original
mission to Spain.[6]

* * *

In December, Peter, with the King's leave, travelled to
Coimbra to see the Jesuit community there. The Jesuit college in this university town, delightfully settled on the chalk
hills of the Serra de Lavrao and skirted by the River Mon-
dego, was the first glow of what was to be the golden age
of Jesuit growth in Portugal. Seven years before Peter went
there, the University had been moved from Lisbon in one
of the many transfers of location in its long history since
1290, which gave it the distinction of being the most mobile
university in the world, exception being made for the university attached to the papal court.[7] The Rector of the Jesuits
at Coimbra, Father Santa Cruz, and his subjects received
Peter, "not as a guest," as he told Ignatius, "but as the father,
lord and master of all." [8]

The two months that Peter stayed at Coimbra, December, 1544, and January, 1545, were in some respects a repetition of the Louvain story, but this time *à la portugaise*. Peter
and Francis Strada again worked together, Peter preparing
the sermon material and Strada emblazoning it by the fire of
his eloquence. Students of the University beat a path to
Peter's door to seek his spiritual direction. Several of these
became Jesuits. In that number were the eminent scripture
scholar, Manuel de Sa, and the famous missionary to Brazil,
John Azpilqueta. Another was the unfortunate Antonio
Gomez, a man of great natural gifts who, after a period of
success as a preacher in Portugal, went to India where he
failed miserably as Rector of the College of Saint Paul.
Francis Xavier dismissed him from the Society in 1552. In

218

1554, on his way to Rome, Antonio was lost at sea when his ship foundered.[9]

Of all the Portuguese vocations to the Society of Jesus that felt the touch of Peter's influence, none could quite match that of John Núñez Barreto for the unusual way in which it developed. Núñez was a priest in the little town of Freiris near Braga. Gifted with a striking facility in prayer and a strong inclination to contemplation, he was experiencing, at the very time that Peter was in Portugal, an intense interior conflict of the soul. He felt an insistent desire to follow his brother Melchior into the Society of Jesus, but at the same time he feared that Jesuit life would demand as a price the surrender of the sweetness he enjoyed in prayer. His irresolution was aggravated by a dream in which he saw himself acting as the deacon of a Mass celebrated by a priest whose identity he did not know. At the point in the Mass when the *Pax* is given, the celebrant and the deacon differed in their ideas about the rubrics. The Deacon, in the usual way, offered the *deosculatorium* at the celebrant's right, but the celebrant insisted that it be presented at his left.[10] In the midst of this little rubrical tussle at the altar, Núñez awoke. He made an attempt at dream-analysis and worked out an interesting interpretation. A life of peaceful contemplation was symbolized by the right side, a life of apostolic activity by the left. The celebrant's insistence on receiving the *deosculatorium* at his left side was a sign that the deacon was to find his peace of soul not in contemplation alone. Núñez, however, wanted more than a dream to guide him in his decision. His attachment to the purely contemplative life was weakened a bit more by a letter he received from his brother Melchior. Melchior urged John to come to Coimbra, see at first hand just what Jesuit life was like, and talk over his problem with Father Favre, who was expected at the College. John turned to Our Lady for help. On the feast of the Faithful Departed, she appeared to him in his oratory, not alone but with the unknown priest he had seen in his dream. Our Lady told him to go to Coimbra and there he would find a servant of hers who would put an end to his doubts. John arrived at Coimbra in early November, and when Peter Favre arrived the next month, to his amazement, he recognized him as the unknown priest of his dream and visit from Our Lady.[11]

John threw himself at Peter's feet and told him the story of the tension in his soul, of his attraction to the Society of Jesus that was overshadowed by the fear of losing in the active life the sweetness of prayer. If anyone could appreciate the appeal of prayer it was Peter. But he also knew that sweetness in prayer is not the essence of the spiritual life. He explained to John the basic lesson of the high holiness there is in detachment from spiritual consolation and in the dedication of self to the fatigue and weariness of apostolic action. He emphasized the lesson of sanctity attained in the full surrender of self-will through religious obedience. Here Peter was touching the very heart of the spiritual teaching of Saint Ignatius, a doctrine of service of the Divine Majesty in a spirit of love (*mystique de service par amour*) rather than a doctrine of desire for divine union (*mystique d'union et de transformation*). It was what Père de Guibert has called the Ignatian message, an apostolic service of God in imitation of and in union with Christ Our Redeemer. With a profound sense of God's Infinite Majesty, even amid the tenderest outpourings of love, and with an ardent attachment to Him Who was the Servant of God *par excellence,* Ignatius regarded prayer, habitual union with God found in all things, familiarity with Christ, not as ends in themselves. All these attractive and magnificent things were means to

220

release the soul, purify it, strengthen it, inflame it so that it might render with perfection its service for the greater glory of God. His central preoccupation was ever the accomplishment of God's Will. This was the badge of a soul's fidelity.[12]

Then Peter made a startling prediction. "From now on," he told Núñez,

you shall no longer enjoy tranquillity in your place of retreat. Your soul will be harassed by constant afflictions because you turn your back on toil and the Cross, because you do not follow in the footsteps of the Savior, taken up as you are with the desire of your own comfort and personal peace.

Núñez, caught up short by these words, placed himself entirely in Peter's hands. Peter instructed him to rise during the night for prayer, as was his custom, give himself without reserve to Almighty God, defy the devil to bring on the temptations he would endure should he enter the Society, say Mass and then make his decision. Núñez met the challenge nobly. Severe were the trials he experienced, but he found them more than outbalanced by the blessings and unusual graces given him during the night and at Mass. And his decision was to enter the Society.[13]

Then began a life of extraordinary toil as apostle among the Christian slaves of Morocco, as Patriarch of Ethiopia, as missionary in Goa, where he died in 1566. The din of Goa was a far cry from the serenity of Freiris. Núñez had grown in spiritual stature ever since the day he met Peter Favre at Coimbra eighteen years before.

In early January, 1545, Peter sent a letter to Rome which brought him within the shadow of one of the most regrettable episodes in the history of the early Society. Peter gave Ignatius a glowing account of the religious fervor he found at Coimbra, such as would gladden the heart of any superior.

The scholastics were open and candid, disclosed to him the secrets of their interior life and showed great seriousness of purpose in their progress toward perfection. "Great peace and concord prevail among all," he told Ignatius.

> There is fraternal charity and humble obedience in all things to Superiors. The spirit of order in their external occupations is universal. So is it also in their literary and spiritual exercises. In relating this to you I wish you to know that I am not taking measure by the norm of my own personal want of regularity. . . . The order here strikes me as being just what Your Reverence would want.[14]

At the conclusion of the letter, however, a few sentences slip in which, to say the least, are ambiguous and seem to indicate that Peter, despite his encouraging report, felt somewhat uneasy about the Coimbra community.

> Inasmuch as Father Araoz has been in this area longer than I, his discernment of the deficiencies that exist here is much clearer and better than mine. Nevertheless, what I say is not meant to be an objection to Your Reverence's taking this matter into account in the presence of Christ Jesus. You know how we are all subject to extreme sentiments and divers inclinations; you also know how different things are in their objective reality and in our subjective comprehension of them. All the things that could appear to me as gold might very well be lead to someone else.[15]

Was Peter raising a storm signal forecasting the whirlwind that would be started on its way by the indiscretions and inconstancy of Simon Rodrigues? Six months later, when Peter was already in Spain, letters came to him from both the Rector of Coimbra, Father Santa Cruz, and Hermes Poen with an account of the scholastics' conduct that would make any normal religious take pause. The distracted Santa Cruz recited for Peter a litany of the bizarre manifestations of piety by his subjects, ordered in many instances by Simon Rodrigues. To send the scholastics to classes in the University wearing ill-fitting clothes and coats without sleeves was tolerable enough, but to have them go into the streets ringing a bell and shouting "Hell fire to all in mortal sin" was coming close to the absurd. One day at table Father Simon made one of the scholastics rise, go to the church to get some holy water. When the scholastic returned, he sprinkled each of his brethren, one by one, all the time reciting the *Miserere.* On another occasion two scholastics entered the refectory, one ringing a bell while the other incensed the diners. The refectory seems to have been one of Father Simon's favorite places for such *experimenta,* for at another time he ordered a scholastic to come down on the table with his hand and proclaim, "That will settle the Manichees," and then to start an argument. All the ascetical eccentricities that went on at Coimbra cannot be laid to Father Simon's doing, such as when a scholastic took a skull to class and for two straight hours stared at it while the professor held forth at the rostrum. Rodrigues disapproved of the latter episode, but enough was allowed by him to upset Santa Cruz and several others.[16]

Peter, in Spain by this time, let it be known that he was displeased with the stories from Coimbra. Still more, he was afraid lest the news of the unusual mortifications spread and become "a source of mortification to him in Castile." [17] A rift developed between Father Rodrigues and Father Santa Cruz, and the latter appealed to Favre's authority on the side of moderation and prudence. These were but the beginnings of the great crisis in the life of the Portuguese Province. Peter, however, did not become further involved, since the full strength of the danger was not revealed until after his death.

✻ ✻ ✻

King John, Father Rodrigues, the scholastics at Coimbra, the students of the University, many as they were, did not crowd from Peter's mind his attention to his *Memorial*. A few selections will show that his concern for the life of prayer continued apace with his various activities while in Portugal.

On the feast of the Three Kings in 1545, these thoughts came to mind as ideas for sermons. Jesus Christ hid His Divinity in the lowliness of human flesh so that the innermost attitudes of men toward Him might be made manifest. For this reason He willed to hide beneath the lowliness of His Humanity all His treasures of Divine Wisdom and Knowledge in order to give us the opportunity of meeting the test of our appreciation of those riches we receive and which have their source in His Divine Majesty. And so He brought it about that the Three Kings at the sight of His poverty should open up their own treasures to Him. Then there were these thoughts. In the very act of hiding His Power, He had the Angels come to earth to proclaim it. At the very time He hid His Holiness and asked to be baptized by John, He moved the Father to reveal that Holiness through the words, "This is My Beloved Son." When at the marriage feast of Cana He chose to conceal His charity He inspired His Mother to say "They have no wine," and this drew from Him the manifestation of His glory even before His hour had come.

The Magi offered to Christ a little gold in their wish to ease His poverty and at the same time they confessed that all they owned they owed to Him. They offered Him incense in the hope of comforting Him in mind and heart and, nevertheless, they were firm in their belief that without Him they themselves could not have a single good desire or noble thought. And finally, they offered Him myrrh as an expression of their hope that His Infant

Body would not see corruption, and yet it was through His Passion that the glory and final incorruption of our bodies was to be won.[18]

On the octave of the Epiphany I took as the text of my sermon the words: "John saw Jesus coming to Him." When I was about to say Mass, I was filled with an intense desire that during the Holy Sacrifice the affections of my heart might be inflamed and that the eyes of my soul might be opened to see Jesus coming to me in the Holy Eucharist. I had simply to admit that He had come to me entirely too often without my being alert to His coming. I asked God, the Blessed Virgin and a number of saints that to me, my brethren, and in fact to all who receive Holy Communion, the grace be granted of seeing Jesus coming to us, of being properly reverent and worthily prepared. While I was putting on the vestments I prompted myself to assume the bearing that one should have who beheld Jesus coming to him.[19]

On the feast of the five holy martyrs, Bernard, Peter, Acurtius, Adjutus and Otho, while I was present at the recitation of the Divine Office in the Church of the Holy Cross in Coimbra where the bodies of these saints are laid to rest, I had feelings of deep compassion for all in general who are clearly in danger of eternal damnation. Among the number that came to mind were Luther, the King of England, and the Turk. But then my thoughts turned to God's mercy that allows these men and many other sinners, of whom I am the first, to live on in order to have time for repentance. . . . Then it occurred to me that it could very well be that God not only grants time for penance, but also awaits for someone to rise up with a willingness to pray for these men and to labor for their change of heart. . . . It is therefore incumbent on us to whom is entrusted the power of preaching and teaching that we be vigilant lest great numbers die eternally because of our fault and negligence. Many on all sides are yearning for us. . . . The blood of these martyrs is calling to us to care for these people among whom and for whom they laid down their lives. May it come about that one day some of our Society might have the opportunity as well as the desire of going to the land of those Mohammedans where these five martyrs were sown as seed for the eternal salvation of the infidels. They were the living words of God Himself and His Christ. And because they could not find soil that would receive the words of the Gospel, they themselves as the choicest of seeds elected to fall into the ground and die. Therefore, if the fruit of their martyrdom has not yet been gathered, the time will come nevertheless when other faithful workers for Christ will enter into the harvest.[20]

Toward evening of the Saturday after Ash Wednesday as I was leaving the King's palace, I happened to fall in with a cavalcade of gentlemen who had come to escort some duke or other. A great throng of people gathered to see this elaborate and brilliant sight. I turned aside from the uproar and the crowd and went into the church nearby. Still, no little impulse of curiosity tempted me to go again into the street and review precisely that which I was avoiding. Then it was that my eyes fell on the Image of the Crucified and immediately my curiosity was checked. With flowing tears I thanked my God for giving me the grace to look upon His Image. I realized that this was the only true and strength-giving object of contemplation, the recollection of how God Omnipotent willed to take on human life and then lay it down as a public spectacle hanging between two thieves.[21]

As the weeks passed, Favre and Araoz were chafing at the bit because they could not forget that the primary purpose of their current mission was the establishment of the Society in Spain. Yet King John could not bring himself to make a definite decision as to whether or not he would give them permission to leave Portugal. At one moment he gave consent; at the next he retracted. Then he worked out a compromise. Araoz was to remain in Portugal; Favre was to go to Spain alone or accompanied by some third Jesuit. At this point Simon Rodrigues pleaded the cause of the two royal captives and brought the King and the Queen to agree to let Favre and Araoz leave for Spain together. The reluctance of the King had been very great. Peter, explaining to the Coimbra Jesuits what had happened, used a forceful expression: "We wrested, *extorsimus,* from the King what he who sent us wanted, permission to go to Spain." [22]

Before his departure, Peter sent one of the heads of Saint Ursula's companions to Father Santa Cruz with the request that it be fittingly venerated at Coimbra and that the history of those saints be read at table thrice over. Father Santa Cruz was exceptionally successful in propagating devotion to Saint Ursula and her companions, and with obvious delight he wrote to Peter the following October about the enthusiastic way that the Portuguese took to the Rhineland saints.

> Since I know how devoted Your Reverence is to the Eleven Thousand Virgins, I want you to know that we ran a great festival in their honor, or rather, to express it more aptly, they did so for us. We exposed the relic to the entire city. A great number of the students came to hear the sermon preached by Strada, who, I think, was better than I have ever heard him.[23]

This devotion, which was solemnized each year on October 21st at Coimbra until 1759, when it fell a victim of one of Pombal's attacks in the name of the "Enlightenment," explains the error made by some authors, including recent ones, of referring to the Jesuit College as the "College of the Eleven Thousand Virgins," whereas the name given by Simon Rodrigues was *Colegio de Jesus.*[24] On the feast of Saint Matthew, a week before his departure for Spain, Peter gave the heads of two of the Cologne virgin martyrs and two bones of the members of the Theban Legion to the King and Queen. To the Prince he gave a bone of one of the Ursuline saints. The King and Queen very graciously had Peter place

227

the relics into a case and then set them in the Queen's oratory.[25]

One of the last things that Peter did before leaving Evora was to send a farewell message to the young Jesuits at Coimbra. It was an echo of the voice of Ignatius teaching the primacy of the interior life and the principle of seeing all in Christ.

Because business is very pressing we cannot gratify the hope and earnest desire we had of going by way of Coimbra. . . . God knows how much I would like to spend some days with you, but this pleasure must be sacrificed so that God's Will might be accomplished. . . . I find myself forced, therefore, to say Farewell by letter when it would be much more pleasant to do so *viva voce*. All success to you. Serve Christ Our Lord in joy always. Never withdraw from Him Who is our entire Strength. Be wholehearted in your attachment only to Jesus, Who cannot ever be taken from you. The company of men, sometimes of advantage to us, is more often a hindrance, and we must therefore accustom ourselves to that interior life which is rooted in the things of heaven. Dealing with the things of time is indeed a help to us as long as it leads us to the things of eternity and does not tie us down to what is transitory. The living, human voice, for example, has its complete meaning for us so long as it turns us to that interior voice that speaks within our heart. I would say the same about the other senses. These help us most when through them we are drawn to the interior perception of spiritual things. . . . I am putting these ideas to paper for the sake of those who usually become sad when the company of their friends is withdrawn from them. If it was expedient for Christ's Apostles that the presence of Him Who was accomplishing the salvation of the world be withdrawn from them, is it not essential in our relationship with one another that everyone of us be prepared to take leave of the others, even if it means a complete and utter separation? One thing alone should remain common to us, Christ the Mediator of men and Who is All in All. Let us therefore ever keep Him present to us. Let each one of us learn to seek himself and his brother in Christ, the Source of all we are. Let us look for each other, contemplate each other in Him Who is our Origin, our Cause, our First Principle. If there is anyone who would wish that I were with him, let him see and discern me in the Price by which I was bought. If those who are redeemed happen not to be visible to you, let the Redeemer Himself be present to you. . . .[26]

On March, 4, 1545, Father Favre and Father Araoz left Evora for Valladolid, where Prince Philip and his Portuguese wife, Doña Maria, were holding court.

❈   ❈   ❈

The high point of the two week journey between Evora and Valladolid was the stopover at the interesting old city of Salamanca. There the two Jesuits received a gracious welcome from the Doctors of the University, especially from the Franciscan theologian, Alphonsus de Castro, and the Dominican whose name will ever have a place of honor in histories of international law, Francisco de Vittoria. The two travelers were assured that the Society could count on the University's professors for help in its work. Anything like a permanent Jesuit residence in Salamanca, however, would have to wait three more years until 1548. But by that time the great Vittoria had died and his chair of theology was taken by that watchdog of the flock who saw in every Jesuit a preying wolf, Melchior Cano.[27]

When the two Jesuits presented themselves at the Spanish court in the city once called Medînat al Walid by the Arabs, they found a regimen all decked out in the glorious trappings of the duchy of Burgundy, for Chièvres and the other Burgundian ministers who had accompanied Charles into Spain had brought with them the rich, ornate and elaborate ceremonial that had made the land of the Order of the Golden Fleece the most magnificent in fifteenth-century Europe. It would take Philip considerable time to restore the simplicity of the court ceremonial of the Catholic sovereigns.[28] But all the Hapsburg importations could not hide the many currents of Spanish feeling that crossed and recrossed at Philip's court. There were men like the stiff, unbending Duke of Alba, herald of the Spain of the immediate future and its struggle in the Netherlands. Then there was Hernando Cortes of the Spain that looked beyond the seas to the lands of the new world. There were Medina-Sidonia of the Spain wrapped in the mantle of the conquest of Granada, and Cervillo of the Spain that was the pillar of the traditional dignity and integrity of the Castilian nobility.[29] But the court was more than just a convenient place for gathering together the strands of Spanish feeling in the sixteenth century. It was the citadel of the new spirit of the absolute state. With the waning of the Middle Ages "there had been thrust into the life of Christendom a force very well aware of its own nature, very clear about its objective, and which now began to impose upon the whole of that life its own peculiar pace and rhythm." [30] This spirit of the national state was proud, jealous of its prerogatives, ambitious to enter every phase of a country's life. Like a tree bending before a storm, the Papacy was forced to yield to many of its demands, as when Sixtus V in 1478 gave Ferdinand and Isabella extreme control of the Inquisition, and when Leo X in 1516 gave Francis I a practical strangle hold on the French hierarchy. Father Araoz, unwittingly perhaps, showed himself to be an accurate reader of the signs of the times when he called the Spanish court *fons universalis regni totius* and expressed the judgment that nothing more profitable could be done for the Society of Jesus in Spain than to have some of its members at the court.[31] The sun that rose over sixteenth-century Spain was the Absolute Monarch and men did their utmost to be sure that they could bask in its favor. ". . . it was not uncommon for men brought up on the field of battle or in the austere solitude of learning to die of actual grief on losing the royal favor." [32] Banishment from the royal presence was likened to the pain of loss that the damned feel in their rejection by Almighty God. If the Society of Jesus would live and flourish in Spain it, too, had to be sure that it was within the range of the rays of the royal sun.

Prince Philip, eighteen years old, an expansive, optimistic, and joyous prince, so different from the stern, melancholy, serious King of the Escorial of later years, and his delightful Princess, the same age as himself, were to the Spanish people a symbol of the affection that the Emperor had for Spain. Two things the Spanish people wanted of Charles: the appointment of a prince of the blood as regent and a marriage alliance with Portugal. Charles gave them both in the persons of Prince Philip and Doña Maria.[33]

The arrival of Fathers Favre and Araoz at Valladolid on March 18, 1545, despite the character of their mission, did not mark the actual beginning of the permanent and stable settlement of the Society in Spain. Events had been running ahead of the two emissaries. At the very time they were on the road between Salamanca and Valladolid, Ignatius was writing from Rome a letter of acceptance to Francis Borgia, who had offered to erect a school for the Jesuits in Gandia. To staff the school Ignatius assigned two Jesuits from Coimbra, Andrew Oviedo and Francis Onfroy, and five from Rome. On November 16, 1545, almost eight months to the day after Favre and Araoz arrived at Valladolid, Oviedo reached Gandia.[34] The community at Gandia probably enjoyed a certain primacy of honor, organized as it was under the aegis of the Borgias, but *ratione antiquitatis* it had to yield to Valencia where a Jesuit community of four had settled on July 1, 1544. The idea of a Jesuit residence in Valencia came from the mind of Father Jerome Doménech, who had been a canon there before he met Favre and Laínez in Parma in 1539. Ignatius approved Doménech's plan to use his extensive possessions to set up a house of the Society and then called on Coimbra to supply the man power.

Two Jesuit communities, therefore, one already set up and the other in the blueprint stage, predated the arrival of Peter and Antonio at Valladolid. When they presented at the court the letters from King John, they were received in a friendly and gracious way by Prince Philip and Doña Maria, and the warm reception augured well for the future of Valencia, Gandia and other places where the Society might take root. The Prince and the Princess gave orders that the two Fathers be lodged next to the Church of Señora la Antigua.[35]

That Philip would be sympathetic to the Jesuits was almost inevitable. His young wife had brought with her the good will of the Portuguese royal family for the Society. Araoz likened her affection for the Society to that of a mother for her child.[36] Estephana de Requesens, wife of Philip's major-domo, Juan de Zuñega, came to know the two Fathers, and in her personal reflection of their teaching helped to create the spiritual ambient in which Philip lived. Her special interest in the Society was understandable since she and her mother, the Countess of Palamós, had known Ignatius in Barcelona in the early days after his conversion. How considerably her way of thinking was shaped by the Jesuits was manifest in the Ignatian concepts and even phraseology that went into the texture of an *Instrucción* she

gave her son Luis when he left Spain for Flanders.[37] Another
who helped create the spiritual climate about Philip was
Doña Leonor Mascarenhas, devoted friend of Ignatius and
his *Compañía*. It was to this woman, as well as to his aunt
Doña Juana, that Philip entrusted the education of his son
Don Carlos.

Araoz made his mark at the court by his preaching. Peter
gave his time to the confessional and personal spiritual direction. Interest in the new Order spread rapidly among the
prelates and noblemen, and the two priests were hard put
to find time for all who wanted to speak with them. A month
after their arrival, Araoz gave Ignatius an enthusiastic picture of developments.

> A nobleman, a friend of mine, was telling me that there is
> considerable complimentary talk about us. It seems that our
> sermons are making a particularly good impression. Some call us
> *Iniquistas*, others, *papistas*, others *apostoles*, others *teatynos*. . . .
> Master Favre has heard the confessions of more than fifteen of
> the ladies-in-waiting, not to mention other persons, both in and
> outside the palace. The confidence in the Society that is manifest
> among the courtiers, and the understanding they have of its
> nature make one pause to give thanks to God. Good Doctor
> Ortiz has preached much about the Society and is still going
> strong. . . .[38]

Among the more important people who confessed to
Peter was Philip's secretary, Gonzalo Pérez, famous father
of a still more famous son, Antonio.[39] Doctor Ortiz was not
the only familiar face that Peter saw at the court, for the
Papal Nuncio there was the very man who tried his hardest
to keep Peter from being sent to Spain in the first place, John
Poggio. Araoz could easily sense Poggio's closeness to the
Society and wrote to Ignatius, "He is ever tagging after us
and wants us never out of his sight." He placed himself

entirely at the disposition of the two Jesuits, and to help them in whatever financial needs they might have, he gave them a ducat a week.[40] Ironically enough, among those who gave Peter and Antonio assurance that they were well thought of by Prince Philip was the man who in later years became one of the most formidable enemies with whom Ignatius had to deal. Juan Martinez Guijarro was the Prince's tutor and therefore in a particularly good position to know Philip's likes and dislikes. He assured the Fathers that all was well at the focal point of the court. "The Prince, the Princess and the Cardinal of Toledo," wrote Peter to Ignatius after two months at Valladolid, "are conversant with what we are doing here and are deeply impressed by our achievements." [41]

* * *

The new field of work, the new experiences, the new people to know, all paved the way for a return of Peter's old temptation to diffidence and timidity. He wrote to Ignatius of the trouble he was having in the preservation of an interior tranquillity between the extremes of high hope and dispiriting anxiety.

May Your Reverence intercede with Jesus for me in my serious need of your prayerful assistance. The biggest temptation at the moment is in imagining that I am possibly held in disfavor. . . . At other times I have such an overflow of confidence in the opposite direction that it reaches the point of being a real defect and becomes actually a temptation of another sort. And so I carry on, caught between hope and fear, and this because I am not firm in Him Who is ever unchangeable.[42]

Less than a week after his arrival at Valladolid, while he was still somewhat unknown there, Peter had an experience which he recorded in his *Memorial.*

234

One day I went to the palace with the idea of listening to the sermon being preached in the Prince's chapel, and it happened that the porter, not knowing who I was, would not let me in. I stood outside for some time and reflected on how frequently I had allowed evil thoughts and suggestions to gain entrance into my soul and how frequently I let Jesus and His Spirit stand outside and knock. I also reflected on how Christ is so ill received throughout the world. I prayed for the porter and myself that we might not have to wait long outside the gates of heaven in the punishments of purgatory. A number of other thoughts came to mind to prick my conscience as I stood there. For that reason I felt great affection for that porter, who was the occasion of my experiencing this devotion.[43]

Peter made a number of notations in his *Memorial* for Holy Week, which was in the third week of March that year. What he noted about Good Friday follows:

On Good Friday, while hearing the confessions of the children of a certain nobleman, one of my spiritual sons, certain proud thoughts came to mind as well as the spirit that put certain questions to me such as these: Did you come here to spend your energies on these youngsters? Would it not be more profitable to be where you could hear the confessions of the grown-ups? I resolved then and there, if God should so will it, to spend my entire life on nothing else except on such works as these which in themselves seem to be so lowly and insignificant. Great consolation, born of the spirit of humility, followed on this resolve, and my eyes were opened to see, as I never saw before, the value of work done with a right intention for God's little ones. . . .[44]

Juan Luis Vives, eminent citizen in Europe's republic of letters, was Spain's proud answer to Boccaccio's contempt for things Castilian and his derisive judgment that Castilians were a half barbarous people. Nor was Vives the exception that proves the rule, for in the sixteenth century Spain saw a

235

tremendous boom of college and university expansion as the love of learning spread from the Asturias to Andalusia and from Catalonia to Estremadura, paced by the magnificent enterprise of Cardinal Ximenes at Alcalá. Jesuit enthusiasm for this intellectual revival in Spain had its beginnings in the college residences at Valencia and Gandia, and in those started by Favre and Araoz at Alcalá, Valladolid and Barcelona.

In May, 1545, Peter, during a visit to Madrid and Galapagar, went to Alcalá to see a Jesuit who had been a student there since April 1543. Francisco de Villanueva, one of Ignatius' own novices, had become unwell during his studies at Coimbra and was directed by Ignatius to go to Alcalá. Doctor Ortiz, ever ready to help a Jesuit, obtained a scholarship for Villanueva in the College of Saint Isidore. One of the things Peter talked over with Villanueva was the advisability of a Jesuit college residence being formed at Alcalá. He decided it was a promising project; another student at the university named Pedro Sevillano wanted to join the Society; sentiment in the university was favorable; the elder Infanta, Doña Maria, and Doña Leonor Mascarenhas both made contributions. A start had been made and Peter wrote to Ignatius,

> Villanueva and his companion are doing well at Alcalá and we have the wherewithal to support them and three or four others. Having found these stones of promise to start the building at Alcalá, may it please Our Lord to give us additional men for this enterprise.[45]

Peter also dreamed of setting up a college residence at Valladolid. He had a deep affection for this city, and he told Simon Rodrigues why. "I shall say this that, nowhere—and I am taking into account Paris, Rome and Parma—nowhere have I come to know so many people responsive to conversation on spiritual things as here in Valladolid." [46] But to start a community there Peter needed men. To obtain them he turned to the man power reservoir of the Society, Coimbra. Simon Rodrigues had already sent four of his subjects the previous year to Valencia, and now he sent another group of four, Francis Onfroy, and three whom Peter knew from the Louvain days, Andrew Oviedo, Hermes Poen and Maximillian Capella. The Jesuits of Coimbra were on the move eastward, not only by sea to the Indies, but also by land into Spain. The first four colleges of the future Province of Spain were founded, at least in part, by men from Coimbra. Onfroy and Oviedo were sent to the college opened by Borgia in Gandia, Capella was sent with a recently admitted novice named Lopez to Alcalá. Poen was designated Superior at Valladolid with two new Spaniards as subjects, a priest named Diego Mendez and a Bachelor of Arts named Juan Gonzalez. Father Araoz was not to be outdone in this kind of work. At the very time that Peter was bringing his stay at Valladolid to a close, he was organizing a community at Barcelona with four priests, Juan Queralt, Montserrat Soler, Louis Cistero and Bernard Casillos. [47]

Peter was back in Valladolid from his visit to Madrid about a month when the entire court and country were thrown into mourning. Four days after she had given birth to her son, Don Carlos, Princess Doña Maria died. It was the 12th of July. Peter felt the loss of the young Princess deeply, and in his appreciation of what the news would mean to her parents, he immediately sent King John a letter filled with the tenderest sympathy.

MOST EMINENT AND POWERFUL LORD:

May the grace and peace of Christ Our Lord ever shield

Your Highness' most serene heart and give it strength to drink this new chalice which our Eternal and Almighty King Jesus Christ has prepared for you.

His Divine Majesty is wise in what He does, telling us by the mouth of His Apostle Paul that, "to them that love God, all things work together unto good." Nonetheless, despite the truth of this, counsel is necessary for us so that we might be able to recognize and correctly interpret those things that are entirely the work of His hand. . . . Your Highness knows that the bitterest of medicines are the most efficacious. Therefore we believe that the most severe afflictions sent by Christ, our Source of Glory, are the clearest signs and the most certain proofs of the secret and ineffable love with which God loves us and governs us. . . .

All of this present sorrow is as nothing when we recall Who it is Who has brought it about and when we reflect on the happiness of her whom we all mourn. If so kind and merciful a Lord has now willed to send such immense distress and sorrow by the simple act of giving peace and eternal rest to one who means so much to Your Highness, who would dare censure Him? And how can Your Highness be but content in seeing the Lord of the universe intent on serving your sons and daughters at His very own table? If you should show yourself to be distressed she would be able to say to you, "If you loved me, you would indeed be glad because I go to the Father. . . ."

Who would be able to describe the tears that were shed at the court and in the city of Valladolid? It would be an unending story and would only add to the sorrow of Your Highness. May Christ Jesus turn all to the greater good, not only of ourselves, but also of all who have given so generously of their love and loyalty to Her Highness. Lamentation in this palace has been so profound that it seems as though all Spain has died and as though no comfort is to be found in this life.

Blessed be He Who has brought pain to our hearts and Who has been pleased to remove from us so great a consolation. . . .

238

If it is the Lord's wish to glorify her and give her rest at the price of our sorrow and desolation, may He be blessed and praised by everyone of us and by Your Highnesses for ever and ever. Amen.[48]

In his grief Philip decided to move his court from the city filled with so many happy memories of Doña Maria. In September he went to Madrid, at the same time arranging that Fathers Favre and Araoz should also transfer their residence there.

*　*　*

Busy as Peter was at the court—from Madrid he wrote to Antonio Araoz, who had gone to Valencia from Barcelona, and asked him to return to the court because of the amount of the work to be done there—he could not forget Germany and Belgium, and he frequently confided to Ignatius his hope to see the Society firmly established at Cologne and Louvain.[49] Cologne remained the big source of anxiety. The unchanging theme in the letters from Canisius, Kessel and Kalckbrenner was the horrible uncertainty of living behind dykes that at any moment might crumble before the waves of hatred for the Society. In Spain, where at every corner Peter met encouragement and respect, the messages from Germany were like a voice from another world. On July 28th, a little over two weeks after Peter had left Cologne for Portugal, Canisius was visited by some city officials who transmitted the startling information that the Jesuits were ordered to quit the city without delay.

A wave of confused and emotional thinking swept over the populace of Cologne. There seem to have been two reasons for this. First, there was an old ordinance on the law books of Cologne which forbade new religious orders in the city, filled as it already was with so many ecclesiastical institutions. The Archbishop, in a burst of civic zeal and love of law, called this edict to the attention of the city government. Second, there were the orders of the Emperor, who quite obviously had the Protestants in mind, that members of new religious sects should be expelled from the city. The consciousness of von Wied's power, the strange confusion of the Jesuits with heterodoxy, the frayed nerves that must have existed after years of contention between Catholics and Lutherans, all contributed to the unreal situation of fervent Catholics repudiating those who would be their comrades in arms in the battle for the Faith. It was this precise point that impressed Canisius as he wrote to Favre about the cruel injustice being perpetrated

not by buffoons, but by men who in the eyes of all are superior in their discretion and who are the very best throughout all Germany in their devotion to the faith. Their unanimity of opinion gives the argument against us an aura of greater plausibility.[50]

The antipathy of the Senate filtered down into the homes, the shops, the street corners of the city until practically the entire body of citizens echoed the sentiments of their leaders. The popular imagination was caught by the crusading idea of cleaning out of their midst any and all organizers of a new sect. When men gathered together, the popular thing was to damn the Jesuits. Songs that loaded contempt on the men in the house *auf dem Burgmaur* were the fashion of the hour. As Canisius wrote to Favre,

So it is that we pass through good report and evil report. . . . It is an amazing thing how hateful we are to our Archbishop, whose beliefs give off such an offensive smell to all Catholics. He has in person and with severity admonished the Consuls of Cologne not to bear with us in the slightest way, adherents of a

240

devilish sect and a bane to the Republic as we are. He claims that he can see through the objective of our efforts and that we are here in no other role than that of spies. Consequently, he will not let up until he has certainty that all of us will be ousted from his diocese.[51]

Then Lambert de Castro became ill, so seriously that he was unable to travel. To add to the difficulties, their financial resources were practically depleted. Three of the community, Canisius, Kessel and Alfonso, stayed at Cologne to care for the dying Lambert; the others left to join Claude Jay at Augsburg. These were but some of the details that cascaded from Canisius' long letter—it fills eleven pages of the *Monumenta Fabri*—and fell upon an anxious Peter at Valladolid.[52]

Another letter from Canisius followed three months later. It struck a note that Favre could readily appreciate from personal experience, the sense of loneliness and isolation created by the spell of complete silence that seemed to have fallen over fellow Jesuits in other parts of Europe. Months had passed in Cologne and not a single word from other Jesuits was received. Favre himself in April, 1545, told Ignatius that he had not seen any letter from him since the previous July.[53] "If it be difficult for a son not to be able to see his father nor to greet him face to face," wrote Canisius to Favre,

it becomes doubly hard to carry on without any news whatsoever of him. It has been both very hard for us and very strange that up till now we have not had the happiness of receiving at least some few letters dictated by your paternal spirit.[54]

Then Canisius broke the news of the death of Lambert de Castro and of his burial in the Carthusian monastery.

He whom you loved has been sick and his sickness has been unto death. His death, precious though it was in the sight of the

241

Lord, cannot help but be mourned by us, since it was the passing of one who was dearer to us than any brother and who meant more to us than any friend. . . . In his life he had given himself completely to Christ and in death he held back nothing. Up to the very end he kept up his spirited manner and conversation. When the church bells sounded at Vespers time and summoned those who would celebrate the feast of the Angels, he sweetly went to sleep. . . . Happy soul that in union with the Angels has come to its joy! Happy body that has merited to find a burial place that is a source of joy to the Carthusians! For they, our dearest friends, are happy to have among themselves this unusual pledge of their love for us. . . .

All that remains, Reverend Father, is for you to bless us and by your prayer lead us to Christ. . . . Desolate children we are indeed, but we shall judge ourselves to be singularly consoled if you plead our case before God and His saints. If you regard as sons those who have ever confessed you as our father, look upon us now as we lie prostrate with outstretched hands, tear-filled eyes and sorrowful voice. . . . We salute with every feeling of affection all our brothers, your spiritual sons now with you. Forgive, Father, forgive your son and his ramblings. But the rules of formality should not inhibit a son when he wishes to pour out his soul to his father. . . .

Your Reverend Paternity's son and least servant,
PETRUS KANISIUS QUEM CHRISTO GENUISTI.[55]

Favre's answer had the glint of steel. Cologne must not be abandoned. Come what may, the Jesuits must remain in that city, so important in the touch-and-go struggle between the Catholics and Lutherans. The only acceptable exception would be an order of holy obedience. "At long last," wrote Favre,

your letters, which I looked forward to so eagerly and which are now so welcome, have finally reached me. I have read and reread them in their entirety, and I cannot say which was greater, my joy or my sorrow. For who would not be grieved by the news that you and your companions, one as you are, are not permitted to live under one roof? On the other hand, I rejoice in the news of your constancy. I am glad to know that Master Lambert's illness made his departure from Cologne an impossibility and that by reason of his dying condition some of you had to stay on in the city. For you have correctly interpreted what my mind on this matter was and still is: by no means leave Cologne. . . . Already I have placed the good of many souls ahead of your intellectual pursuits, realizing full well that all of you would make far greater progress if you were enrolled in universities other than Cologne's. But so strong is my intense love for Cologne that I surrender you to its dangers and prefer to see you there as unlettered men than eminently learned somewhere else. I hope that this zeal of mine is guided by His wisdom Who surrendered His Only Begotten Son into the hands of sinners. . . . My thought in this whole affair is that I would more willingly hear that all of you are dead (and I speak especially of you, Master Peter and Master Alvaro) and buried with Master Lambert than that you are alive amid congenial surroundings some place outside Cologne.[56]

As quickly as the storm in Cologne had arisen so did it subside. A new grouping of the city government brought in an administration friendly to the Jesuits, the pendulum of public opinion swung the other way, and the metropolitan chapter challenged von Wied. But the fact that it was ultimately an empty purse that made the withdrawal of some of the community a necessity annoyed Peter, and he seemed to feel that Nicholas Bobadilla and Claude Jay, both in Germany at the time and in the company of Bishops, had failed their brethren. "I am displeased to learn of the failure of Master Nicholas, Master Claude and their Lordships to take care of you. But, enough said on this point." [57] Of course the problem of expenses could not simply be wished away, and Canisius suggested to Favre, "Perhaps glorious Portugal in her spirit of duty to God or Spain, renowned as a leader in human kindness, will come to our aid. Yet it is only right that the servants of Christ should long for poverty rather than run away from it." [58] Favre sent funds from Spain, Ignatius sent them from Rome. Jay delayed no longer and obtained help from Cardinal Farnese. Bobadilla did his share too. Canisius rented a house of five rooms next to the Dominican Convent, not far from the Montanum. Like Favre he appreciated the city's strategic importance. "Should Cologne fall," he advised Favre, "Geldern, Jülich, Cleves, Brabant and Holland will in turn fall as a consequence." [59] Canisius' tenacity checked the tide that was running against the Society, and nineteen months after he first wrote to Favre of the uncertain situation, the Jesuits were still at Cologne and Favre was able to send his commendation,

I am deeply consoled by the constancy that binds you to the people of Cologne, a constancy that is motivated by devotion to Christ alone and the salvation of souls. May the grace of Our Lord Jesus Christ be with you in all that you undertake. . . ."[60]

X. With Sails Furled

IN SEPTEMBER, 1544, five ships, flying the pennant of
Portugal and laden with treasures from the Far East,
dropped anchor in the harbor of Lisbon,

> *Her image floating on that noble tide,*
> *Which poets vainly pave with sands of gold,*
> *But now whereon a thousand keels did ride . . .*

Of all that precious cargo nothing was more precious than a
long letter from Francis Xavier to his Jesuit brothers in
Rome, a letter that was to open the eyes of many a European
to the empire of souls that was coterminous with the empire
of pearl fisheries and silk marts in the Indies. Francis wrote
in part:

Multitudes out here fail to be converted to Christianity
because there is no one who will undertake the holy and pious
work of teaching them. Many are the times I have felt impelled
by the thought of breaking in on your universities, especially the
Sorbonne at Paris, and, like a man out of his mind, calling out to
those men of more learning than generous will to see to it that
their learning bring forth fruit. I would cry out about the countless number of souls that fail to win heaven and instead go to hell
because of their negligence. If these men, immersed in literary
pursuits, would study with like seriousness what God Our Lord
will demand of them and the talent they have received from
Him, many of them would be moved to enter into making some
spiritual exercises in order to discover and realize interiorly just
what is the Divine Will. They would then bring themselves into
conformity with the Divine Will rather than be guided by their
personal preferences, and they would exclaim: "Lord, here I am.
What is it that You want me to do? Send me wherever You will,

even if it means the Indies." . . . So tremendous is the number being won to the Faith of Christ out here that often my arms are weary from the constant pouring of the waters of Baptism and my voice often fails me because of the repetition of the Creed and the Commandments. . . .[1]

Peter Favre was with Simon Rodrigues and Antonio Araoz at Evora when the letter arrived in Portugal. It caused a sensation at the court of John III. Everybody wanted to read it and as a consequence its delivery to Rome was delayed. The Jesuit collegiate residences of Europe stayed in close contact with each other in those days—there were seven in Europe at the end of 1544—and Simon Rodrigues saw to it that letters from the Indies were translated at Coimbra and copies sent to the other communities.[2] Peter, who had used to such great advantage in Germany letters from his Jesuit brothers, took a copy of this long letter from Xavier along with him in May, 1545, when he visited Galapagar. There he had the opportunity of showing it to the Cardinal of Toledo and Doctor Ortiz. Nine months after the letter was received Father Araoz told Ignatius that in his judgment Xavier was accomplishing as much in Portugal and Spain by his letter as he was achieving in the Indies by his preaching.[3] In the face of suspicions in some quarters about the new religious Order, the story of the former Paris regent, toiling amid the vast expanse of paganism, became an effective and masterful *Apologia Societatis*.[4]

In September of the following year more letters arrived from Francis aboard the S. *João*. It was stirring news that Francis sent back to Europe, the story of how he baptized in a single month ten thousand persons at Travancore, of the heroism of six hundred recently baptized natives of the island of Manar slaughtered by a reckless Ceylonese king, of the staggeringly vast regions that yet awaited the word of

246

Christ. King John had this news announced from the church pulpits and made provision for the sustenance of up to eighty Jesuits at Coimbra. Soon after, he raised this number to a hundred and arranged that twelve Jesuits would be sent to India at the beginning of 1546.[5] Again copies of these letters were written out and sent around to the Jesuit communities. Names of such places as Goa, Travancore, Manar, Ceylon, began to have a familiar ring in European ears. Xavier's zeal was infectious. Father Santa Cruz, the Rector at Coimbra, wrote to Peter, "I really believe that there would be little objection to moving this entire community to the Indies." [6] Peter received from Rodrigues the original copies of two of these letters and, before sending them on to Rome, had Latin translations made, and these he sent to Cologne and Valencia. Valencia then supplied Gandia with a copy.[7] Peter could not remain so close to that fire of enthusiasm without himself being touched by its flame. In November, 1545 he wrote to Rodrigues,

The spiritual joy here manifested on the reception of the good news from our brother Master Francis is every bit as great as the news itself. Our Lord knows with what willingness I would send men to cooperate in this field of labor, and how even more deeply I desire to go myself.[8]

When Peter wrote to Rome at the close of 1545 about the stir that Xavier's letters were causing at the Spanish court, he told the story with an eagerness and almost breathlessness, like that of a little boy so proud of the prowess of his big brother.

We are sending you copies of the letters received from our Master Francis in the Indies. May it work out that Our Lord will use them as instruments for His glory in Rome. Here we have every reason to praise God Our Lord because of the

247

abundant consolation and spiritual strength derived by those who read them. I have sent copies to Toledo and Valladolid. . . . Likewise to the Bishop of Calaharra, the Bishop of Pamplona, the Prior of Roncesvalles, Señor Juan de Silveira. During a conversation with the Prince a few days ago, when I was giving His Highness the news from the Indies, he told me that he wanted to see the letter to which I was referring. In the group at the time were the Bishop of Cartajena, the Major Domo and one time Captain General at Perpignan, Don Juan de Zuñiga, as well as Don Antonio de Rojas. It was the latter who later on procured the letter to read it to His Highness. The Licentiate, Aguirre, key man and Senior on the Council of the Inquisition, was so delighted with it that he ordered his chaplain to make a copy with the idea of personally seeing that it received a wide audience. Before my arrival here Monsignor Poggio had showed it to I do not know how many. Fray Vincent, nephew of Master Salmerón, kept it more than just a few days in order to read it at his leisure and in order to let the Cardinal of Seville see it. . . .[9]

In January, 1546, when he happened to be in Cologne, Nicholas Bobadilla was witness to the inspiration the Jesuits there, as well as Gropper, Kalckbrenner and others, received from reading the letters of Xavier that Peter had forwarded.

Xavier's *cri du coeur* was the desire that his voice would be heard in the lands he had left behind in 1542. In a way he could never have guessed, his desire was realized, for his voice sounded across Europe like a clear, challenging, thrilling call to arms. It reverberated from Lisbon to Gandia, from Valencia to Cologne, from Coimbra to Rome. Certainly Francis' dear roommate from the Paris days could have given him no greater happiness, save perhaps to join him personally in the Indies, than to carry the part he played in the spread of the gospel from the Far East.

✻　✻　✻

This point in the story of Peter's work in Spain is probably as good as any to bring together some loose strands, especially those that have something to tell about Peter's friends in different parts of Europe. First of all, there was Father Cornelius Wischaven, who was making quite a name for himself in Flanders as an exorcist. Cornelius had written to Peter Canisius about his adventures with the devil, a story filled with all sorts of marvellous details, and Peter in turn passed on the news to Favre. Not only that, but Peter added his own personal testimony as an eyewitness to the exploits of Father Cornelius. "In a short time," wrote Canisius,

he drove out eight devils which would not be budged by the exorcisms of other priests. It was a tremendous thing to behold. If I had not been on the spot to see it, I would have pooh-poohed the whole story rather than give it any credence.[10]

Favre was not in the least impressed and promptly proceeded to say so. In his reply to Canisius he wrote,

I in no way approve of the mode of Master Cornelius' devil-ousting activities. Let him put his mind to the work that is proper to a priest and banish the devil from the souls of men. I would have him leave the work of exorcism in the hands of men who have been designated for that office. Has not Master Cornelius already burned his fingers more than once through the illusions of the devil?[11]

Hermes Poen ever remained one of the most devoted of those whom Peter received into the Society of Jesus. In 1545 he had been sent by Simon Rodrigues to Valladolid to help staff the college residence that Peter was organizing there. His days at Valladolid were marked by poor health, and Peter, in his desire to help him as much as he could, suggested that, once he had convalesced, he either travel to

Madrid or remain at Valladolid, as he would wish. In January, 1546, Hermes wrote to Peter,

> To put your mind at rest I want to assure you that in God's Goodness I have my old health back again, except that my feet are not yet quite what they should be. They are still too weak to use. On the feast of Saint Paul I left the house for the first time to do some walking and to get some recreation. When I left the house I was in fine shape, but on my return I had reached the point where I was unable to stand any longer. . . . In your letter you told me that after my recovery I could stay here if I so wished or I could go to Madrid. You know what is best for me and I leave the matter to your judgment and decision. If you want me to stay here, that I shall do. If you want me at Alcalá, I shall go there. If you choose Gandia, Gandia is agreeable to me. I am ready, it making no difference to me, to set out for Flanders, Brabant, Portugal, Italy, France, India, Arabia, should you so wish. And if I cannot walk, I shall crawl.[12]

About six weeks later Hermes reported that he had his health back and that he had taken on some teaching.

> In a few days I shall start prelecting either the *De Officiis* or the *De Senectute* of Cicero. On feast days, however, I think that I shall use the letters of Saint Paul. Meanwhile, I wait to hear what you think of this project of mine.[13]

Despite Hermes' optimism about his ability to carry on his work, his health failed and he died at Valladolid before the end of the year. He was one of the three novices whom Peter received at Louvain who died within two years after their admittance into the Society. Lambert de Castro had died toward the close of 1544 and the younger Wischaven was drowned in 1546. There were also others of Peter's younger Jesuit friends who met premature deaths. Aemilian de Loyola died in 1547. Peter de Smet, one of the Louvain

250

novices, died in 1548 as Rector of the college residence in Pavia.[14]

A man whose early admiration for Peter grew with time was Prior Gerard Kalckbrenner of the Cologne Charterhouse. In the spring of 1544 the Carthusians held a general chapter of their order at La Grande Chartreuse, the Prior of which, Peter Marnef, also held the office of General of the entire Order.[15] Gerard Kalckbrenner went down from Cologne—it was during his absence that the storm of opposition broke over Canisius and his companions—and at this solemn assembly of his fellow religious he told them the story of the Society of Jesus and its accomplishments in Germany. He then made the proposal that the Carthusians receive the Jesuits as participants in the fruit of all their prayers and good works. Nothing in the long and selfless life of Prior Gerard more strikingly revealed the depth of his insight and the magnanimity of his spirit. Formed in the traditions of an Order founded in the eleventh century, he nevertheless had the discernment to see in the sixteenth century an age that demanded of the Church new forms of expression in its unending care for souls. He saw that the Cologne and the Germany of his day were worlds apart from the Cologne and Germany known to previous Priors at Saint Barbara's. The mission of Peter Favre in the Rhineland, the example of Peter Canisius, Lambert de Castro, Leonard Kessel and the others, convinced him that the Society of Jesus was an instrument peculiarly apt to meet the demands of the new era. With a complete absence of anything like the petty jealousy that has all too often greeted the appearance of a new religious community in the Church, Gerard showed himself to be in complete sympathy with the Jesuit ideal.[16] The sincerity of his conviction made its mark, and the assembled Carthusians at La Grande Chartreuse ratified his proposal

251

and thus opened up the floodgate of untold graces that helped carry the Jesuits on the tide of success in their apostolic works. Who can tell but that without the great reservoir of spiritual power placed at their disposal by the sons of Saint Bruno, the Jesuits might never have established their outposts as far forward as they did.

When Peter heard what his Carthusian friend had done, he sent him a letter filled with expression of tenderest affection for him and his monks. This letter was Peter's last to Prior Gerard, sent from Madrid in March, 1546.

You should not fear, dearest Father, that I shall forget you. Continue to make yourself daily more and more disposed to receive the Divine Spirit, Who intercedes for you in the hearts of your friends. He watches over you and unceasingly calls you to mind. Then, too, your memory is kept fresh by the favor you have shown me and my brothers. Not least among the things you have done is to make our Society a sharer in all the good works of your Order. That is indeed a telling reason why the memory of you and your monks will be kept vividly alive in the thoughts of my brothers.

Last year I wrote to Master Francis [Xavier], now in India, about what you had done and I exhorted him to ever keep you and your community in mind. Right now ten of our Portuguese brethren, conversant with the story of your kindness and aware of the love I have for your monks and for all Germany, are being sent out to join him. They are taking to Master Francis still another letter of mine in which I speak of you and our other friends at Cologne and in which I also make the point that he should realize his indebtedness to you. . . . I am truly overwhelmed by the generosity and favor of God to me, a very wretched sinner. To think that so many each day make an offering of themselves as my advocates before the throne of God to help me attain to my eternal salvation!

Why, for a while I felt as though I were in the presence of

252

all the brothers of your monastery and I therefore expressed myself as though such were the case. May they, for their part, preserving unity of mind and heart, keep me as one in their midst.
May the grace of Our Lord Jesus Christ, His Presence and Benediction be ever with you and manifest itself in your persons and
in your works.

Your Brother in Christ,

PETER FAVRE [17]

The Jesuits in turn through Ignatius assured Kalckbrenner that the members of his order were made participants in the merits of the Society of Jesus. Like Wisdom in
Holy Scripture, this mutual charity "hath built herself a
house," and of the pillars she has hewn for the house the two
principal ones were the figures of Gerard Kalckbrenner,
Carthusian, and Peter Favre, Jesuit.

One of the great problems that faced the nascent Society
of Jesus, as indeed it faced all the forces of the Catholic
Reform in the sixteenth century, was that of shaping an
attitude toward heretics. Up to 1544, Peter Favre was the
Jesuit with the most experience among the Protestants. To
Peter, then, James Laínez turned for help and requested that
he make some suggestions on how to win heretics back to
the Church. Almost two years after he had left Germany for
the last time, Peter finally managed to send his answer to his
friend. Before he went into detail, Peter first laid down two
more or less basic principles for any apostolate among the
Protestants.

The first thing to keep in mind is that if anyone would be of
help to the heretics in this day and age, he must look upon them
with great charity and love them in truth. And he must close his
mind to all thoughts that would tend to lessen his affection for
them. The second thing to be remembered is the need of gaining
their good will so that they in turn shall love and think kindly of

253

us. This can be accomplished by dealing with them in a friendly way on those subjects about which we are in agreement and by avoiding those disputed points in which one side might give the impression of lording it over the other. *Rapprochement* should be established with them in those areas in which there is concord between us rather than in those which tend to point up our mutual differences.[18]

The great compelling force, Peter told Laínez, which would cause a Lutheran return to the Church had to be the winning and attractive portrayal of the beauty of virtue and the ideal of holiness. The appeal, in brief, had to be made primarily to the affections.

The man who has the knack of speaking with the heretics on holiness of life, virtue, prayer, death, hell, and those other truths closely related to moral reawakening, will accomplish far more good with the heretics than the man who, armed with the pronouncements of authority, makes it his aim to confound them. Briefly then, these people are in need of being counselled and encouraged to embrace a high code of morality, to rise to the fear and love of God and an appreciation of the dignity of good works as their best safeguard against the spiritual languor, the coldness, the dissipation of mind, the disgust with spiritual things, and in fact, all those evils with which they are afflicted and which in the main do not arise in the understanding. . . .

At first glance, these might look like the sentiments of a man who announces that he would rather feel compunction than be able to define it. That Peter placed the emphasis on the moral and affective side of the question is clear enough. But he did so not with any misgivings or distrust in the dignity and power of man's reason. In a different milieu, argued Peter, say during the age of the infant Church in the Roman Empire, stress of necessity had to be placed on

254

reasoning and dialectics. Peter synthesized the German situation for the Prior of the Monastery at Reposoir:

I find that here in Germany a great number of people are returning to their first faith and are beginning to open their eyes to the fact that the heresies of the age are proving to be nothing else except a dearth of piety, humility, patience, chastity and charity.[19]

Protestantism was still young and the Catholic conscience with its age-old attitudes and convictions, formed by centuries of teaching by the Church, was still bound to be a force in German life and make its voice heard, if but the stifling effects of immoral living could be removed. The German people as a whole were not turning their backs on the Church because of any logical force in the theology of Martin Luther. Peter insisted that he was not speaking *in vacuo* and pointed to his own success in vindication of his principles.

For example, a priest happened to come to me, asking that I prove to him the error of his beliefs, especially of that one in particular by which he held that it was entirely proper for priests to marry. I spoke to him in such a way that he opened up to me the story of his past and revealed how for several years he had been in serious sin because of a life of concubinage. I did not get into any disputes with him on matters of faith, but I adopted an approach designed to win him away from this manner of life. As soon as he gave up his sinful habit and with God's grace was able to live without the woman, his illusions were dissipated and he spoke not a word more of those errors which were nothing more than a sequel to an evil life.[20]

Peter never intended that these reflections of his should be lifted from their context and moulded into universal principles, applicable in exactly the same way in every age

255

and clime. Even within the framework of contemporary Germany he as much as admitted that he might be over-sanguine about his ideas, and he granted that their application did not carry an absolute guarantee of success with those who might be called the more advanced heretics. Luther, he felt,

by breaking the evil habits which have held him in their grip, would *ipso facto* cease to be a heretic, and this without another word of disputation. It must be admitted, however, that he would need a spiritual fire of great intensity to give him strength for such a course of action. Spiritual energy of an uncommon sort would be demanded of him if he would walk the path of the profound humility, patience and other virtue so requisite in a man who would rise up from a fall and moral destruction of such magnitude as his has been. Without God's help it is improbable, nay impossible, that such a change of heart be realized in men who have suffered moral ruin. It is not easy therefore to hope to win back this brand of heretics.[21]

Without an attempt to give an all-embracing speculative formula and with the reality of contemporary Germany before his eyes, Peter simply passed on to Laínez some *ad hoc* hints which he had found to be practicable and fruitful. The affective approach might have its limitations but, in Peter's mind at least, it was the most efficacious of any he had yet witnessed.

The convictions he formed at Worms and Regensburg in 1540 and 1541 about the futility of legislation as the way to reform, and about the pitiful inadequacy of the negative mentality that would wipe out heretics by force, were in no way lessened in 1546. His last letter to Prior Gerard was in some ways a cry of lament.

I am grieved that the men in power are attempting nothing

256

else, are planning nothing else, think that nothing else is necessary in their conduct of affairs except the extirpation of public heretics. This is, as I have often personally said here, a situation where both hands of the builders of the city are engaged in brandishing the sword against the enemy. Why is it, O Good God, that we do not keep at least one hand free for the positive work of construction? Why is it that not a finger is being lifted to bring about a reformation, not in dogma of course or in the doctrine of good works, since in these nothing is wanting, but in the moral temper of our Christian people? Why is it that by the path of the dogma, which is ever old and ever new, we do not return to the practices of the early Christians and holy Fathers? [22]

Peter's letter to James Laínez found itself in select company when years later Father Jerome Nadal, in an instruction to the Jesuits at Vienna on the manner of treating with heretics, listed three things to be kept before their eyes: the decrees of the Council of Trent, Ignatius' "Rules for Thinking with the Church," and this letter of Father Favre's.[23]

❊   ❊   ❊

On the Third Sunday of Advent in the year 1545, in the Tyrolese town of Trent, a solemn procession of Bishops and priests chanting the *Veni Creator Spiritus* proceeded from the Church of the Holy Trinity to the Cathedral, where they attended the Solemn Mass celebrated by Cardinal Giovanni del Monte. It was the solemn opening of the Council of Trent. Under the guidance of the three Papal Legates, Cardinals Reginald Pole, Marcellus Cervini and del Monte, and with the assistance of such learned theologians as Girolamo Seripando, the Augustinian, and Dominico Soto, the Dominican, the assembly, finally called together by Paul III after years of diplomatic duelling with the Catholic sover-

257

eigns of Europe, plunged into the questions of dogma and ecclesiastical reform.

No Jesuits were present on the opening day of the Council, but three days later Claude Jay arrived as representative of Otto Truchsess, Cardinal of Augsburg. The following February, Paul III asked Ignatius for more of his men for the work at Trent. Ignatius chose Fathers Laínez, Salmerón and Favre. The question of bringing Peter all the way from Spain was not an easy one for Ignatius to decide, and he turned to the other Fathers at Rome for advice. Before they expressed their opinion, special prayers were said for three days and each priest offered three Masses, asking God for light to know which would be more to His Divine Service, Peter's attendance at Trent or the continuance of his work in Spain. With Ignatius voting last and fully aware of the traveling difficulties involved, the decision was unanimous that Peter should bring his Spanish mission to an end.[24] On February 17, 1546, Ignatius wrote to Doctor Ortiz and Prince Philip requesting that Peter be allowed to leave Spain.[25] The order from Rome came as a jolt to Peter. It meant the repetition of what he had gone through so many times before, the abrupt termination of work that was just about under way and so full of promise. But, as he told Simon Rodrigues, the thing that redeemed all was the fact that his changes all originated with orders from his superiors.

You may already know of my summons from Spain to the Council. May Our Lord be praised because of the mercy which His Divine Majesty has shown me in giving me a command that has the approbation of the Holy See.

If it were otherwise and if you recall the many journeys and the amount of travel in foreign lands that I have done, I could not but be judged an inconstant soul. I would not be able to be at peace, except that holy obedience has so disposed. I say this

258

especially in view of the brevity of my sojourns, my departure being ordered at the very time when human reason would have me endeavor to prolong my stay. If it is for me to sow and for another to reap, I would be happy, but there is a lurking fear in my heart that it is my sins that are the cause of these transfers. My needs are great. Because of them, and now that we shall no longer be near to each other, I ask you to remember me more often. I shall not forget you, nor your harvest, nor your flock. I would like to have time to send a letter to each of our brothers at Coimbra, Almeirín, Lisbon, the Indies, and other places scattered about, but you can obtain from them for me what I desire, a remembrance of myself and the Council in their prayers. . . . I close this letter with the hope that this journey may turn out to be a quest for another Favre who will have less thought of self and more of you in Christ.[26]

Peter's instructions were to visit the Jesuit communities at Valencia and Gandia before he embarked at Barcelona for Italy. When he left Madrid on April 20th, Antonio Araoz accompanied him a way down the road. "After we said Goodby and parted the other day," Peter wrote to Araoz from Valencia,

I observed that you stopped near the flock of sheep and waited until I disappeared from view. Even though I kept walking and did not stop, I nevertheless looked back several times, in fact very frequently, until it was impossible for you to see me any longer. . . .[27]

These two Jesuit pioneers in Spain who had worked together so smoothly were never to be together again. Two weeks later Araoz wrote to Father Bartholomew Ferron.

What Our Lord has accomplished among the *señores* here through Master Favre I shall not attempt to relate. But believe me, *hermano mio,* if you knew Master Favre as did this poor

259

person who must now carry on without him, you would thank God for such a grace. He is a soul filled with loving kindness.[28]

On Thursday of Easter Week Peter arrived at Valencia and on the following Sunday reached Gandia, where he was to enjoy for a few days the generous and princely courtesy of Francis Borgia.

About a month before this, Doña Eleanor had died. Francis felt the loss of his wife deeply. She had been failing for some time and early in the previous March the Duke had written to Peter to ask his prayers for her. One day while praying before a crucifix in his palace the soul of Francis was suddenly illumined and he heard an interior voice: "If you desire that I allow the Duchess to live for a long time, the matter is in your hands. But I advise you that this is not the right thing for you." Francis placed all in the Providence of God. Doña Eleanor confessed to Father Andrew Oviedo, received the Last Sacraments, had the Passion of Our Lord read to her and died on the 27th of March. A month later, the day Peter came to Valencia, Francis wrote a letter to Father Araoz filled with a most refined sense of God's Goodness, in which he mentioned how much he was looking forward to the coming of Peter to Gandia.

I am anxiously awaiting the arrival of Father Favre. He will be here in a few days. If he gives me but a few hours of his time I shall use them in the realization that I am unworthy to enjoy his holy conversation.[29]

Peter spent two full days at Gandia, part of the time with the Jesuits who had come to Gandia in November, 1545, and part of the time with the nuns of the Convent of Saint Clare, whose Abbess, Sister Francesca de Jesús, had been commended to him by Father Araoz. Most of his attention, however, he reserved for the Duke. Francis charged Peter to carry to Ignatius the news that he had decided to ask admission into the Society of Jesus.[30] The crowning event of Peter's stay at Gandia was the laying of the cornerstone for the college that the Duke was erecting for the Society near the hermitage of San Sebastian, against the walls of the city. A simple but impressive ceremony was organized for the occasion. On May 4th Peter celebrated Holy Mass at San Sebastian's in the presence of the Duke and his sons. After Mass they all went to the site of the new building, where Peter recited some Psalms and the prayer *Visita quaesumus*, sprinkled holy water, and then laid the first stone. The Duke laid the second stone, Father Oviedo the third, Don Carlos, Francis' eldest son, the fourth, and then each of the other sons followed in turn. Other stones were laid in the name of each member of the Society, one for Ignatius, and then for the others. This ceremony in a way had more meaning for the future history of the Society than even the thrilling enterprises of Francis Xavier in the Indies, for Francis' exploits flowed from the very initial concept of the Society as a group of men ready to move to any part of the world at the wish of the Pope. To teach in schools and universities with its implied fixity of residence was something very new. The school at Gandia was a pathfinder, and on that May morning in 1546, when its first stones were being laid, the foundations were being outlined for all the future Gandias in so many of the great civilized centers of the world, Paris, Vienna, Lima, New York.[31]

Peter left Gandia that same day, and on the 5th he was back in Valencia, where he stayed until the 11th, receiving visitors and calling on those whose social position gave them every right to expect the courtesy of a visit from him. One person he was especially glad to see was his confessor at

Paris, Juan de Castro, now the Prior of the Carthusian monastery of the "Valley of Christ."

After Peter arrived in Barcelona in the middle of May, a combination of sickness and transportation difficulties held up his departure until early in July. The enemy of many an early Jesuit, the tertian ague, laid him low for several weeks, but by the 12th of June he was well enough to try to find passage across the Mediterranean. On the 21st of June he wrote Ignatius that his efforts to book passage in a galley had been unsuccessful, but that he would keep trying for about a week longer, and that if he were still without success he would resort to looking for passage on one of the smaller and lighter craft. In Rome, meanwhile, Ignatius was eagerly awaiting Peter's arrival. He wrote to Canisius on June 2nd that he was hoping to see Favre within fifteen or twenty days. Canisius had asked Ignatius' advice about his activity in Cologne, and Ignatius, desirous of first having authoritative information from one who knew Germany so intimately, deliberately held off from giving a decision until he should have time to confer with Peter. Peter, meanwhile, during the days of waiting after his recovery from the fever, did some preaching in the churches of Nuestra Señora del Py, Santiago and Santa Clara.[32]

One day in early July he sailed out of the great harbor of Catalonia's capital and on the 17th, a little over seven years since he started out with James Laínez for the Legation of Parma, he arrived back in the Eternal City. During those seven years, by land and by water, he had travelled 7,000 miles, measured by straight and direct lines. Unrecorded journeys and the windings of the road would no doubt double that. Peter found the Jesuit community no longer living in the house of Antonio Frangipani at the Torre del Melangolo which he had known, but in a new Professed

262

House which they had occupied in September, 1544, and which was built near the Chapel of Santa Maria della Strada. The responsibilities of his Roman brethren had multiplied during his absence, charged as they now were with the care of this chapel and its parish. Pietro Codazzo, the first Italian to enter the Society, had received the pastorate of della Strada in November of 1540 and on June 24, 1541, he made his renunciation of the church in favor of the Society. The same day Paul III turned it over to Ignatius and his companions. On December 15, 1542, the Pope suppressed three parishes, S. Andrea delle Fratte, S. Nicolao, and SS. Vincenzo e Anastasio, joined them and their churches to della Strada, and placed them under the care of the Society. Not far distant was the Casa Santa Matha, started by Ignatius in January, 1544, for girls who had been living sinful lives and who were determined to reform. These were signs that spoke to Peter of some of the things that Ignatius and the other Jesuits at Rome had accomplished during his absence.

The details of what must have been an affectionate welcome by Ignatius and the other Roman Jesuits, if ever recorded, have been unretrieved. The man who returned to Ignatius was a different Favre from the one who had set out for Parma seven years before. Peter now stood before Ignatius as the living embodiment of so many of the hopes that he, Ignatius, had entertained for his Society in the Empire, the Netherlands, Portugal and Spain. In his mind and heart Peter carried back with him the impress of the timeless, beautiful Rhine flowing past Worms, Speyer, Bonn, Cologne, of the mist and frost of a Netherlands winter settling on the plains of Brabant, of the enchantment of lovely Lisbon reflected in the tides of the Tagus, of the jagged peaks of the Guadarrama, of the stern, dry plain of Castile. Into the room about Peter crowded the figures of the vocal John Eck, the magnanimous Gerard Kalckbrenner, the gracious Prince Philip, the stormy Hermann von Wied, the saintly Peter Canisius, the tireless John Gropper, the generous King John, the stolid Albert of Brandenburg, the slippery Martin Bucer, the faithful John Poggio, the courteous Francis Borgia. Like ivy clinging to brick and stone with a tenacity that would make it to be almost a very part of the building itself, the epic of the Society's beginnings clung to Peter, the tale of the rebirth of Eucharistic fervor in Parma, of the battlefield whereon forces were contending for the soul of Germany, of Belgian and Portuguese youth gathering beneath the standard of Ignatius, of colleges full of promise in the glow of the Spanish Renaissance.

At Rome there was work to be done. The business of Germany was hanging fire and demanded some important decisions. Peter looked over Canisius' letters and discussed with Ignatius the various knotty problems that faced the Church and the Society of the Empire.[33] With his eye on his assignment to the Church Council, he wrote to James Laínez, then at Trent, that his departure from Rome was being held up by the excessive summer heat. Laínez' father had died some months before, and Peter took advantage of this letter to tell his friend what he had done once he had heard of his father's passing.

I do not know whether you have received the news of your father's death. I myself learned of it through a letter from your sister Doña Maria while I was still in Madrid. I answered her letter and I tried to give some comfort to those whom your father has left behind, your mother, your two sisters and your brother, Christopher. Do not delay in writing to them yourself so that they might have the consolation you can give. . . . Here at Rome I have had the Fathers of the house say Mass for him. I had the same thing done in Spain at a much earlier date, writing,

264

if my memory serves me right, to Portugal, Valladolid, Alcalá, Valencia and Barcelona, not to mention in passing other places where there are people who are grieved by such happenings as your father's death, happenings which should, I think, be felt through the entire Society, and by its friends too.

If you do not already know about it I must break the news of the death of Father Hermes, who passed away suddenly at Valladolid after I left there, and of the death of the youth Cornelius, who met his end while on a journey from Portugal to Castile in obedience to the orders of his superior. I am passing on this information so that you may show your brotherly spirit and do for them what you would want others to do for you when your time comes to be in like need of prayer.

May the Holy Spirit and the spirit of all those holy Fathers who were ever summoned to the past councils of the Church be with you and all those accredited to this Holy Council of Trent.[34]

Of Peter's letters that have come down to us, this was the last he wrote. When he arrived at Rome on the 17th, he was feeling well. Eight delightful days followed among old friends. Then the fatal fever struck. On the 25th, probably debilitated by the heat he had mentioned to Laínez, he fell ill. On July 31st, a Saturday, he made his confession. The next day he was able to hear Mass and receive Holy Communion. He then received the Sacrament of Extreme Unction. Father Ferron, Ignatius' secretary, observed that Peter, realizing that his life in this world was drawing to a close, showed in many ways that he was looking forward to life eternal. That afternoon, sometime between midday and Vespers, surrounded by the Jesuits of the community and many of his other friends, he gave up his soul to the Lord he had served so well. It was August 1, the feast of St. Peter in Chains.[35] Father Polanco entered the event into his *Chronicon* of the Society as follows:

Since the Divine Goodness called His Favre to the Council of Heaven rather than to the Council of Trent, *ad coeleste concilium potius quam ad Tridentinum,* it came about that on the feast of Peter in Chains he was freed from the chains of his earthly life and went to the liberty of the life of heaven.[36]

His body was laid to rest in the Church of Santa Maria della Strada alongside the body of John Codure—Savoyard and Dauphinois together as their homelands lie adjacent to each other in the western Alps.

During Peter's last days, in far away Portugal, King John was cutting the pattern for a mantle of honor he intended Peter to wear. Approached by an embassy from the Negus of Ethiopia with a request for a Patriarch and some missioners to instruct the Abyssinian people, King John spoke to Simon Rodrigues about the matter in March, 1546, and decided to ask the Pope to designate Favre for the office of Patriarch. The King wrote to Ignatius, but Peter was dead even before the letter left Portugal.[37] Peter Canisius was in Cologne fighting the good fight when he received the news of Peter's death. "The death of my father, Master Favre," he wrote to Ignatius,

is in itself not a reason for grief. Yet I must confess that for me it is a most painful thing, indeed so deeply so that the sorrow of my soul drives me to the point of giving voice to my feelings of affliction. I beg you to help me in my weakness by your prayer just as he, as I hope, will never be unmindful of his friends in Germany whom he was ever deeply desirous of seeing.[38]

The long years of labor in the Empire, the seeing of books through the press, the founding of colleges, the responsibilities of a Jesuit Superior, all of these things never effaced from Canisius' mind the vivid and tender memory of his Favre. Thirty years after his death, in obedience to Father

266

Mercurian's instructions to list suggestions for a revision of Ribadeneira's *Vita Ignatii Loyolae,* Canisius was able to give detail after detail about Favre's work in Germany, his lectures at Mainz, his sermons at Cologne, his love for the Chapel of Saint Ursula, his *mira sedulitas* in prayer for the German people.[39] When he wrote to Father Nadal in 1572 about the need of developing the College of Cologne, and when he sent a letter of encouragement in 1574 to Cologne's hard-pressed Rector, Father Leonard Kessel, he spoke of the Jesuit foundation in that city with a special reverence and affection because it had its beginnings in the labor of Peter Favre. *Non negligenda sunt fundamenta quae in urbe sancta iecit P. Faber piae memoriae.*[40]

In the October after Favre's death, Father Andrew Oviedo wrote to Ignatius.

We were no less consoled by the happy entry into the celestial city of our good Father Favre. If those at Rome press their claim on him on the score of having his body, we here at Gandia likewise have a claim on him because in our College we have the first stone which was laid by his own hand. So just is this claim of ours that if we but keep our good will and place no impediments in the way, we shall certainly have, as long as we live, an efficacious patron, arrived as he has in the port of heaven. And there his charity, which in this world was so great, will without doubt not only not be constricted, but rather will be made even more expansive in the Lord. . . .[41]

Out in the Indies in December, 1547, Francis Xavier, on a voyage between Malacca and India, ran into a storm that lasted three days and nights, the worst he had experienced up to that time. In his prayer for help he called upon the Jesuits who had died, "especially the blessed soul of Father Favre." [42]

Among the Jesuits at Rome there were mixed feelings of

joy and sorrow. They rejoiced in what they saw to be the eternal triumph of their dear friend. Through his secretary, Father Ferron, Ignatius expressed these feelings to Canisius. "He will now help all of us more than he could have ever done here below. This is the hope and the joy that the Lord has poured into our souls." [43] The sentiments were the same in his report to the Jesuits in Spain and Portugal.

> After Master Peter's departure from this sorry world for the next, we here at Rome have been filled with a certain hope. In fact, to be more accurate, I should say that we have been filled with a certain sureness and joy that from his place in heaven he will help us far more than he has helped us here below in the past, or would be able to do if he had remained among us.[44]

Yet the natural sense of loss was very great and several of the Roman community could not see how Peter's place could possibly be filled. Ribadeneira recalled that Ignatius comforted his brethren with the assurance that God would repair the loss. Ignatius, of course, had learned through Favre that Francis Borgia had decided to enter the Society. "The Lord will provide another in place of Favre," said Ignatius, "and this man will bring an increase to the Society and shed a lustre on it even greater than that given by Favre." When Borgia learned of Peter's death he wrote to Ignatius and asked that no one be received into the grade of professed until he himself had taken the place of Father Favre. And so it was accomplished. Francis made his profession on February 1, 1548, the first to do so since Peter's death.[45]

In the colorful and dramatic story of Saint Francis Borgia may very well be found the clue to the question why Peter has suffered the eclipse that has been his historical lot. Peter died young, when he was but a few months over forty years of age. In the half-century or so after his death, there were giants in the Society of Jesus, who by their natural and supernatural gifts captured the imagination of the world. Francis Xavier lived six years more than Peter to become the lovable model of future generations of missionaries. Ignatius lived ten more years to be at his death the font of wisdom and inspiration for over a thousand Jesuits in twelve Provinces.[46] Twelve years after Peter's death, Francis Borgia shared with Philip II the office of executor of the will of the recently deceased Emperor Charles V. Fourteen years after, Father Anthony Possevino began his long series of diplomatic missions. Eighteen years after, Father John Maldanado began at Paris his brilliant lectures on Theology and Holy Scripture. Twenty-one years after, the innocent Stanislaus Kostka entered the Society in Rome. Twenty-four years after, Ignatius de Azevedo and his thirty-nine companions were butchered by Calvinists off the Canary Islands, and the same year Robert Bellarmine began teaching Theology at Louvain. Thirty-four years after, Blessed Edmund Campion and Father Robert Parsons landed in England. Thirty-five years after, Father Claude Aquaviva was elected General of the Society. Thirty-six years after, Father Matteo Ricci set out for Macao. Thirty-nine years after, the heir to the Duke of Mantua, Aloysius Gonzaga, became a Jesuit novice. Fifty-one years after, Father Francis Suárez began lecturing at Coimbra, and in the same year Father John Gerard escaped from the Tower of London. These saints, martyrs, theologians, missioners, appeared on the roster of the Society before the end of the sixteenth century, and it was their names, in the company of many others, that spelled out the greatness of the young Order. Peter lived when Europe was only first becoming aware of the stirrings of a new spiritual force in the world, and he died before the word "Jesuit" had become a commonplace name at international religious

269

disputations, in the classrooms of the universities, in the widespread printing plants of the continent. Peter lived at the time of the dawn in the Society's history, a beautiful dawn indeed that gave promise of a glorious day, but which was drowned in the very brilliance and splendor of the day it announced.

During the Generalate of Saint Francis Borgia, the small chapel of Santa Maria della Strada was torn down to make way for the impressive and elaborate Gesù Church. When the body of Ignatius was moved to the new edifice in July, 1569, efforts were made to recover Peter's remains, but it was found to be impossible to pick out his bones from those of the others who also had been buried there. All were gathered up together and reburied just in front of the main portal of the Gesù.[47] Year after year, thousands of the faithful enter through the great doors of this church, kneel in prayer before the rich altar of Saint Ignatius, cross the wide breadth of the edifice to the altar where the arm of Saint Francis Xavier is enshrined, then leave, reflecting on the early Society of Jesus as the story of two gentlemen from Guipuzcoa and Navarre, and not giving the slightest thought to the gentle Savoyard who with such engaging holiness placed for the first time the signet of the Society on so many places of Europe. From his place in heaven Peter sees all and he must smile with content. It is just the way he would want it to be, for he ever thought of himself as Ignatius' *hijo minimo.*

Epilogue

I N THE conclusion of his *La Spiritualité de la Compagnie de Jésus*, Père de Guibert endeavors to depict what he judges to be the characteristic note of the spirit of Saint Ignatius.

Saint Ignatius' conversion was essentially the discovery of the greatest and most attractive of all leaders, Our Lord Jesus Christ, the renunciation of all service to an earthly king in order to vow himself in a matchless and ardent way to the service of the one and only King of Kings and Lord of Lords. . . . This desire, so ardently expressed by Ignatius to the Virgin Mary, that she obtain for him the grace to be "placed with Jesus," this thirst for service which inspired his entire life, forms, it seems to me, the twofold element in the spirituality of his sons: companionship with Jesus as the servant of His Divine Majesty, *être avec Jésus pour servir*, following Him and imitating Him in order to serve Him and His Mother, in order to serve in Him and with Him the Holy Trinity, in order to serve souls ransomed by Him, and all this under the most exacting direction of His visible representative here below.[1]

Blessed Peter Favre's meeting with Saint Ignatius was in turn his own personal discovery of the attractiveness of Christ the King, to Whom is due a complete, wholehearted and never-ending service. This fact is the clear line of demarcation between two clearly diverse phases of Peter's life, the initial phase of the shepherd boy in Savoy and student in Paris—prayerful, docile, idealistic but perplexed and uncertain—and the latter phase of the Jesuit priest—mature, assured, dedicated. But more than that, this fact

271

must be the starting point of any consideration of what might be called the spirituality of Blessed Peter Favre. The salient features of Peter's interior life were formed to the point that they were a reflection of Ignatius' very own. Ignatius looked to the lessons of Loyola, Montserrat and Manresa and built the hesitant, uncertain soul of Peter into the uncompromising, selfless servant of the King of Kings. As for Ignatius, so for Peter the ideal became: companionship with Jesus as the servant of His Divine Majesty. Peter's journey out of Rome to the north and the west and back to Rome was an extension of the Ignatian desire for service. At the disposal of Cardinal Filonardi in Parma, of Doctor Ortiz and Cardinal Morone in southern Germany, of Albert of Brandenburg at Mainz, of John Poggio in northern Germany and Spain, of John III in Portugal, Peter was the tireless servant *par excellence*. The concept of service became a part of Peter's thinking. In one of the last entries that he made in his *Memorial,* he wrote:

On the feast of the Exaltation of the Holy Cross, when I was on my way to say Mass, someone spoke to me on the road and asked me to hear his confession. I told him that it was my wish to be a broom in the hands of Christ for the cleansing of his conscience. Then it was that the desire rose up within me to be looked upon and actually to be a broom of Christ. . . . I could see that I shall certainly be used up the way brooms are wont to be, and yet I found deep devotion in offering myself to Christ for use in cleansing His spiritual home, the souls of men.[2]

Under Ignatius' direction, Peter learned to blend the two concepts: the service due to God and an ardent love for the Person of Christ. Devotion to the Person of Christ as He is manifested in the Gospels is, of course, not the exclusive property of the Society of Jesus. The Society's attachment to

Christ is traceable, as far as human sources are concerned, to the tender and ardent love for Our Lord of Saint Bernard, Saint Francis of Assisi and their sons. Père de Guibert, putting aside any pretense of comparing different schools of spirituality, poses the question: what is, considered in itself, the most essential and interior note of Jesuit spirituality? "Considered in this way there is no question but that for the sons as well as for the father the center of their spirituality is truly in the tender devotion to Christ." [3] Throughout the pages of his *Memorial*, Peter mentions his meditation on the mysteries of Our Lord's life wherein he came to know and love Christ more surely and more completely.

While meditating on the place in Scripture that tells of the shepherds who came to Jesus at His birth, I asked the grace that the Lord would deign to renew me completely and raise my mind to higher things, just as He had wrought a change in the shepherds, whose desires had tended toward lower things.[4]

On the feast of Saint Praxedes, while going over the mysteries of the life of Christ, it occurred to me to ask God for certain graces through the merits of the Annunciation and Visitation, such as the grace to know exactly how I might praise, love and be intent on serving Him. . . .[5]

On the feast of Saint Cerbonius, Bishop and Confessor, while I was reflecting on the life and death of Our Lord Jesus Christ, certain colloquies suggested themselves to me as with tenderness of spirit I prayed: O Christ Jesus, may Your death be my life, Your labor my repose, Your human weakness my strength, Your confusion my glory. . . .[6]

On the feast of Corpus Christi, the grace was given me to desire to imitate completely in body and soul Christ Himself, and this in a twofold way. First, that I might know how utterly to spend myself and consume myself in good works out of devotion to Him; and second, that I might cultivate the bearing of suffer-

273

ing in all parts of my body just as He, in all parts of His Body, suffered for me and all men even to the death of the Cross.[7]

It is this spirit of personal attachment to Christ, derived from the Meditation on the Kingdom in the *Spiritual Exercises,* blending with the spirit of service, derived from the consideration of the Principle and Foundation, that creates the ideal of *être avec Jésus pour servir* and produces that particular spiritual temper peculiar to the Society of Jesus. There are, of course, any number of ways in which a soul may show its love for Christ. There is the love of the spouse uniting herself to the Beloved in the silence of prayer, the love of the artist and poet singing of the Most Beautiful of the Sons of men, the love of the victim completing by its self-immolation the Sacrifice of the Head of the Body, of which it is a member.

Among all these forms of love, as well as others that can be added, that which is paramount in the Jesuits' attachment to Christ is the love of the servant, vowed without reserve to toil and suffer for the Person, works, interests of the Master, in accordance with His aims and purposes, where He wills, how He wills and to the extent He wills.[8]

This union of the logic of The Foundation and the *élan* of The Kingdom found a happy realization in Blessed Peter. When he was on an arduous journey, or when taken up with the affairs of a religious colloquy, a city, or a court, it was the very time when he fed his soul with thoughts of his Master and revealed to those to whom he wrote his preoccupation with the task of making himself more like to Christ.

For the achieving of his ideal of "companionship with Jesus as servant of His Divine Majesty," Saint Ignatius relied on certain virtues as essential aids, among which the primacy of honor is held by self-abnegation, especially as practiced in the virtue of obedience. The very nature of Ignatius' purpose, according to Père de Guibert,

is one of the main reasons for insistence on total self-abnegation: abnegation is the virtue peculiar to the servant, who, by definition, is not out for himself but for his master; it is the virtue of complete and unconditional service. This will therefore be the great Jesuit virtue, practiced above all in obedience, the most complete manifestation of this abnegation. . . .[9]

So usual is it to think of Blessed Peter in his gentleness and attractiveness that it is possible to miss the decidedly Ignatian character of his interior life in its esteem and zeal for self-abnegation and obedience. The shield of the medieval knight was a thing of beauty with its varied colorings, its paintings of lilies and leopards and other symbols that make up a coat of arms. But it was also a thing of strength in the firm and unbending steel of which it was made. Beneath Peter's amiability and sweetness of temper was the strong steel of total self-abnegation and obedience. His delicacy of feeling never meant compromise with what was fundamental in Ignatius' teaching.

The chronology of his life once he left Rome is a rapid succession of changes of assignment, all of which demanded that he leave the carefully furrowed field for another to gather the harvest. Between May, 1539, and March, 1542, he was in the Legation of Parma a little over a year, in Germany eight months, in Spain five months. Back in Germany in April, 1542, he was in Speyer only about seven months when he was ordered to Mainz, where he labored for ten months. The rest of his life was very much the same: a month and a half in Cologne, three months in Belgium, back to Cologne for six months, followed by five and a half months in Portugal and fourteen months in Spain. Peter was not insensitive to the implications of these many changes and how they worked against anything like permanence and stability in his work. Nor, in his affective nature, was he impervious to the feelings of regret when he had to take leave of the friends he had made. To rise above a spirit of querulousness required the surrender of all self-interest and a preoccupation with the interests of his Divine Master. It was Peter's experience that this self-abnegation brought its own rewards in the wider fields that opened up before him with each successive move. To Ignatius he wrote from Mainz in November, 1542:

> Our Lord knows why I have not deserved to remain in one place for any length of time, and why it is that I am usually withdrawn at the very time when the harvest is ripe for the gathering. And yet I can see that all has been for the best. Consequently, for nothing in the wide world would I have entertained the wish to stay in Rome rather than go to Parma, or to stay in Parma rather than go to Germany. Never shall I feel regret because I was called from Germany to Spain, and still less because I was summoned from Spain to Speyer, and then from Speyer to Mainz.[10]

The principle of self-abnegation had its part in Peter's life of prayer, especially in detachment from interior sweetness and consolation. On the feast of the Epiphany in 1545 Peter experienced heaviness and dullness in his prayer and then noted in his *Memorial:*

> This is the day of the Three Kings and their adoration of the True King. Suffer therefore this burden of dryness in the realization that you will now better know whether or not you are master of yourself. For it is not a great accomplishment to conquer and have dominion over oneself when we have the fervent feeling of being near to Christ. The really true victory and effective rule

276

over ourselves is recognized with greater certainty at that very time when Our King seems far removed from us. . . .[11]

This was but another expression of the same basic point that Peter made with John Núñez, that love of God is measured by the extent of the surrender of self-interest.

But it is in the virtue of obedience that self-abnegation is carried to its most perfect form. It was obedience that Ignatius desired to see as the cardinal virtue of the Jesuit and on the practice of which he would have the whole good of his Society depend. The roadway through those seven years of Peter's travel after he left Ignatius was illumined by the lamp of obedience that Ignatius had lighted for him. Time and again, as has been pointed out, Peter kept after Ignatius to send him directions because it was his conviction "that there is a difference between being moved by the dictates of self-will and being prompted by the way of holy obedience."[12] And near the end of his days Peter reflected that the exterior changes of his life, in themselves so suggestive of instability, actually enjoyed an interior unity and intelligibility that was given by the practice of obedience.[13] It was his insistence on obedience that Gerard Kalckbrenner remembered as one of the noteworthy features of Peter's teaching. By failure in obedience

we would to our hurt lose the influx of divine grace which as sons of obedience we receive from God through our superiors. We would fall little by little in smaller things and then eventually in greater things. . . . For he who withdraws himself from obedience withdraws himself from the grace which God sends through superiors. . . . Nor must this be allowed to happen on the excuse of winning the heretics and saving the faith of some particular locality, lest we actually turn it over to the devil.[14]

❖   ❖   ❖

One of the things that Peter Canisius noticed particularly about Father Favre was his "wonderful application to prayer." [15] This is not surprising when one realizes both Peter's natural bent toward contemplation and his training in the school of Saint Ignatius. Ignatius understood with the clarity of a mystic that without prayer there is no spiritual life. Each of his sons was to be an "instrument in the hands of God," an ideal to be achieved in large measure through prayer. This lesson Peter learned well. Phrases such as these appear frequently in the *Memorial:* "I prayed with much devotion of spirit"; "I asked God's mercy on Germany"; "When I rose in the silence of the night to pray"; "I was reflecting on the mysteries of Christ's life"; "I offered an earnest prayer to Our Lady."

In its docility to the inspirations of the Holy Spirit, Peter's prayer had the freedom of the sons of God, a freedom that stands as a refutation of those who would see Ignatius as the spiritual guide insistently drawing up minute rules and regulations that inhibit and restrain the response of the soul to grace. Peter's devotion to the angels was characteristically his own. He was ever devising little schemes to help make his prayer the more fervent.

About this time I took up a devotion inspired by God to help me to recite the Breviary better. With a view to recollecting my spirit, this devotion was to say between psalms this brief prayer which I took from the Gospels: "Heavenly Father, give me Your Good Spirit." I have found this practice to be very helpful.[16]

On the feast of Saints John and Paul, I received a certain light which is a help to me for the better recitation of the Divine Office. It was to set up, as it were, certain limits beyond which I would be out of bounds at the time of saying the Office. These quasi-boundaries beyond which my attention should not be allowed to stray were: first, the predetermined physical place of recitation; second, the persons and saints who appear in the Office; third, the words of the prayers; fourth, the external actions connected with the recitation of the Office. When beginning the Office, it is worthwhile to recall these four points as a means to resist distractions that might come to the memory, the mind, the senses and the affections from other places, people, words and actions. . . .[17]

At times Peter's prayer was of an extraordinary kind. Wilhelmine d'Arenthon had witnessed him wrapped in ecstasy. Gerard Kalckbrenner could write of the special gifts from God which Peter managed to keep hidden. But overshadowing all else and permeating his entire activity was the prayer which has received its classic description in Ignatius' "seeking God in all things." Peter's life was an intensely active one; it was also an intensely prayerful one. His labor fed his prayer, and, in turn, his prayer fed his labor. Everything could be turned into a means of union with God, such as a journey through the lands of heretics.

During the journey from Spain to Germany Our Lord bestowed uncounted blessings on me. . . . Many were the sentiments of charity and hope that the Lord gave me in regard to the heretics, and indeed the entire world.[18]

Or it might be a reflection on the four seasons of the year.

With a holy desire I hoped to see the four seasons of the year re-enacted in a spiritual way in my soul during the course of the New Year. I longed for a spiritual winter so that the divine seeds, planted in the soil of my soul, might become embedded and take root; a spiritual spring that this soil might bring forth fruit; a spiritual summer so that the fruit might ripen unto a wonderful harvest; a spiritual autumn so that the ripened fruit might be gathered into the granaries of heaven and there be preserved against the possibility of perishing.[19]

279

A liturgical ceremony led Peter to think of the apostolate.

On that holiest of nights when Jesus Christ Our Lord was born, while I was in the cathedral looking upon the relics during the recitation of Matins, I was filled with intense devotion and I shed an abundance of tears from the very beginning of the ceremony to the end. The words of Jeremias that are read in the first nocturn touched me deeply. In the great desires that were given me, I was moved to wish with all my heart to be born of God, and "not of blood, nor of the will of the flesh, nor of the will of man." I also desired that on that same night there might be born some good and efficacious means of combating the evils of our age. . . .[20]

In his own imperfections and weakness Peter found stepping-stones to prayer.

On the feast of Our Lady's Purification, I felt a definite joy in reflecting on my spiritual destitution and need because it gives the Blessed Virgin Mary occasion to have pity on me as she beholds my shortcomings.[21]

In another's lack of consideration Peter found reason to lift his mind and heart to God.

One day I was awaiting a young man who had promised to come to me for confession and who had twice before disappointed me. While I awaited, my soul filled with distress because it looked as though six hours had been wasted on this young man. Then it was that I received great comfort from the Lord because it was in His Name I was making this sacrifice. This reflection crossed my mind: if for the love of God you are wont to spend several hours outside the doors of lords and princes and feel no tedium in the knowledge that the Lord has stored up a reward for you, why are you annoyed when one of Christ's least makes you wait? Do you feel that in such circumstances God will give you a lesser reward? How often have you made Jesus stand at the door of

280

your heart . . . ? Do that which you know He would do if He should be here in His Humanity.[22]

Meditation on the mystery of the Incarnation led Peter to feel the need of more activity in his apostolate.

While I was reflecting on the feast of the Annunciation, that on this day Christ became Incarnate and so began by deed and action the work of our salvation, I prayed to the Lord that He give me the grace to begin by deed and action the work that up till now I have merely desired. Let this be the beginning, O My God, of a change-over on my part from desires and hopes to deeds and actions.[23]

To the scholastics at Portugal Peter had written,

Dealing with things of time is indeed a help to us as long as it leads us to the things of eternity. . . . Let each one of us learn to seek himself and his brother in Christ, the Source of all we are. Let us look for each other, contemplate each other in Him Who is our Origin, our Cause, our First Principle.[24]

Gerard Kalckbrenner made this note of Peter's teaching: "Thus it is that, at any time we can walk among creatures and turn all to the glory of God and the salvation of souls." [25]

Thus Peter's life, as it unfolded, had the unity of a beautiful landscape. Each wearying journey, each "light" in prayer, each confession heard or sermon preached, each interior response to grace, threw into relief some other feature of his life, somewhat the way a clear sky sharpens the outline of a mountain, or the gentle roll of a field softens the roughness of an overhanging crag. His work and his prayer were but parts of one grand view.

✿   ✿   ✿

A man's character, above all when the man is one of no common mould, cannot be analysed by picking up an action or a characteristic here and there and tying them in a bunch. No one passes through time and its accidents and remains unchanged. A man has free will and he can, indeed he must, exercise it. . . . No one remains the same in virtue and love; not to go forward is to go back.[26]

Now, it is clear enough that the Peter of Montmartre was not the same as the Peter of the Valley of the Borne and the classroom of La Roche. Ignatius had come into Peter's life at Sainte-Barbe, and with him he brought to Peter's docile and receptive nature a clarity of vision, poise of judgment and resoluteness of purpose. Less dramatically and less perceptibly, but nonetheless truly, from his days at Paris until his final rendezvous with Ignatius at Rome, Peter grew and developed in his understanding and love of the things Ignatius taught him. With Ignatius and under his sure personal direction at Paris, Vicenza and Rome, Peter of course experienced the meaning of poverty, abnegation, obedience, zeal for souls, but never to the extent during the seven years when he was on his own. New challenges, new demands, unforeseen crises, ever-changing circumstances, all these unloosed deep reserves of charity, self-sacrifice, patience, brought out latent powers of endurance and doggedness, so that the Peter who came back to his father in Christ in 1546 was a person far greater, far nobler, far dearer than the one who had left him in 1539.

The *Memorial* is in many respects a record of Peter's growth in his vocation. The pages are replete with delicate nuances suggestive of the widening breadth of his spiritual experience and education. A surer grasp of the meaning of suffering in the soul's purification, a more assured mastery of the rules for the discernment of spirits, a deepening sense of God's Majesty, an enhanced sympathy for the weakness of men, all these subtle and ofttimes almost intangible changes betoken the growth of Peter's spiritual stature. A few excerpts from the *Memorial* may show this.

A thought which I have had frequently before again came to mind. A man, in order to keep his soul in a state of preparedness for the good spirit, should concentrate his energies primarily on the things of God. It is in this attention to the things of God that a man makes spiritual progress, and not, as I have done heretofore, in simply seeking relief from perplexities, temptations and sadness. For the man who would seek God and His blessings primarily in order to get rid of temptations and sadness would show himself to be spiritually immature and little appreciative of the grace of devotion except in periods of trial.[27]

On the feast of Saint Dominic, while I was walking through the streets, I took no joy in the things I saw. Rather did I find in them a source of distraction and temptations to vanity and evil thoughts. As a result I was filled with sadness. Then an interior voice spoke to me: "You have reason indeed to feel sad in not finding peace in these empty things, and precisely because of this you should be grateful and happy. Sadness is justly your lot because you do not endeavor to discover your peace and consolation in prayer, holy exercises and in that conversation which is in heaven. In your lack of concern for spiritual things you would have the company of many a man if peace were to be found in absorption in the things of this world." [28]

On Good Friday I was blessed with a certain insight into spiritual things and of this I made note. First of all, during the entire period of Lent I was troubled by all kinds of thoughts and feelings which seemed to reopen the wounds of my miseries and imperfections. . . . My mind was totally distracted by the very things in which I was wont to find peace. My body was drawn to the things which from my earliest days have ever spelled distress and spiritual death. Disorder, sloth, ignorance, seem to have risen up to color all my actions. All my evil inclinations which I had thought were quite dead seem to have come to life again during this Lenten season. I had every reason in the world to feel grieved. . . . When Good Friday came around and I began to recall these afflictions, it happened that I grew strong in spirit and I came to the realization that all this suffering had been for my good. For these are the days and this is the season dedicated to the memory of the Passion of Christ Jesus, His bodily wounds, afflictions and death, the blame, ignominy and opprobrium which He endured. I concluded that there was a benefit, therefore, in the reopening of my spiritual wounds and the scars of my infirmities during the season when we recall the memory of the Passion of Christ.[29]

On the feast of the Resurrection I began to rise somewhat out of my preoccupation with myself to the attitude of attention to Christ, with the result that it became my desire and my joy to find in Him the cause of consolation. Up to the present I have gone too far in making the measure of my sadness or joy to be the good or the evil I have discovered in myself. From now on may I recognize whatever worth is in me, not in the light of my achievements and the changing details of my life but in the light of Him Who is the Price of my redemption. May I rise to the point of fearing the loss of my soul, not because it might suffer eternal punishments and separation from the company of the blessed, but rather because it was purchased by the precious Blood of Christ.[30]

Of his early days in Savoy Peter had written: "When I was about seven years of age I several times felt an especially strong attraction to a devout life." [31] It is a simple statement of acknowledgment of God's invitation to a life in His service which might be made by many a young soul raised by pious parents amid beautiful surroundings that naturally lift the mind and heart to the supernatural world. Such a grace sometimes proves to be in the history of a man's life merely the mark of what might have been. With Peter it proved to be a promise of noble achievement, for in him this "unusual attraction to the fervor of a consecrated life" steadily grew until it permeated all the years of his life, extended into all his varied works, colored his relations with God and neighbor, comprehended the thought, desires and affections of his soul.

❀   ❀   ❀

One certain reaction to a reading of Peter's letters, and even his *Memorial,* is a sense of regret that he did not do all his writing in French, his native tongue. Peter wrote the greater number of his nearly one hundred extant letters in Spanish, a language which he never completely mastered and which he handled with awkward and often annoyingly obscure results. Frequently enough, when at a loss for the Spanish idiom, he fell back on Latin, so that many a page was not completed before it received a generous sprinkling of Latin phrases. Saint Ignatius did not want to receive letters from his sons that gave the impression of carelessness, and he admonished Peter to do considerably better in the future. Poor Peter! In Germany at the time and with his hands full, he told Ignatius—in clumsy Spanish—that he would try to keep the admonition in mind.

Yet it seems that I am at a loss on just how I might bring myself to act in conformity with your directions, because in the rapidity of my writing I cannot always hit upon the Spanish phrase. The result is that my letters become obscure, poorly arranged and replete with Latin. If you can bear with it, please excuse such a way of writing. If you find it intolerable, I shall try to apply myself more and reflect more on what I put to paper. . . .[32]

Peter tried hard, and in the two extant letters to Ignatius from the last year of his life not a single Latin phrase seems to have crept in among his sentences. Peter's few letters in

Italian were just as bad as those in Spanish. The letters he wrote in Latin and his *Memorial,* also in Latin, show a far greater control and grasp of that language, but the firmness of this hold, sure as it might be, is not crowned with the finesse and urbanity that one finds among his humanistic contemporaries such as Melanchthon, Erasmus and More. In fairness to Peter, however, it should not be forgotten that normally he did not pick up his pen in the tranquil and recollected surroundings of a Vivarium or a Bobbio. His were the efforts of a man who was bearing the heat of the day, and the wonder is that he ever wrote as much as he did.

Only one letter in French remains, written from Mainz to the Carthusian Prior of Reposoir. Its grace, its simple directness, its ease and lucidity underscore the great loss that is ours in being deprived of that more accurate and truer expression of Peter's thought and sentiment which would certainly have been conveyed if he had not abandoned French for the use of Spanish, Italian, and even Latin. In this letter Peter recounts for the Prior how he has made friends with the Carthusians of Mainz, how he has been invited to Cologne by Gerard Kalckbrenner, his personal analysis of the basic evils in Germany and some suggestions for making progress in the spiritual life.[33] Père George Guitton discerns in this letter the characteristics that would distinguish the school of Saint Francis de Sales.

These pages, written in French, enable us to form an idea of the place Peter would have acquired in our literary history if circumstances had placed him in the region between the Seine and the Rhône. Do not these pages anticipate the rhythm and charm of Saint Francis de Sales?[34]

At least once in after years, the memories of La Roche and its lessons in the conscious development of a literary

286

style rose up and produced a letter that smells very much of the lamp. In July of 1546 Peter wrote from Madrid to the Jesuits at Coimbra. As he passed each member of the community in review before his mind's eye, he fell back on the rhetorical tool called *"enumeratio,"* with rather stuffy results. "I request the cook of the community," wrote Peter,

that he ask God to make me to be an excellently prepared spiritual nutriment on which others might feed; the porter, that I may deserve to hear the sentence "Enter into the joy of your Lord"; the keeper of the dispensary that I shall not dispense the words of God and His saints in an unworthy manner; the superior, whom I should have mentioned first, that I may be able to give a good account of those subject to me; the refectorian, that I may see Christ walking among His holy ones and waiting on them; the infirmarian, that I may be counted among those to whom it is said: "Blessed is he that understandeth concerning the needy and the poor: the Lord will deliver him in the evil day"; the buyer, that when I shall go in and go out I shall find pastures; the keeper of the wardrobe, that I may hear the word of God correctly and keep it; the sacristan, that in carrying the vessels of the Lord I may be made clean; the minister of the house, that I may imitate Saint Joseph, of whom it is written: "He made him master of his house and ruler of all his possessions." [35]

This pretentious bit of writing is very much the exception, in fact, the solitary instance of Peter's reliance on an exaggerated rhetoric. What is typical, however, is the frequent and felicitous use of Holy Scripture. In his letter of condolence to King John III on the death of Princess Doña Maria, Peter causes the Princess, gone to her reward, to address the King in words from the Gospel of Saint John: "If you loved me you would rejoice because I go to the Father." [36] Shortly after Christmas of 1545, Peter wrote to the Jesuits of Coimbra asking prayer for himself in words

287

taken from Isaias: "Ask the Lord for the grace that I may one day be able to write to you and tell you the good news, that a Child is born to us and a Son is given to us, not in the Person of Christ only, but in my own person also." [37]

Peter was one of those men who cannot help but reveal themselves in almost every line they write. There have been men of intelligence far superior to Peter's, like Robert Grosseteste, or of historical import far more significant, like Saint Thomas Becket, who gave in their written word little or no insight into their intimate life of thought and love. Such silence and walled-in human feeling were entirely foreign to Peter.

*　*　*

The place where the memory of Blessed Peter Favre has been kept most alive among the faithful is his own Savoy. Of the many persons who, in the course of four centuries, have promoted the cause for Peter's canonization, most credit probably is due to Wilhelmine d'Arenthon, daughter of Mark d'Arenthon, Peter's host in Savoy in the summer of 1541. Wilhelmine, it will be recalled, was the one who, as a girl, observed Peter so closely and saw him in what was apparently a state of ecstasy. As an old woman Wilhelmine remonstrated with her son, Peter Critain, then a priest, because so little was made of the holiness of a man who was the honor of Savoy. She urged him to make an inquiry into the life of Favre while there were people still alive with personal recollections of him. Père Critain did so in October of 1596, assisted by two other priests, Juste Balliat and Jean Fournier. The three priests questioned inhabitants of the immediate neighborhood of Villaret and gathered much information about Peter's boyhood and his visit of 1541, which otherwise would have been lost. Throughout the testimony there occur in reference to Peter the words "*saint*" and "*bienheureux.*" [38]

Four years later, a second cousin of Peter, a priest named Jean Favre, who had been laboring for thirty years at Joinville in Champagne, returned to Villaret. He had heard that Peter was considered "Blessed" and decided to erect a chapel in his honor. He put up the chapel on the site of Peter's original home and was assisted in defraying the expenses by still another relative, Jean Favre, a doctor.[39] In 1605 Peter Critain, again assisted by two other priests, examined some few people who recalled Father Favre's visit to Villaret in 1541. Critain has merited the gratitude of all interested in the early history of the Society of Jesus because it was during the course of this particular questioning that the few details we have of Peter's personal appearance were recorded.

In 1607 Saint Francis de Sales, Bishop of Geneva, stopped at Villaret while on a tour of visitation of his diocese. There he consecrated the altar in the recently erected chapel and preached a sermon almost completely dedicated to the praise of Father Favre.[40] A year later, when he published his *Introduction to the Devout Life,* Francis used his fellow Savoyard as an example of one who practiced devotion to the angels.

The great Peter Faber, the first priest, the first preacher, the first lector of divinity in the holy Company of the Name of Jesus, and the first companion of the blessed Ignatius, its founder, returning one day from Germany, where he had done great services to the glory of our Lord, and traveling through this diocese, the place of his birth, related that, having passed through many heretical places, he had received innumerable consolations from the guardian angels of the several parishes, and that on repeated occasions he had received the most sensible and convincing proofs of their protection. Sometimes they preserved him from the ambush of his enemies; at other times they rendered several

289

souls more mild and tractable to receive from him the doctrine of salvation. This he related with so much earnestness that a gentlewoman, then young, who heard it from his own mouth, related it but four years ago, that is to say, about threescore years after he had told it, with an extraordinary feeling. I had the consolation last year to consecrate an altar on the spot where God was pleased that this blessed man should be born, in a little village called Villaret, amidst our most craggy mountains.[41]

Father Nicholas Polliens of the Jesuit College at Chambéry loaned Saint Francis a small volume on Father Favre— more than likely a copy of Peter's *Memorial*. Francis expressed his gratitude as follows:

It is high time that I return to you the small book on the holy life of our Blessed Peter Favre. I have been careful not to attempt to make a copy of it, since, when you sent it to me, you made clear that, for the present, it is reserved to your Society. Nevertheless, I would very much like to have a copy of the history of such a holy life. . . . I like to think that the Society is determined to do no less for the honor of this first companion of its founder than it has done for the others. Although the story of his life, both because of its brevity and because details were not too carefully recorded in those days, cannot supply biographical material to the same extent as other lives, nevertheless, what it will give, when written, will be all honey and sweetness of devotion.[42]

Francis wrote this letter on January 10, 1612. Later the same year his hope to see a life of Favre was fulfilled in the work by Father Nicholas Orlandini. The printer, Pierre Regand of Lyons, aware of Francis' devotion to Peter, dedicated the *Vita Petri Fabri* to the Bishop.[43]

In 1626, on instructions from Father Mutius Vitelleschi, General of the Society, Father Louis Serran, Rector of the Jesuit College at Chambéry, requested Jean François de

Sales, successor to his brother in the See of Geneva, to create an official and authoritative process of inquiry into the life of Father Favre. The Bishop granted the request and authorized three priests, Jean Roland, Claude Prumaz and Philippe Ducrest, to carry out the inquiry. The witnesses, led by good Père Critain, then about sixty years old, all testified to the devotion to Peter Favre that flourished among the Savoyards. The people referred to Peter as Blessed, and even Saint; they held processions in his honor. Some testified to extraordinary cures in his name. "Each morning," said one witness, "all the people of Villaret go to the door of the chapel . . . to pray to Blessed Peter Favre—for so they refer to him—and to recommend themselves to his prayers." [44] For some reason or other the authorities at Rome did not act on this inquiry. But this did not dampen the devotion in Savoy. In 1705 the Bishop, Monsignor de Bernex, at the request of the parishioners of Saint-Jean-de-Sixt, approved a vow that they had taken to keep August 1st, the day of Peter's death, as a day of rest from work. [45]

During Easter week of 1794 the chapel became one of the casualties of the French Revolution. It rose again between 1823 and 1826 through the devoted efforts of some priests and François Favre, a descendant of one of Peter's cousins. In 1869 Father Joseph Boero, Postulator General of the Society of Jesus, delegated Father Anthony Maurel, S.J. to request the Bishop of Annecy, Claude Marie Magnin, to conduct an official Process with a view to obtaining pontifical approval of the public cultus rendered Peter for over two centuries. Many witnesses testified to the existence of the public cultus and to the general practice of calling Peter Blessed. Miracles, such as the sudden cure of a six-year-old child paralyzed since birth, were attributed to the intercession of Father Favre. The Bishop, in reaching his decision, had to keep in mind the decrees of Urban VIII that forbade, before proper official approbation had been given, the public veneration to persons reputed to have died in the odor of sanctity. Urban somewhat alleviated the rigor of his decrees by a threefold exception: first, where there has been a *de facto* public cultus from "time immemorial"; second, where the cultus is based on the writings and testimony of the Church Fathers or the saints; third, where the cultus has been permitted for a long time by either the Holy See or diocesan bishops. By virtue of these excepting provisions of Urban VIII, Bishop Magnin declared that the veneration paid to Father Favre, as well as the use of the title Blessed, was proper and legitimate. The Bishop had in mind, among other things, the testimony of three saints, Saint Francis de Sales, Saint Peter Canisius, Saint Francis Xavier. His decree was dated July 23, 1869.[46] Three years later, September 5, 1872, Pope Pius IX gave pontifical approval of the public devotion to Blessed Peter Favre.

Abbreviations

I. Volumes of the *Monumenta Historica Societatis Jesu:*

Chron. S.J.   *Vita Ignatii Loiolae et Rerum Societatis Jesu Historia Auctore Joanne Alphonso de Polanco.*

EB   *Epistolae Paschasii Broeti, Claudii Jaji, Joannis Coduri et Simonis Rodericii.*

EM   *Epistolae Mixtae.*

EX   *Epistolae S. Francisci Xaverii.*

FN   *Fontes Narrativi de S. Ignatio de Loyola et de Societatis Jesu Initiis.*

MB   *Sanctus Franciscus Borgia.*

MF   *Fabri Monumenta.*

MI   Series I —*Sancti Ignatii de Loyola Epistolae et Instructiones.*

     Series II —*Exercitia Spiritualia.*

     Series III—*Sancti Ignatii de Loyola Constitutiones Societatis Jesu.*

     Series IV—*Scripta de Sancto Ignatio de Loyola.*

MN   *Epistolae P. Hieronymi Nadal.*

MR   *Patris Petri de Ribadeneira Confessiones, Epistolae Aliaque Scripta inedita.*

II. Other Volumes:

AHSJ   *Archivum Historicum Societatis Jesu.*

AS   *Acta Sanctorum.*

CR   *Corpus Reformatorum.*

EC   *Beati Petri Canisii Epistolae et Acta.*

Footnotes

I. OF BOOKS AND OF SHEEP

[1] R. Avezou, *Histoire de la Savoie* (Paris, 1949), pp. 5–9.

[2] Villaret is a most common name for communities in Savoy. In 1897 there were twenty-seven hamlets in the Département de la Savoie called Villaret. There was a Villaret at Thônes, another at Faverges, another at St. Martin-en-Genevois, another at Mageve, etc. Peter's Villaret, as has been said, lies in that region which is the valley of the Borne River and which is referred to in general as the valley of Le Grand Bornand. Some authors contend that Geneva, and even Belgium, was the place of Peter's birth. Le Grand Bornand is the name not only of the valley through which flows the River Borne, but also of a particular parish. Peter himself speaks of being born *"in magno Bornando,"* but he refers not to this parish but to La Vallée du Grand Bornand. St. Jean-de-Sixt has a variety of spellings: des Sits, Sixts, d'Essits, Sitz, Lessit. (Cf. F. Pochat-Baron, "À Propos du Bienheureux Pierre Favre dit Lefèvre. Quelques notes sur sa Paroisse natale et sur le lieu de ses premières études," *Congrès des Societés Savantes de la Savoie*, XVII [1906], 462–465.)

[3] Peter's family name appears in a variety of spellings, the three most common in English publications being Faber, Lefèvre, Favre. Which is the most correct is by no means certain. *Favre* is used in this volume, chiefly because that is the original form of the name, a fact confirmed by considerable documentation. When he wrote in French, his native tongue, Peter signed his name as *Favre*. Those who would prefer *Faber* have an argument in the fact that in the 1598 *Processus* for Peter's beatification the witnesses spoke of *Pierre Faber*. It is possible that Peter, following the Renaissance custom, had adopted the Latin form of his name after he had arrived at Paris. Yet his letters show that he did not always insist on using *Faber*. He changed the spelling of his name according to the language he happened to be using, his Latin letters being signed *Petrus Faber*, his Spanish letters *Pedro Fabro*, his French letter (only one is extant) *Pierre Favre*. Usage is certainly no argument for the form *Faber*, because there is no such thing in this case that can be called common usage. Father William Young, S.J. in his translation of Père Dudon's *St. Ignace de Loyola* uses *Faber*. Paul Van Dyke in his *Ignatius Loyola* uses both *Faber* and *Fabro*. *Lefèvre* is the form preferred by H. D. Sedgwick in his *Ignatius Loyola*. Father James Brodrick, S.J. in all his volumes in which Peter appears uses *Favre*. Father William J. Read, S.J. in his *The Industry Prayer of Blessed Peter Favre* concurs with Father Brodrick. In French the same arbitrariness is evident. A Belgian Jesuit, Father H. P. Vanderspeeten, insists on the use of *Favre* against such

295

forms as *Lefèvre, Lefèbrve,* etc. It was only in the beginning of the seventeenth century that forms such as *Lefèvre* took root. (Cf. "Le Bienheureux Pierre Favre de la Compagnie de Jésus. Quel est son véritable nom?" *Collections de Précis Historiques et Mélanges Religieux, Littéraires et Scientifiques,* XXI [1872], 496–474.) Even the editors of the *Monumenta Historica Societatis Jesu* have not been consistent. In the indices of various volumes *Faber, Favre, Lefèvre* are found.

4 F. Pochat-Baron, *op. cit.,* pp. 472–476.

5 *Ibid., Le Bienheureux Père LeFèvre ou Pierre Favre* (Paris, 1931), p. 3, n. 2.

6 *MF,* p. 804.

7 *Ibid.,* pp. 761, 799.

8 André Hamon, *Vie de Saint François de Sales* (Paris, 1896), II, 269.

9 *FN,* I, 29.

10 *MF,* pp. 768–779, 804.

11 *FN,* I, 29.

12 *MF,* p. 774. Around the turn of this century two good Abbés of Savoy were in disagreement in the learned journals of their country. The question on which they differed was that of Peter's schooling. The Abbé J. Mercier claimed that Peter did not attend school at Thônes. He based his position on his belief that there was no school to go to until the Collège de Thônes was opened in 1676. Peter's entire schooling, therefore, must have been at La Roche. ("Le Bienheureux Pierre Favre dit Lefèvre, Son Culte et sa Chapelle," *Mémoires et Documents publiés par L'Académie Salésienne,* VI [1883], 53, n. 2.) The Abbé Pochat-Baron, on the other hand, came to the defense of Thônes. Admitting that there was no Collège in the strict sense of the word at Thônes until after Peter's death, he claimed, nevertheless, that this did not necessarily rule out the existence of a school on more modest lines and geared to the teaching of grammar and the rudiments of Latin. The Abbé cited an array of historical records to show that such schools actually did exist in Thônes' history. For example, in 1389 there was *"Magister Amidius de Thono, rector scholarum Thoni."* Besides, one of Peter's nephews, also named Peter Favre, testified in the Process of 1596 that his uncle had gone to the school at Thônes. It would seem that the Abbé Pochat-Baron has gained the *plume de victoire.* (*Congrès des Sociétés Savantes de la Savoie,* XVII [1906], 478–481.)

13 Unedited document in the Bibliothèque Publique et Universitaire de Genève. Notes on the *Modus Componendi Epistolas* of P. Veillard by Théophile Dufour. Veillard's name is sometimes spelled Velliard or Veliard.

14 *MF,* p. 491. See also I. Iparraguirre, S.J., "Influjos en la espiritualidad del Beato Pedro Fabro," *Revista de Espiritualidad,* XX–XXI (1946), 438–452.

15 G. Schurhammer, S.J., *Franz Xaver, Sein Leben und Seine Zeit* (Freiburg im B., 1955), I, 248–249.

16 *FN,* I, 30.

17 *Ibid.,* 31.

[18] *MF*, p. 778. See also Jean Falconnet, "La Chartreuse du Reposoir au Diocèse d'Annecy," *Mémoires et Documents publiés par l'Académie Salésienne*, XVIII (1895), 1–8.

[19] *Ibid.*, pp. 593–595.

[20] *FN*, I, 31.

[21] F. M. Nichols, *The Epistles of Erasmus from His Earliest Letters to His Fifty-First Year Arranged in Order of Time* (New York, 1904), II, 505.

II. A Decade in the Land of The Fleur-de-lys

[1] S. D'Irsay, *Histoire des Universités* (Paris, 1933), I, 62. "*Mens humilis, studium quaerendi, vita quieta, scrutinium tacitum, paupertas, terra aliena.*"

[2] Hilaire Belloc, *Paris* (London, 1929), p. 201.

[3] *Ibid.*, p. 293.

[4] Philip Hughes, *A History of the Church* (New York, 1947), III, 475–477.

[5] D'Irsay, *op. cit.*, I, 267.

[6] H. Hauser and A. Renaudet, *Les Débuts de l'Age Moderne* (Paris, 1946), pp. 289–290.

[7] Charles Homer Haskins, *Studies in Medieval Culture* (Oxford, 1929), p. 36.

[8] *Chron. S.J.*, I, p. 48.

[9] *MF*, p. 104.

[10] Schurhammer, *Franz Xaver*, I, 61.

[11] *Fondo Gesuitico*, 2b, 2–7.

[12] *MB*, p. 453.

[13] *Chron. S.J.*, I, 48.

[14] *FN*, I, 33.

[15] *Ibid.*, 724–725.

[16] *MF*, pp. 103–104.

[17] Schurhammer, *op. cit.*, I, 103.

[18] St. Augustine, *The Confessions*, translated by F. J. Sheed (New York, 1943), p. 116.

[19] *FN*, I, 365.

[20] *Ibid.*, 407.

[21] J. de Guibert, S.J., *La Spiritualité de la Compagnie de Jésus* (Rome, 1953), p. 56.

[22] *Ibid.*

[23] *FN*, I, 169.

[24] *MI*, series IV, I, 490–491.

[25] *FN*, I, 33–36.

[26] Schurhammer, *op. cit.*, pp. 139–177; *FN*, II, 314–315.

[27] Feliciano Cereceda, S.J., *Diego Laínez en la Europa Religiosa de su Tiempo* (Madrid, 1945), I, 49–51.

[28] *FN*, I, 541.

[29] *Ibid.*, 704–705.

[30] *MF*, 1–4; *FN*, I, 36. On the document of Peter's subdiaconate the date is given as February 28, 1533. The editors of the *Monumenta Historica Societatis Jesu* show that this is a mistake, since the ordination took place on the Saturday of the *Quatuor Tempora* of Lent, and it was in 1534 and not 1533 that this particular Saturday fell on February 28th. *MF*, 2, n. 4.

[31] *EB*, 457–458.

[32] *Ibid.*, 459.

[33] *Ibid.*, 547.

[34] *FN*, I, 102–103.

[35] *Ibid.*, 104–105.

[36] *Ibid.*, 658.

[37] *MN*, I, 2–3; IV, 661–662.

[38] Pierre Suau, S.J., *Saint François de Borgia* (Paris, 1905), I, 53. The wounds of de la Vega were critical and he died three weeks after the attack on Muy.

[39] *EB*, 462.

[40] *FN*, I, 108; *EB*, 463.

III. DECISIONS IN ITALY

[1] *EB*, 462–463.

[2] Schurhammer, *Franz Xaver*, I, 265, n. 5.

[3] *Ibid.*, 271, n. 3.

[4] *FN*, I, 40.

[5] Schurhammer, *op. cit.*, I, 288–290. Diego, already a priest, entered the Society in 1540. Cf. *FN*, I, 110, n. 3. Estaban was probably the first coadjutor brother in the Society of Jesus.

[6] *EB*, 483–484.

[7] *Ibid.*, 486.

[8] Pietro Tacchi-Venturi, S.J., *Storia della Compagnia di Gesù in Italia* (Rome: Edizioni "La Civiltà Cattolica, 1950), II, I, 104–105.

[9] Ludwig Pastor, *The History of the Popes from the Close of the Middle Ages,* translated by F. I. Antrobus, R. F. Kerr, & E. Graf (London, 1912), XI, 38.

[10] *EB*, 486–487.

[11] *MF*, 7–11; Schurhammer, *op. cit.*, I, 322, n. 2; 323, n. 1. Father Schurhammer attributes the omission of the names of Broet and Jay from the faculties to hear confessions to the fact that they did not understand Italian.

[12] *FN*, I, 495; *Chron. S.J.*, p. 60.

[13] *EB*, 489.

[14] *FN*, I, 495; *Ibid.*, II, 84.

[15] P. Leturia, S.J., "Importancia del ano 1538," *AHSJ*, IX (1940), 188–207. Father Leturia in this article argues for computing the year they would

be obliged to wait from the spring of 1537 to the spring of 1538. Father Tacchi-Venturi in the latest edition of his *Storia della Compagnía di Gesù* takes cognizance of Father Leturia's viewpoint but says the evidence still makes him prefer the traditional view which we have followed (II, I, 63, n. 3.).

[16] *FN,* I, 204; *Ibid.,* II, 595–596.

[17] *Ibid.,* I, 313, n. 37. This narrative of the famous vision of Saint Ignatius is based on Father Nadal's account, the oldest testimony aside from Ignatius' own brief allusion to it in his autobiography. The words heard by Ignatius are presented in different ways by different authors. Nadal in his exhortation of 1554, as well as in that of 1561 at Coimbra, used the words: *"Ego vobiscum ero."* In his annotations to the Examen he wrote that the words were: *"Ego vobis ero propitius."* Father Laínez in his exhortation at the Roman College in 1559 used the words: *"Ego ero vobis Romae propitius."* There is also divergence of judgment as to which of the Divine Persons, the Father or the Son, said the words. Nadal in one place attributes them to the Father, and in another, to the Son. Ribadeneira attributes them to the Son; Laínez to the Father.

[18] *FN,* II, 260, 377, 585; Tacchi-Venturi, *op. cit.,* II, I, 90.

[19] *MI,* ser. I, VIII, 427.

[20] Tacchi-Venturi, *op. cit.,* II, I, 93.

[21] *FN,* II, 585.

[22] *MI,* Ser. IV, I, 548–550.

[23] *EB,* pp. 503–504.

[24] *Chron. S.J.,* I, 69; *EB,* pp. 504–507.

[25] *FN,* I, 42.

[26] F. Rodrigues, S.J., "O Dr. Gouveia e a entrada dos jesuitas em Portugal," *Broteria,* II (1926), 267–274.

[27] *MI,* Ser. I, I, 132–134.

[28] *EB,* pp. 499–500.

[29] Pastor, *op. cit.,* XV, 352–353.

[30] *EB,* pp. 499–500.

[31] *Ibid.,* pp. 201–203.

[32] *MI,* Ser. III, pp. xxxvii–xxxviii. The editors of the *MHSJ* have on these pages an interesting discussion of the difficulty of discovering with certainty the secretary of the proceedings.

[33] *MI,* Ser. III, I, 1–4.

[34] *Ibid.,* 4–8.

[35] *Ibid.,* 8.

IV. PARMA DONS AN AUREOLE

[1] Pastor, *History of the Popes,* XI, 504–508.

[2] Tacchi-Venturi, *Storia,* I, I, 269; II, I, 223–224.

[3] *Ibid.,* II, I, 220–223.

[4] *Ibid.,* 223–224.

⁵ P. Galtier, "La Confession et le Renouveau Chrétien," *Revue d'Ascétique et de Mystique*, XXV (1949), pp. 18–44; J. Duhr, "Communion Fréquente," *Dictionnaire de la Spiritualité*, II (1953), p. 1246.

⁶ *ML*, I, 4; Tacchi-Venturi, *op. cit.*, II, I, 241.

⁷ *Ibid.*, 372–375.

⁸ *MF*, p. 251.

⁹ *MF*, p. 569.

¹⁰ Tacchi-Venturi, *op. cit.*, II, I, 227–232.

¹¹ *MF*, pp. 15–17.

¹² *Ibid.*, p. 30.

¹³ *Ibid.*, pp. 25–26.

¹⁴ *Ibid.*, p. 499.

¹⁵ *EM*, III, 334–335; *MF*, pp. 33–34.

¹⁶ Tacchi-Venturi, *op. cit.*, II, I, 235.

¹⁷ *Ibid.*, 244. Father Boero and Father Cornely, by making a mistake in dates, have been unintentionally unfair to Laínez. They state that Laínez left the city of Parma for Piacenza not long after he and Favre arrived there with Cardinal Filonardi. Thus Peter was left alone at Parma to bear the heat of the day for over a year. Actually Laínez stayed at Parma only about two and a half months less than Peter. And it should be remembered that during Peter's three month illness it was Laínez who was the mainstay of the work in Parma. Cf. Tacchi-Venturi, *op. cit.*, II, I, 250, n. 1.

¹⁸ *MF*, pp. 39–44.

¹⁹ Tacchi-Venturi, *op. cit.*, II, I, 253–256.

²⁰ *Ibid.*, I, I, 568–570.

²¹ *MF*, p. 36, n. 6.

V. The Voices of the Two Germanies

¹ Pastor, *History of the Popes*, XI, 393.

² *MF*, pp. 48–49.

³ *Ibid.*, p. 57.

⁴ *Ibid.*, p. 54.

⁵ *Ibid.*, p. 56.

⁶ L. Cardauns, "Zur Geschichte der Kirchlichen unions und Reformbestrebungen von 1538 bis 1542," *Bibliothek des Kgl. Preuss. Historischen Institute in Rom*, V (1910), 145–150.

⁷ *MF*, p. 70, n. 4.

⁸ *Ibid.*, p. 202.

⁹ *Ibid.*, pp. 59–60.

¹⁰ *Ibid.*, p. 196.

¹¹ *Ibid.*, pp. 45–46.

¹² *Ibid.*, pp. 57, 63.

¹³ *Ibid.*, pp. 63–65.

¹⁴ *Ibid.*, p. 63.

[15] *Ibid.*, pp. 63, 67.
[16] *Ibid.*, p. 65.
[17] *Ibid.*, p. 70.
[18] G. Guitton, S.J., *L'Ame du Bx. Pierre Favre*, p. 247.
[19] *MF*, pp. 499–500.
[20] *EN*, IV, 637.
[21] Pastor, *op. cit.*, XI, 433–434.
[22] *CR*, IV, 184–185.
[23] Pastor, *op. cit.*, XI, 440.
[24] *MF*, pp. 91, 96.
[25] *Ibid.*, pp. 108, 112.
[26] *Ibid.*, p. 108.
[27] *Ibid.*, p. 90.
[28] *Ibid.*, pp. 90, 107–108; A. Astrain, S.J., *Historía de la Compañía de Jesús en la Asistencia de España*, I, 232.
[29] *MF*, p. 89.
[30] *Ibid.*, pp. 91–92.
[31] *Ibid.*, p. 82.
[32] *Ibid.*, pp. 77–78.
[33] *Ibid.*, p. 107.
[34] I. Iparraguirre, S.J., *Práctica de los Ejercicios de San Ignacio de Loyola en Vida de su Autor* (Rome, 1946), pp. 2 ff.
[35] *MF*, pp. 119–125.
[36] Dom David Knowles, *The Benedictines* (New York: The Macmillan Company, 1930), p. 2.
[37] *MF*, p. 51.
[38] *EX*, I, 26.
[39] *EB*, p. 519.
[40] *Ibid.*, pp. 418–419. Ignatius, excluding himself, gave his vote to the one whom the majority of his companions would choose.
[41] J. Janssen, *History of the German People*, VI, p. 142.
[42] *MF*, p. 88.
[43] *Ibid.*, pp. 113–114.
[44] *Ibid.*, pp. 117–118.
[45] *Ibid.*, p. 112.
[46] *Ibid.*, p. 50.

VI.   Weighing the Needs of Spain and Germany

[1] I. Le Masson, *La Vie de Messire Jean d'Arenthon d'Alex, Évêque et Prince de Genève* (Lyon, 1895), p. 6, n. 1. The families of Alex and Arenthon were joined in marriage as far back as 1383, when Pierre d'Arenthon married Marguerite d'Alex. Through the centuries the Arenthons were united to other famous houses of Savoy, such as the Meuthon, the Lucinque, the Gerbais, the Des Clets, the Sussel.
[2] *MF*, pp. 773–779.

[3] *Ibid.*, p. 502.
[4] *Ibid.*, p. 503.
[5] *Ibid.*, p. 127.
[6] *Ibid.*, p. 129.
[7] *Ibid.*, p. 131.
[8] *Ibid.*, pp. 133, 137.
[9] Astrain, *Historía de la Compañía de Jesús*, I, 235; *MF*, p. 136.
[10] *MF*, pp. 135–136.
[11] *Ibid.*, p. 138.
[12] *Ibid.*
[13] *Ibid.*, p. 502.
[14] *Ibid.*, p. 135.
[15] *Ibid.*, p. 138.
[16] *Ibid.*, p. 150.
[17] *Ibid.*, p. 140.
[18] *Ibid.*, p. 142.
[19] *FN*, I, 472, n. 14; José March, S.J., *Niñez y Juventud de Felipe II, Documentos ineditos* (Madrid, 1941), I, 354–355; II, 448, n. 11.
[20] *MF*, p. 151.
[21] *Ibid.*, pp. 442–443.
[22] *Ibid.*, p. 151.
[23] *Ibid.*, pp. 152–153. The Infantas, Cifuentes and Doña Leonor agreed to a plan by which both chaplains were to stay with the Jesuits for a year or two in order to get a grasp of the *Spiritual Exercises* and the other means they used in their ministry. The chaplains were then to return to Spain to teach what they had learned in the event that it was impossible to have any Jesuits themselves there. Father Astrain makes Father John and Father Alfonso the first Spaniards admitted into the Society in Spain; however, their original plan was not to enter the Society but simply to act as understudies to Favre and other Jesuits in order to carry their spirit and methods back to Spain. It was not until they were well along in their thirty-day retreat at Speyer that Favre intimated to Ignatius that the two retreatants might take the step of entering the Society. (*MF*, p. 164.) Father Astrain is in error when he speaks of both chaplains as being Spaniards. Father Rodrigues in his *História de Companhia de Jesus na Assisténcia de Portugal* shows that Alvaro Alfonso was a Portuguese who had accompanied the Empress Isabelle from her country into Spain. And Peter himself speaks of him being a Portuguese. (*MF*, pp. 226, 333; Astrain, *Historía de la Compañía de Jesús en la asistencia de España*, I, 235–236; Rodrigues, *op. cit.*, I, 202, n. 2.)
[24] *MF*, p. 154.
[25] Astrain, *Historía*, I, 237–238. Father Bartolomé Alcázar, an eighteenth-century author, has in his *Crono-historia de la Compañía de Jesús en la Provincia de Toledo* turned the story of Peter's stopover at Barcelona into a scene filled with wonder and excitement. According to Alcázar, Favre, travelling from Madrid, and Araoz, travelling from Rome, arrived in Bar-

celona on the same day. Their joy at this unexpected meeting was intense. The next day Antonio preached in the Church of Santa Maria del Pino and Favre spoke at the Chapel of a monastery of nuns. Among those who heard Peter was Doña Leonor, Francis' wife, who made a point to see Peter after Mass. She then carried back to her husband a glowing account of the unction and virtue of the visiting preacher. Later that day Araoz called on Doña Leonor and gave her an account of the aims of the Society of Jesus. This, too, she reported to her husband. The next day Francis himself, along with his entire court, went to the Chapel to hear Peter preach. So great was the impression made by Favre on the Viceroy that the latter invited Peter to dinner and learned from him about the Jesuits and their work in Italy, Germany and Portugal. This was the beginning of Borgia's attachment to the Society of Jesus. Alcázar's account can be read in *MB*, I, 567–569. Father Boero in his *Vita del Beato Pietro Fabro* presents substantially the same account. Both Father Astrain and the editors of the *Monumenta Fabri* rather brusquely deflate the whole story by the simple process of comparing the dates of Peter's departure from Barcelona and Araoz' departure from Rome and showing that the two men could not possibly have met at Barcelona in 1542. Father Astrain has a remark or two to make about Father Alcázar's historical work. Father Alcázar "admits in his introduction that he has taken entire pages from Ribadeneira. This is very true, as one can see if he but takes the trouble to compare the two works. Father Alcázar's own personal contribution was the lenient, or more accurately, the easy-going standards of critical judgment by virtue of which he endeavored to cover up the failings of others and to use on everything the gilded paintbrush with the result that a number of times he has achieved a lamentable falsification of history." (*Historía*, I, xi.)

[26] *MF*, pp. 156–157.

[27] *Ibid.*, p. 159.

[28] *Ibid.*

[29] *Ibid.*, p. 161.

[30] *Ibid.*, p. 162.

[31] *Ibid.*, p. 160.

[32] *Ibid.*, p. 166.

[33] *Ibid.*, pp. 165–166.

[34] *Ibid.*, p. 174; *Chron.* I, 101.

[35] *MF*, p. 164.

[36] *Ibid.*, pp. 176–177.

[37] *Ibid.*, pp. 515–516.

[38] *Ibid.*

[39] H. Grisar, S.J., *Luther*, translated by E. M. Lamond (London, 1913–1917), IV, 292.

[40] F. Reiffenberg, S.J., *Historia Societatis Jesu ad Rhenum Inferiorem* (Cologne, 1764), I, 6.

[41] *MF*, pp. 183–184.

[42] *Ibid.*, p. 185.

43 *Ibid.*, pp. 185–186.
44 *Ibid.*, p. 186.
45 *Ibid.*, p. 175, n. 2.
46 *Ibid.*, p. 171.
47 *Ibid.*, pp. 187–189, 485.
48 *Ibid.*, p. 192.
49 Grisar, *loc. cit.*
50 *MF*, p. 191.
51 *Ibid.*, pp. 597–598.

VII. ALONG THE PRINCE BISHOPS' HIGHWAY

1 *EC*, I, 10–12.
2 For this reason he is frequently called Hammotanus.
3 *EC*, I, 76–77.
4 *MF*, pp. 198–199.
5 *EC*, I, 78.
6 B. Duhr, S.J., *Geschichte der Jesuiten in den Ländern deutscher Zunge im XVI Jahrhundert* (Freiburg im Breisgau, 1907), I, 33.
7 J. Janssen, *History of the German People*, VI, 224, 233.
8 *Ibid.*, 295.
9 Conrad Varrentrapp, *Hermann von Wied und Sein Reformationsversuch in Köln* (Leipzig, 1878), pp. 35–38.
10 *Ibid.*, pp. 120–123.
11 *Ibid.*, p. 37.
12 P. S. Allen, *Opus Epistolarum Des. Erasmi Roterodami* (Oxford, 1906), I, 52.
13 Varrentrapp, *op cit.*, p. 70, n. 1.
14 Walter Lipgens, *Kardinal Johannes Gropper und die Anfänge der Katholischen Reform in Deutschland* (Münster, 1951), pp. 137–138.
15 *Kirchenlexicon* (Freiburg im Breisgau, 1883), II, 836–837.
16 Joseph Greven, *Die Kölner Kartause und die Anfänge der Katholischen Reform in Deutschland* (Münster, 1935), pp. 88 ff.
17 Greven, *op. cit.*, p. 91, n. 9.
18 *AS*, I, xxii.
19 Janssen, *op. cit.*, VI, 233.
20 *MF*, pp. 198, 202. How Peter and Gerard came first to write to each other is not clear. It may have been at the suggestion of the Carthusians of Mainz, whom Peter used to visit.
21 *Ibid.*, pp. 194–200.
22 *Ibid.*, pp. 447–448.
23 In the course of studies with which Peter was familiar the students of rhetoric and logic were more advanced than the students of grammar and dialectics respectively. Peter's idea is that any spiritual advice he would give would serve only to make Gerard retrace steps he had already covered.
24 *MF*, pp. 208–209.

25 *Ibid.*, p. 574.

26 *Ibid.*, p. 576.

27 *Ibid.*, pp. 589–590.

28 *Ibid.*, pp. 611–612.

29 *Ibid.*, p. 619.

30 *Ibid.*, pp. 619–620.

31 Lipgens, *op. cit.*, p. 140.

32 *CR*, V, 123.

33 *Ibid.*, 100.

34 Lipgens, *op. cit.*, p. 139.

35 *MF*, p. 198, n. 10.

36 *Ibid.*, p. 215.

37 *Ibid.*, pp. 215–217.

38 Raynaldus, *Annales Ecclesiastici ab anno quo definit Card. Caes. Baronius MCXCVIII usque ad annum MDLXV . . . auctore Odorico Raynaldo* (Cologne, 1727), XXI, pars I, 201; *MF*, pp. 216–217.

39 *MF*, p. 217.

40 This episode, which should be one of the most interesting of Peter's life, is one about which least is known. Even this minutia owes its preservation to a single sentence of Peter Canisius in which he recalled that Favre had effectively argued for the Catholic position. (*EC*, VII, 261–262, 270–271.) Until Father Braunsberger published his seventh volume of the *Canisii Epistolae et Acta* in 1922, it was disputed whether Favre had actually debated with Bucer. The German scholar, J. Hansen, in his *Die erste Niederlassung der Jesuiten in Köln, 1542–1547* (Beiträge zur Geschichte vornehmlich Kölns und der Rheinlande, Köln, 1895, pp. 168–184) claimed no such meeting had occurred. Thus the conclusion that what was affirmed by Ribadeneira, Orlandini and Reiffenburg was simply a myth. This particular bit of editing by Father Braunsberger, wherein he brings Canisius' record of the event to light, should write *finis* to the dispute. It is interesting to note, however, that Ribadeneira in his *Vita Ignatii Loyolae*, while following Canisius in substance, actually let the fervor of his imagination run beyond the strict text of Canisius' written word. Canisius' words are: "Several times he [Favre] did not hesitate to debate with Bucer and other heretics and he was able to prove to them the truth of the faith he himself professed." Ribadeneira's version is, "He [Favre] vigorously repressed the raving of the heretics and again and again disputed so strongly and so steadfastly with their leaders and masters, especially Bucer, that he could easily have proven the faith which he professed if they had not become obdurate." Ribadeneira should be taken to task for his elaborations on the debates between Favre and Bucer. But it must also be granted that he did not manufacture the basic fact of the disputations. Americans will be interested to know that Father Braunsberger dedicated his seventh volume to the students and Alumni Sodality of Canisius College, Buffalo, who had helped him to carry the financial burden of publishing that particular volume. (*EC*, VII, 261–262, 270–271.)

[41] *MF*, p. 219.

[42] *Ibid.*, p. 220.

[43] *Ibid.*, pp. 451–452.

[44] *Ibid.*, pp. 219–220.

[45] *Ibid.*, p. 453.

[46] Rodrigues, *História de Companhia de Jesus*, I, 373–378; p. 398, n. 1. Father Simon Rodrigues is normally thought of as one who caused Ignatius many troubles. It is a pleasure, therefore, to be able to add a few bright lines to the usual darkly shaded portrait. Father Francisco Rodrigues, modern historian of the Portuguese Province, argues cogently for his sixteenth-century namesake and shows that it was a zealous and apostolic Father Simon who fathered Favre's mission to Spain. He shows, for example, that several writers, including the historian of the Spanish Assistancy, Father Astrain, suppose that the main reason Favre was ordered to Spain was simply to accompany Doña Maria, and that it was King John who was the first to ask for Jesuits for this purpose. In the spirit of giving credit where credit is due, Father Rodrigues proves, first, that it was Father Simon who, in a disinterested love for the Society and zeal for its expansion, broached the subject to King John; and second, that Simon's master idea was the introduction of the Society into Spain. This was to be effected with certainty through the kind protection of Doña Maria at the court of Prince Philip.

[47] Lipgens, *op. cit.*, p. 153.

[48] *MF*, p. 219.

[49] *Ibid.*, p. 490.

[50] The best treatment in English of the problems created by the various texts of the *Memorial* is in William J. Read, S.J., *The Industry in Prayer of Blessed Peter Favre* (Rome, 1950), pp. 57–62.

[51] P. Leturia, S.J., *Inigo de Loyola*, translated by A. J. Owen, S.J. (Syracuse, 1949), p. 114.

[52] *EC*, VIII, 128.

[53] *MF*, p. 651.

VIII. Jesuit Roots in Belgian and German Soil

[1] Alfred Poncelet, S.J., *Histoire de la Compagnie de Jésus dans les Anciens Pays-Bas*, I, 40.

[2] S. D'Irsay, *Histoire des Universités*, I, 254 ff.

[3] Alfons Kleiser, S.J., *Ein Seelensoberer: Lebenserinnerungen des ersten flämischen Jesuiten Kornelius Wischaven* (Paderborn, 1930), pp. 18–64. The Louvain episode in Blessed Peter's life presents a maze of difficulties because of several divergences among the primary sources. Father Kleiser wrote his charming little life of Cornelius Wischaven with all these sources before him and has created, despite the reluctance of the material to be brought into order, a clear-cut portrait of his subject.

[4] *Ibid.*, pp. 64–70.

⁵ Francis Strada, Andrew Oviedo and John of Aragon were to go to Portugal with Peter. Aemilian de Loyola, Anthony Strada and James Spech were to go to Rome. In February, 1543, Doménech had already taken Ribadeneira and Lawrence Dels to Rome. Usually Wischaven is spoken of as the first Belgian Jesuit. It is true only in the sense that he was the first Belgian Jesuit to persevere. Dels was a Belgian and had entered before Wischaven, but was dismissed by Saint Ignatius in Rome for some ideas that were hardly in keeping with the Jesuit way of life. (*MF*, p. 474, n. 20; p. 453, n. 6.)

⁶ Kleiser, *op. cit.*, p. 72.

⁷ *Chron. S.J.*, I, 115.

⁸ *MF*, pp. 226, 458–459; *EM*, I, 146–147.

⁹ *MF*, p. 234, n. 7; *Chron. S.J.*, I, 116–117.

¹⁰ *MF*, pp. 459–461.

¹¹ *Ibid.*, p. 228.

¹² *Ibid.*, pp. 228–229.

¹³ *Ibid.*, pp. 233–234; *Chron. S.J.*, I, 136–137.

¹⁴ *MF*, pp. 461–462.

¹⁵ *MF*, pp. 455–458; *EC*, I, 95, n. 2.

¹⁶ There is disagreement in the various accounts of the Louvain episode about the number of students who asked to be received into the Society. Father Poncelet says that nineteen presented themselves to Peter, that nine were accepted and that the remaining ten were told to stay with Wischaven for further testing. (*Op. cit.*, I, 44.) The number nineteen is borne out by *MF*, pp. 462. Father Kleiser maintains that Wischaven was left alone in Louvain. (*Op. cit.*, p. 77.) The smaller number, which we accept, fits in with what Father Polanco wrote in *Chron. S.J.*, I, 136–137.

¹⁷ *MF*, p. 232.

¹⁸ Poncelet, *op. cit.*, I, 44, n. 3.

¹⁹ *MF*, pp. 235, 463; Kleiser, *op. cit.*, p. 76.

²⁰ *MF*, pp. 230–232.

²¹ *Ibid.*, pp. 235–236.

²² *EC*, I, 102; 103, n. 3. Reiffenburg, *Societatis Jesu*, I, 16.

²³ *MF*, pp. 254–255.

²⁴ *Ibid.*, p. 263.

²⁵ *EC*, I, 288, n. 4. Kannegesser was to join the bewilderingly large number of pioneer Jesuits to whom death came early in their careers. Peter died at Cologne in 1548 and was buried in the church of Saint Agatha.

²⁶ *MF*, p. 256.

²⁷ *Ibid.*, p. 264. Peter's letter of May 10, 1544, to Francis Xavier in which these events are related had itself an interesting little history. It reached Portugal from Cologne too late for the 1544 fleet that sailed to the Indies and was still in Portugal when Peter arrived there in August of the same year. Peter wrote a more up-to-date letter to Xavier, picked up the one he had written in Cologne, carried it to Rome, where it was found after his death. (*EX*, II, 541, n. 14.)

[28] *MF*, pp. 256–257; *Chron. S.J.*, I, 137–138.

[29] *EC*, I, 671.

[30] *MI*, Ser. I, I, 21, 207, 567–569. One of the old codices of the Exercises is the *Codex Coloniensis Exercitiorum B. Fabri*, a copy of the original. The whereabouts of the original, if it has survived to the present day, is still to be discovered.

[31] J. B. Kettenmeyer, S.J., "Aufzeichnungen des Kölner Kartäuserpriors Kalckbrenner über den sel. Petrus Faber," *Archivum Historicum Societatis Jesu*, Vol. 8 (1939), 86–102.

[32] *MF*, p. 240, n. 3; Kleiser, *op. cit.*, p. 77.

[33] *MF*, pp. 236–239.

[34] *MF*, pp. 244–245.

[35] *Ibid.*, pp. 243–245.

[36] *Ibid.*, pp. 260, 264.

[37] Janssen, *History of the German People*, VI, 242–244, 251.

[38] *MF*, p. 258.

[39] *Ibid.*, p. 265; *Chron. S.J.*, I, 139.

[40] *MF*, p. 257.

[41] *Ibid.*, p. 259.

[42] Rodrigues, *História de Companhia de Jesus*, I, 384.

[43] *Ibid.*, 323–324; Poncelet, *op. cit.*, I, 45, n. 4.

[44] *MF*, p. 271, n. 17; *EC*, I, 103, n. 3; Greven, *Die Kölner Karthause*, p. 102.

[45] As he walked out of Cologne with these seven heads, Peter became the unwitting co-operator in the spread of one of the biggest frauds ever perpetrated in the history of relics. The story of Saint Ursula and the 11,000 virgins, orginating in a simple and unadorned form in the fourth century, gradually grew into one of the most extravagant tales about early Christianity and reached the pinnacle of its absurdity in the great discovery at Cologne in 1155 of countless human remains. These were the supposed relics of the Ursuline martyrs. Not only that, but the excavators had come upon what were purported to be the epitaphs of Saint Papunus, King of Ireland, and St. Picminus, King of England, and prominent figures in the legend as co-martyrs with Saint Ursula. The great discovery was actually the opening of a common burial place, and two Benedictines from nearby Deutz were the operating genii behind the great deception. Peter's seven heads were, more than likely, taken from that collection. Peter's critical faculty on such things would never have met the standards of a Papenbroeck or a Mabillon, but, after all, the age of the Bollandists and the Maurists had not yet dawned.

IX. Clear Iberian Skies

[1] *MF*, pp. 464–467.

[2] Damiao de Gois, *Lisboa de Quinhentos, Descricao de Lisboa* (Lisbon, 1937), p. 17.

[3] *EX*, I, 79.

[4] *EM*, I, 169; Rodrigues, *História de Companhia de Jesus*, I, 381, n. 1. Father Rodrigues shows how Polanco, Orlandini and Astrain are all in error when they suggest that Ignatius decided to send Araoz to Portugal only after he had heard that Poggio was determined to keep Favre in Germany. Through evidence in the Portuguese *Corpo Diplomatico*, Father Rodrigues proves that Ignatius' decision had been made before Poggio's representations reached Rome.

[5] *MF*, p. 267.

[6] *Ibid.*, pp. 310–314; 467–468.

[7] H. Rashdall, *The Universities of Europe in the Middle Ages*, ed. by F. M. Powicke and A. B. Emden (Oxford, 1936), II, 109–113.

[8] *FM*, p. 297.

[9] *MF*, pp. 477–478; *EX*, I, 467, n. 14.

[10] The way of giving the Pax known to Núñez was different from that with which twentieth-century American Catholics are acquainted. In Núñez' time, a gold or silver plate, usually embellished with a figure of Christ or a saint and called the *deosculatorium*, was presented to the celebrant to be kissed and was then passed to the other clergy to be kissed by them in turn.

[11] *MF*, pp. 475–477; Rodrigues, *op. cit.*, I, 432–433.

[12] de Guibert, *La Spiritualité de la Compagnie de Jésus*, pp. 165–170.

[13] *MF*, pp. 475–477.

[14] *Ibid.*, p. 298.

[15] *Ibid.*, p. 299.

[16] *Ibid.*, pp. 342–350.

[17] *EB*, p. 550. Peter's letter with its ambiguous concluding sentences has had its repercussions a full four-hundred years later, for it set off a controversy in our own twentieth century. Father Antonio Astrain, historian of the Spanish Assistancy, found material in those last few sentences on which to base some criticism of his Portuguese brethren of the sixteenth century. In Favre's letter Father Astrain was inclined to see the first reports to Ignatius that all was not gold that glittered in Portugal. "Não, não," exclaimed Father Francisco Rodrigues, historian of the Portuguese Assistancy. Peter may have noticed some tiny faults, some peccadillos, but to infer that Favre was reporting that the religious spirit of the Jesuits in Portugal was badly orientated is to stretch the evidence beyond recognition. On Father Astrain's side is no less an authority than Pedro Ribadeneira, but Father Rodrigues would have any one who reads Ribadeneira make sure that he does so with the utmost caution. Ribadeneira had written in his *Persecutiones de la Compañía de Jesús* that both Favre and Araoz had observed that Simon Rodrigues was governing the Society in Portugal independently of Rome and advised Ignatius of this fact. Modern Father Rodrigues commented: "This accusation of Ribadeneira is very serious. If it is true, we shall be forced to qualify as lies the information which Favre and Araoz sent in their letters to the holy founder. But the classical Castilian

author, in this paragraph which treats of Simon, presents so many exaggerations that his words have to be taken with considerable reserve, notwithstanding the judgment of the authors of *Fontes ita Nati Ignatio* (I, 101) that Ribadeneira is 'autor gravisimo y testigo major de toda exception en esta materia.' Any competent critic is certainly on the side of Favre and Araoz."

[18] *MF*, p. 667.

[19] *Ibid.*, p. 670.

[20] *Ibid.*, pp. 674–675.

[21] *Ibid.*, p. 679.

[22] *Ibid.*, p. 310; *EM*, I, 195.

[23] *MF*, p. 306; *EM*, I, 232.

[24] Rodrigues, *op. cit.*, I, 396, n. 2.

[25] *MF*, pp. 679–680.

[26] *Ibid.*, pp. 311–312.

[27] *Chron. S.J.*, I, 160.

[28] Roger B. Merriman, *Rise of the Spanish Empire* (New York, 1934), IV, 28–29.

[29] Astrain, *Historía de la Compañía de Jesús*, I, 245.

[30] Hughes, *A History of the Church*, III, 435.

[31] *Chron. S.J.*, I, 160.

[32] Gregorio Marañon, *Antonio Peréz* (London, 1954), p. 6.

[33] Karl Brandi, *The Emperor Charles V*, p. 484.

[34] Pierre Suau, S.J., *Saint François de Borgia* (Paris, 1905), pp. 164–167.

[35] *MF*, p. 326.

[36] *EM*, I, 271.

[37] José March, S.J., *Niñez y Juventud de Felipe II, Documentos ineditos* (Madrid, 1941), I, 218; II, 179, 183.

[38] *EM*, I, 212.

[39] *Ibid.*, 226.

[40] *FM*, p. 324; *EM*, I, 226.

[41] *FM*, p. 327. Silicio turned on the Society because Ignatius would not go along with him in his anti-semitic policies. (James Brodrick, S.J., *Progress of the Jesuits*, p. 19, n. 1; p. 120, n. 1.)

[42] *MF*, p. 324.

[43] *Ibid.*, p. 683.

[44] *Ibid.*, p. 686.

[45] *Ibid.*, p. 326.

[46] *Ibid.*, p. 365.

[47] Rodrigues, *op. cit.*, I, 404; Astrain, *op. cit.*, I, 267–268, 276.

[48] *MF*, pp. 333–336.

[49] *Chron. S.J.*, I, 163.

[50] *EC*, I, 105.

[51] *Ibid.*, 109–110.

⁵² *MF*, pp. 266–277. Canisius wrote this letter in August and September of 1544 and it did not reach Favre until July of 1545.

⁵³ *Ibid.*, p. 323.

⁵⁴ *Ibid.*, p. 288.

⁵⁵ *Ibid.*, pp. 290–297.

⁵⁶ *Ibid.*, 330–331.

⁵⁷ The editors of the *Monumenta Fabri* and Father Braunsberger differ widely in their identification of the persons with whom Favre was displeased at the time the Jesuits of Cologne were being persecuted. The difficulty of finding Favre's meaning is accentuated by the need to supply an important word that is missing in the original text. The original reads as follows: "Illud non placet, quod sciam magistrum Nicolaum et magistrum (   ) cum illis Rmis dominis nullam vestri curam habere." Father Braunsberger, whom we follow here, inserts the word *"Claudum"* in the blank space because he thinks that what caused Favre's annoyance was that Nicholas Bobadilla and Claude Jay, both in episcopal retinues, failed to provide financial assistance to the hardpressed Cologne Jesuits. The editors of the *Monumenta Fabri* feel that Peter is talking about Nicholas van Esch and Andrew Herll and their Lordships, Bishop Georg Skodborg and the University Rector, Hermann Blanckfort. They therefore insert the name *"Andream"* in the open space. The editors also think that Favre's remark is a reaction to what Canisius mentioned about the conduct of their friends during the von Wiedian storm. Friends on whom the Jesuits felt they could count for help remained tightlipped and, instead of rising to the occasion and going boldly before the Magistrates, they contented themselves with giving advice on the quiet. It should be stressed, however, that Canisius did not include Kalckbrenner in that number. He was absent from Cologne at the time and Canisius felt sure that if he had been there, "he would not have denied us his help." (*MF*, pp. 332, n. 10; p. 269; *EC*, I, 157, n. 1.)

⁵⁸ *EC*, I, 141.

⁵⁹ *MF*, p. 378; *EC*, I, 141, n. 5; 157, n. 1.

⁶⁰ This was but the first storm of many that the Jesuits weathered in their long years in Germany. One of the most delightful of Peter's biographies is that written by the great scripture scholar, Father Rudolf Cornely, S.J. Father Cornely concludes the Preface of his *Leben des seligen Petrus Faber* with these words: "And so we turn over to the good will of our reader this little work, the last it is permitted us to finish at Maria-Laach, feast of Saint Thomas, December 21, 1872." The previous July, the anti-Jesuit laws were passed by the government of Bismarck. These led to the closing down of all Jesuit activity in Germany and the eventual exile of the Society.

X. WITH SAILS FURLED

¹ *EX*, I, 166–168.

² *Ibid.*, 152–153.

[3] *EM*, I, 225.

[4] *EX*, I, 154.

[5] *Ibid.*, 255, 261.

[6] *EM*, I, 231.

[7] *EX*, I, 264.

[8] *MF*, pp. 372–373.

[9] *EX*, I, 264–265.

[10] *EC*, I, 141–142.

[11] *MF*, pp. 331–332.

[12] *Ibid.*, p. 390.

[13] *Ibid.*, p. 418.

[14] *EX*, I, 264, n. 40; *EC*, I, 104, n. 2.

[15] Charles Van de Vorst, S.J., "La Compagnie de Jésus et le Passage à l'Ordre des Chartreux," *Archivum Historicum Societatis Jesu*, XXIII (1954), 6–7.

[16] Greven, *Die Kölner Kartause*, p. 101.

[17] *MF*, pp. 412–416.

[18] *Ibid.*, p. 400.

[19] *Ibid.*, p. 202.

[20] *Ibid.*, pp. 400–401.

[21] *Ibid.*, pp. 401–402.

[22] *Ibid.*, p. 414.

[23] *MN*, IV, 218.

[24] *MI*, Series I, I, 402.

[25] *Ibid.*, pp. 359–361.

[26] *MF*, pp. 419–421.

[27] *Ibid.*, p. 422.

[28] *EM*, I, 273.

[29] Suau, *Saint François de Borgia*, I, 156.

[30] *FN*, II, 355; *Chron. S.J.*, I, 187. Shortly after Peter's departure from Gandia, Francis made the *Spiritual Exercises* under Andrew Oviedo, and on June 2nd, exactly one month after Peter came to Gandia, he made a vow to enter the Society.

[31] *MF*, pp. 424–425.

[32] *Ibid.*, pp. 425, 433; *MI*, II, pp. 391–392, 409–410.

[33] *MI*, II, 409–410.

[34] *MF*, pp. 434–437.

[35] *Ibid.*, pp. 839–840; I. Iparraguirre, *Obras Completas de San Ignacio Loyola* (Madrid, 1952), pp. 711–712.

[36] No part of Peter's life is more colored by romanticizing than the period between his sickness in Barcelona and his death in Rome. Father Nicholas Orlandini, Peter's first biographer, wrote: "Everything was blistering with fever heat under the hostile Sirius. Ignatius did not approve of his coming to Rome at that time. But when the other Fathers were consulted, they expressed a dissenting opinion. . . . Just as Ignatius yielded to these Fathers, Favre, with the determination to obey blindly, yielded to

them and to Ignatius. Weakened and almost an invalid, he came to Rome, a thing which for those enjoying good health is often enough fatal *mordente sidere.*" (*Forma Sacerdotis Apostolici expressa in exemplo Petri Fabri* [Dilingen, 1647], pp. 96–97.) Père Maurel, a ninetenth-century author, goes a bit further: "The order was given and Favre got ready to leave. On all sides they argued, trying to make him see that in his state of health he was courting death. He answered that there was no need to live but that it was imperative to obey . . ." (*La Vie du Bx. Père Pierre Lefèvre* [Lyons, 1873], p. 199.) Father Boero has substantially the same account, with the added note that Peter left Barcelona on June 21st. (*Vita del Beato Pietro Fabro* [Rome, 1873], p. 207.) According to the version of Père Prat, another nineteenth-century writer, Ignatius left it up to Favre to decide what course to follow, to stay in Barcelona or to set out for Italy. The only norm for Peter was obedience, and since he felt that his sickness did not cancel out the original order that he received when in Madrid, he judged himself obliged to finish the journey without waiting for complete recovery. (*Le Bx. Pierre Lefèvre* [Lyons, 1873], p. 271.) Such embellishments as Ignatius yielding to the wish of the other Fathers at Rome that Peter come there despite the summer heat, the people of Barcelona trying to persuade Peter to give up the idea of attempting the trip to Italy, Peter's reply about the need not to live but to obey, Peter's entry into Rome in an utterly exhausted condition, all are either not mentioned in the primary sources or are contradicted by them. Father Ferron, Ignatius' secretary, writing in Ignatius' name to the Jesuits at Coimbra seven days after Peter's death, said that Peter was well when he came to Rome (*"entrando aqui sano y bueno"*) and that eight days passed before he caught the fatal fever. (Iparraguirre, *op. cit.*, pp. 711–712.) Boero's statement that Peter left Barcelona on June 21st cannot stand in view of the fact that on that very day Peter wrote to Ignatius that he was still looking for passage. Father Orlandini's story about the Roman Jesuits exerting pressure on Ignatius and persuading him to have Favre make the trip to Rome from Barcelona in July is open to serious question on several scores: 1) There is nothing in the original sources to substantiate it. Father Orlandini may have seen Father Ferron's letter of August 7, 1546, to Simon Rodrigues (*MI*, Ser. I, I, 402–403), wherein is related Ignatius' consultation with the Roman Jesuits, and judged that all the events narrated by Ferron occurred in June and July of that year. Actually, however, a number of them occurred in February. As presented by Ferron, there is an *immediate* connection between the instructions of the Holy See that Jesuits be assigned to Trent, Ignatius' request of the Roman Jesuits for counsel about the advisability of bringing Favre from Spain, and the actual command sent to Favre. The whole context of this portion of Ferron's letter to Rodrigues is set in February. This may have been what Orlandini saw when he went astray. 2) While it is true that Ferron in his letter to Rodrigues says that Ignatius had qualms about Peter's making such a long and arduous journey from Spain to Rome, it cannot be argued that the implication was that Peter was

313

unwell. Such a journey was an exhausting one in any case, be one sick or well. 3) It was practically impossible that Ignatius and Peter have all the correspondence implied in Orlandini's story. During the period from the middle of May, when Peter arrived in Barcelona, and early July, when he sailed from Barcelona, the slow mails could not have carried a letter from Peter with information about his sickness, and then a reply from Ignatius, time being allowed for the supposed conference with the Roman Jesuits. 4) Orlandini says that Ignatius disapproved of Peter's travelling to Rome at that time of year. Would the Fathers at Rome be so insistent in view of their respect for Ignatius' wisdom? And would Ignatius have yielded to such unreasonable persistence of the Fathers, that a sick man make a long journey under a broiling summer sun? All these accounts seem to have one aim: to stress Peter's obedience. But so evident was his devotion to this virtue throughout his entire life that there is certainly no need to romanticize it the way these authors have done.

37 *MI*, Ser. I, I, 427–428; *FN*, I, 597.

38 *EC*, I, 223.

39 *Ibid.*, VII, 261–264. In 1572 Pedro Ribadeneira, after a host of difficulties, finally published his *Life of Ignatius Loyola* in Latin. Ribadeneira asked Canisius for a criticism of the work. Canisius wrote to Jerome Nadal, then Vicar General of the Society, that criticism would be without point, since the volume had been written tastefully and piously. There was, however, considerable dissatisfaction among some of the Fathers of the Third General Congregation. In fact, so decided was the criticism that the work was not translated into Italian. One of the points made by the critics was that the author had shown favoritism in his treatment of the Spaniards and the Spanish colleges. Father Mercurian, Fourth General of the Society, then called upon Canisius for suggestions. Peter reversed his former judgment about the absence of reason for criticism, and this time drew up a number of suggested changes. It was the account of the labors of Peter Favre that made up a great part of these recommendations. Ribadeneira in turn incorporated a large number of them in his 1586 edition of the life of Ignatius. (*EC*, VII, 251, 270–271.)

40 *EC*, VII, 96, 235.

41 *EM*, I, 314. After Favre's death, Andrew Oviedo wrote to Ignatius of a report he had heard secondhand. Through a certain party, whom he felt worthy of credence, Oviedo learned of a particular pious person, especially favored by Our Lord, who claimed to have had a vision of Father Favre in the glory of the saints. Oviedo did not identify this person. In the vision, Peter spoke with deep feeling about the obedience of Christ as well as his own personal practice of that virtue; he also manifested an extraordinary joy in having met death by reason of fidelity to obedience. Father Boero claims that it is certain that the person who had the vision was Francis Borgia. His proof is a citation from the *Vida de San Francisco de Borja*, written by Father Alvaro Cienfuegos. Cienfuegos in turn relies on an assertion by a Father Pedro Doménech, who had been a companion

of Borgia. Doménech made the claim that the Duke of Gandia had seen Father Favre in glory after his death. It seems strange that Oviedo, who knew Borgia intimately, who had directed him in the *Exercises* and who was at this time Superior of the community at Gandia, should not have learned of the vision firsthand. And as for the value of Cienfuegos as an authority, Father Astrain does not mince words: "It is usual for some people to refer to the volume of Cienfuegos as the last word of historical science on Saint Francis Borgia. Two observations should be made. First, we do not know if the documents of Cienfuegos are authentic. Some were taken from Vasquez, others we do not know where. The staggering differences which we have discovered between the documents as presented in the text of Cienfuegos and the older copies of the originals make us suspect that this historian has taken the liberty, if not of inventing documents, at least of amending them and dressing them up in an up-to-date style with the consequent risk of falsifying them. Second, although this work is the most complete there is on Saint Francis Borgia, nevertheless, in the light of recently discovered documents, it is in no small way defective." Not only does Father Astrain take Cienfuegos to task for his methods, but also for his style: "It seems impossible that one could write a history in a more abominable style." (*Historía de la Compañía*, I, xli–xlii; cf. Boero, *Vita del Beato Pietro Fabro*, pp. 212–213.) Over and above all this, even if the vision attributed to Francis Borgia were true, it cannot be stretched into a substantiation of the details supposedly surrounding Peter's last days as related by Fathers Boero, Orlandini, Prat and Maurel.

⁴² *EX*, I, 393. This traditional story, recited as late as 1922 by Father Brou, S.J. in his *Saint François Xavier*, I, 438, is that Xavier could not have known by that time through any natural means the fact of Favre's death. Brou claims that this is evidence, therefore, of a twofold blessing: a supernatural illumination received by Francis, and the consequent assurance that Peter was in heaven. Since the appearance of Father Brou's work, Father Georg Schurhammer, S.J. has moved this story into the column of legends that have grown up about the Apostle of the East. By meticulous tracing of such details as the dates of the departure and arrival of the Portuguese ship S. *Felipe,* he has shown that the news of Peter's death could have reached Xavier in a natural way by December of 1547. (*AHSJ*, VII, 317.)

⁴³ *MI*, I, I, 410.

⁴⁴ *Ibid.*, 402–403, 405–406.

⁴⁵ *FN*, II, 355, n. 56.

⁴⁶ If Ignatius had lived one more day, he would have died on the tenth anniversary of Peter's death.

⁴⁷ Tacchi-Venturi, *Storia della Compagnia di Gesù in Italia*, I, 416, 605.

EPILOGUE

¹ de Guibert, *La Spiritualité de la Compagnie de Jésus*, p. 591. Fran-

cisco de P. Solá, S.J., "La Idea de Christo en la Espiritualidad del Bto. Fabro," *Manresa*, LXIX (1946), 329–341.

[2] *MF*, pp. 694–695.
[3] de Guibert, *op. cit.*, p. 592.
[4] *MF*, p. 513.
[5] *Ibid.*, p. 517.
[6] *Ibid.*, p. 562.
[7] *Ibid.*, p. 650.
[8] de Guibert, *op. cit.*, p. 592.
[9] *Ibid.*, p. 593.
[10] *MF*, pp. 187–188.
[11] *Ibid.*, p. 668.
[12] *Ibid.*, p. 162.
[13] *Ibid.*, pp. 419–421.
[14] J. B. Kettenmeyer, S.J., "Aufzeichnungen des Kölner Kartäuserpriors Kalckbrenner," *Archivum Historicum Societatis Jesu*, VIII (1939), 100.
[15] *EC*, VII, 263.
[16] *MF*, p. 505.
[17] *Ibid.*, p. 509.
[18] *Ibid.*, 506–507.
[19] *Ibid.*, p. 596.
[20] *Ibid.*, pp. 590–591.
[21] *Ibid.*, pp. 611–612.
[22] *Ibid.*, pp. 689–690.
[23] *Ibid.*, p. 684.
[24] *Ibid.*, pp. 311–312.
[25] Kettenmeyer, *loc. cit.* Recently there have been some well thought-out efforts to explain in strict theological terms the meaning, implications and practice of the idea of a "contemplative in the midst of work." Cf. Emerich Coreth, "Contemplative in Action," *Theology Digest*, III (Winter, 1955), 37–45; Maurice Giuliani, "Finding God in All Things," *Theology Digest*, IV (Spring, 1956), 93–96.
[26] D. Knowles, *The Historian and Character* (Cambridge, 1955), pp. 10–11.
[27] *MF*, pp. 518–519.
[28] *Ibid.*, p. 527.
[29] *Ibid.*, pp. 624–625.
[30] *Ibid.*, p. 688.
[31] *FN*, I, 29.
[32] *MF*, p. 81.
[33] *Ibid.*, pp. 201–205.
[34] Guitton, *L'Ame du Bx. Pierre Favre*, p. 73. Deserving of special mention because of his rescue of this letter from oblivion is Abbé Silvain Vittoz, curé of Little Bornand in Savoy at the time of the 1869 Process for Peter's Beatification. Abbé Vittoz was untiring in his research work on the devotion to Peter among the Savoyards. This letter, as has been men-

tioned above, had been written by Peter to Claude Périssin, Prior of Reposoir. On July 16th, 1611, the then Prior, Jean-Baptiste Recorder, gave the letter to Doctor Jean Favre of Annecy. Saint Francis de Sales had the opportunity of reading the letter and told a Jesuit Father how consoled he had been by it. The letter was exhibited in the Beatification Process of 1626 and then placed in the corner of the archives in the priest's residence at Saint Jean-de-Sixt, where it lay for two centuries and a half. On June 28th, 1869, during the Process of that year, Vittoz searched through the archives of Saint Jean-de-Sixt and found valuable material for the Process without, however, discovering Favre's letter. On July 9th, the octave of the Visitation, a feast to which Peter had a special devotion because it was the anniversary of his profession as a Jesuit, Vittoz for some reason or other felt impelled to take another look through the archives at Saint Jean-de-Sixt. Even though he had a number of guests in his rectory at Little Bornand, he left them, hired a horse, rode to Saint Jean-de-Sixt, and was rewarded by the discovery of the letter. The letter is now kept in the chapel at Villaret, the only relic that Savoy has of its distinguished Jesuit son. (Jean Falconnet, "La Chartreuse du Resposoir au Diocèse d'Annecy," *Mémoires et Documents Publiés par l'Académie Salésienne* [Montreuil-sur-Mer, 1895], XVIII, 600–602.)

[35] *MF*, pp. 385–386.

[36] *Ibid.*, p. 334.

[37] *Ibid.*, p. 384.

[38] *Ibid.*, pp. 768–777.

[39] *Ibid.*, pp. 797, 880.

[40] *Ibid.*, p. 801.

[41] Saint Francis de Sales, *Introduction to the Devout Life*, translated by J. K. Ryan (New York: Harper & Brothers, 1949).

[42] *MF*, p. 803.

[43] Pocchat-Baron, *Le Bienheureux Père LeFèvre*, p. 186.

[44] *MF*, pp. 760–802.

[45] Pochat-Baron, *op. cit.*, p. 203.

[46] *MF*, pp. 743–746.

Bibliography

PRIMARY SOURCES

Volumes of the *Monumenta Historica Societatis Jesu.*

Epistolae Mixtae, I (Madrid, 1898).

Epistolae Paschasii Broeti, Claudii Jaii, Joannis Coduri et Simonis Rodericii (Madrid, 1903).

Epistolae P, Hieronymi Nadal, I-IV (Madrid, 1898, 1899, 1902, 1905).

Epistolae Francisci Xaverii, I-II (Rome, 1944, 1945).

Fabri Monumenta (Madrid, 1914).

Fontes Narrativi de S. Ignatio de Loyola et de Societate Jesu Initiis, I-II (Rome, 1943, 1951).

Monumenta Ignatiana:
Series I, *Sancti Ignatii de Loyola Epistolae et Instructiones,* I (Madrid, 1903).
Series II, *Exercitia Spiritualia* (Madrid, 1919).
Series III, *Sancti Ignatii de Loyola Constitutiones Societatis Jesu,* I-III (Rome, 1934, 1936, 1938).
Series IV, *Scripta de Sancto Ignatio de Loyola,* I (Madrid, 1904).

Patris Petri de Ribadeneira Confessiones, Epistolae Aliaque Scripta Inedita, I (Madrid, 1920).

Vita Ignatii Loyolae et Rerum Societatis Jesu Historia auctore Joanne Alphonso de Polanco, I (Madrid, 1894).

Acta Sanctorum, new ed. (Paris, 1863 ff.)

Braunsberger, Otto, S.J., *Epistolae et Acta B. Petri Canisii,* I-VIII (Freiburg im B., 1896–1923).

Bretschneider, C. G., *Corpus Reformatorum,* I ff. (Halle, 1834 ff.)

Kettenmeyer, J. B., S.J., "Aufzeichnungen des Kölner Kartäuserpriors Kalckbrenner über den sel. Petrus Faber," *Archivum Historicum Societatis Jesu*, VIII (1939), 86–102.

Velez, José M., S.J., *Cartas y Otros Escritos del B. Pedro Fabro* (Bilbao, 1894).

SECONDARY SOURCES

Astrain, A., S.J., *Historía de la Compañía de Jesús en la Asistencia de España*, I (Madrid, 1902).

Boero, G., S.J., *Vita del Beato Pietro Fabro* (Rome, 1872).

Brodrick, J., S.J., *The Origin of the Jesuits* (London, 1940).

Cornely, R., S.J., *Leben des sel. Petrus Faber*, 2nd Ed. (Freiburg im B., 1900).

Duhr, B., S.J., *Geschichte der Jesuiten in den Ländern Deutscher*, I (Freiburg im B., 1907).

Galtier, P., S.J., "La Confession et le Renouveau Chrétien," *Revue d'Ascétique et de Mystique*, XXV (1949), 18–44.

Greven, J., *Die Kölner Kartause und die Anfänge der Katholische Reform in Deutschland* (Münster, 1935).

Guibert, J. de, S.J., *La Spiritualité de la Compagnie de Jésus* (Rome, 1953).

Guitton, G., S.J., *L'Ame du Bx. Pierre Favre* (Paris, 1934).

Hansen, J., *Rheinische Akten sur Geschichte des Jesuitenordens* (Bonn, 1896).

Iparraguirre, I., S.J., *Practica de los Ejercicios de San Ignacio de Loyola en Vida de su Autor* (Rome, 1946).

———, "Influjos en la espiritualidad del Beato Pedro Fabro," *Revista de Espiritualidad*, V (1946), 438–452.

———, "El concepto de vida espiritual según el Beato Pedro Fabro," *Manresa*, XVIII (1946), 293–307.

———, "El Beato Pedro Fabro–Apóstol de la amabilidad," *Razón y Fe*, CXXXIV (1946), pp. 172–186.

Kleiser, A., S.J., *Ein Seelensoberer: Lebenserinnerungen des ersten flämischen Jesuiten Kornelius Wischaven* (Paderborn, 1930).

Lipgens, W., *Kardinal Johannes Gropper und die Anfänge der Katholischen Reform in Deutschland* (Münster, 1951).

Maurel, A., S.J., *La Vie du Bx. Père Pierre Lefèvre* (Lyons, 1873).

Mercier, J., "Le Bx. Pierre Favre," *Mémoires et Documents de l'Académie Salésienne*, VI (1883), 87–97.

Orlandini, N., S.J., *Vita Petri Fabri* (Lyons, 1617).

——, *Forma Sacerdotis Apostolici expressa in Exemplo Petri Fabri* (Dilingen, 1647).

Plaza, C., S.J., *Contemplando en todo à Dios* (Madrid, 1944).

——, "La doctrina del Cuerpo Místico de Christo en la espiritualidad de Fabro," *Manresa*, XVIII (1946), 308–316.

Pochat-Baron, F., *Le Bx. Pierre Lefèvre* (Paris, 1931).

——, "A propos du Bx. Pierre Favre, dit Lefèvre. Quelques notes sur sa paroisse natale et sur le lieu de ses premières études," *XVII Congrès des Sociétés savantes de la Savoie* (Chambéry, 1906), pp. 461–487.

Poncelet, A., S.J., *Histoire de la Compagnie de Jésus dans les Anciens Pays-Bas*, I (Brussels, 1927).

Prat, J-M., S.J., *Le Bx. Pierre Lefèvre* (Lyons, 1873).

Read, W., S.J., *The Industry in Prayer of Blessed Peter Favre* (Rome, 1950).

Reiffenberg, F., S.J., *Historia Societatis Jesu ad Rhenum Inferiorem* (Cologne, 1764).

Rodrigues, F., S.J., *História da Companhia de Jesus na Assisténcia de Portugal*, I (Oporto, 1931).

Schurhammer, G., S.J., *Franz Xaver, Sein Leben und Seiner Zeit*, I (Freiburg im B., 1955).

Sola, J., S.J., "El problema 'acción-contemplación' en el Beato Fabro," *Manresa*, XIX (1947), 342–367.

——, "La idea de Cristo en la espiritualidad del Beato Fabro," *Manresa*, XVIII (1946), 329–341.

Speeten, H. van der, S.J., "Le Bx. Pierre Favre de la Compagnie de Jésus! Quel est son véritable nom?", *Précis Historiques,* XXI (1872), 469–472.

——, "Le Bx. Pierre Favre, Son culte et sa béatification," *Précis Historiques,* XXI (1872), 492–501.

——, "Encore un mot sur le nom du Bx. Favre," *Précis Historiques,* XXII (1873), 261–264.

——, "Séjour du Bx. Favre à Louvain," *Précis Historiques,* XXII (1873), 357–364.

Tacchi-Venturi, P., S.J., *Storia della Compagnia di Gesù in Italia,* I, Part I (Rome, 1910); Part II (Edizioni "La Civiltà Cattolica," Rome, 1950).

Index

323

A NOTE ON THE TYPE

IN WHICH THIS BOOK WAS SET

This book is set in Caledonia, a Linotype face created in 1939 by W. A. Dwiggins, which is by far one of the best book types created in the last 50 years. It has a simple, hard-working, feet-on-the-ground quality and can be classed as a modern type face with excellent color and good readability. The designer claims Caledonia was created by putting a little of each of Scotch Roman, Bulmer, Baskerville and Bodoni together and producing a lively crisp-like book type. This book was composed and printed by the York Composition Company, Inc., of York, Pa., and bound by Moore and Company of Baltimore. The typography and design of this book are by Howard N. King.